Christ-
Centered
Worship

Christ-Centered Worship

LETTING *the* GOSPEL SHAPE OUR PRACTICE

Bryan Chapell

B
Baker Academic
a division of Baker Publishing Group
Grand Rapids, Michigan

© 2009 by Bryan Chapell

Published by Baker Academic
a division of Baker Publishing Group
P.O. Box 6287, Grand Rapids, MI 49516-6287
www.bakeracademic.com

Printed in the United States of America

Library of Congress Cataloging-in-Publication Data

Chapell, Bryan.
    Christ-centered worship : letting the Gospel shape our practice / Bryan Chapell.
      p. cm.
    Includes bibliographical references and index.
    ISBN 978-0-8010-3640-8 (cloth)
    1. Worship. I. Title.
  BV10.3.C43 2009
  264—dc22
                                                      2009012438

To my wife, Kathy,
whose flute, piano, voice, choir directing, and heart
daily bring the music of worship
into the life
the Lord has graced us to share.

CONTENTS

CHARTS

Acknowledgments

I am indebted to Dr. Robert G. Rayburn, founding president of Covenant Seminary, who laid a foundation of profound respect for worship at the seminary. I am also thankful for the friendship and support of Mark Dalbey, Covenant Seminary's worship professor. Mark has sharpened my thought while leading this seminary (and a new generation of church leaders) into wonderful understanding and expression of gospel worship.

Although the research and thought behind this work have spanned years, I have done most of the writing during a sabbatical provided by the board of Covenant Seminary. I want to express my thanks to Covenant's trustees for granting me this wonderful writing opportunity. Working at an institution governed by godly leaders dedicated to the future of Christ's church is a blessing for which I am daily thankful.

I am deeply grateful for the executive team in place as this sabbatical began: Dave Wicker, chief of staff; Sean Lucas, chief academic officer; Wayne Copeland, vice president of business administration; and Mark Dalbey, vice president of student services. The dedication and skills of these friends allowed me to be out of the office for this extended period of time. My sabbatical was also possible because of the caring skills of my executive assistant, Kathy Woodard.

Finally, I wish to express appreciation for my faculty colleagues at Covenant Seminary. Their wonderful and courageous commitment to the gospel of grace has deepened my understanding of Christ's work, increased my love of his heart, and furthered my devotion to proclaiming his work in every dimension of life.

Part I

GOSPEL WORSHIP

1

THE GOSPEL OF STRUCTURE

Structures tell stories. Martin Luther knew this when he designed the first Protestant church in Torgau, Germany. Prior to the construction of this chapel for the castle of Luther's protector, the Elector John Frederick I, Protestant services were held mainly in churches that were formerly Roman Catholic. The main architectural change that occurred when Protestants took control of such churches was the replacement of a cross on the spire of the church with a rooster, symbol of the new dawn of the Reformation. And it was not rare in the competing tides of Reformation times that if Roman Catholic forces returned to power, they would replace the rooster with another cross.

Each faith movement signaled its control by the changed "hood ornament" most obvious to all in the town or region, but the basic architecture of the church changed little. Thus, when Luther had the opportunity to design a church that would reflect the new perspectives of the Reformation, he made sure that the basic structure of the church would convey the gospel story he wanted to tell. No structural change would have been more obvious to sixteenth-century worshipers than the placement of the pulpit. In deliberate contrast with the Roman Catholic practice of placing the pulpit at the front of the congregation, Luther arranged for the pastor to preach among the people. The pulpit was at the center of the long wall of the worship sanctuary. In addition, the altar, while still located at the front of the church, was no longer separated from the people by screens that had designated sacred space for clergy alone.

Luther preached "the priesthood of believers," and his structures conveyed the same message. The placement of the pulpit silently explained that the preacher was not more holy than the people. He ministered among them because all were fulfilling holy callings as they served God in the occupations for which he had gifted them. The architecture of the altar "said" there was no need for priestly intercession or separation, since everyone had equal and immediate access to God. The early Calvinistic churches of the French Reformation pushed the idea further by putting the pulpit in the center of a circled congregation.[1] This structure not only symbolized the priesthood of believers, but also asserted the centrality of the Word in Christian worship.

Informed, Not Ruled

I do not mention these architectural details in order to mandate designs for church architecture. In fact, the various ways in which the Reformers expressed their views can also argue for the liberties in church architecture that modern Christians have obviously exercised. But such freedom is best applied when we have some sense of the story we are trying to tell, and this requires understanding our place in God's unfolding plan for his church. We should not ignore the wisdom of church forebears just because it's old, or automatically reject it just because we didn't think of it. We consider the history because God does not give all of his wisdom to any one time or people. Slavish loyalty to traditions will keep us from ministering effectively to our generation, but trashing the past entirely denies God's purposes for the church on which we must build. If we do not learn from the past, we will lose insights God has granted others as they have interacted with his Word and people.

Always we are to be informed by tradition; never are we to be ruled by it. The Word of God is our only infallible rule of faith and practice, but an unwillingness to consider what previous generations have learned about applying God's Word discloses either naïveté or arrogance. God intends for us to stand on the shoulders of those faithful before us. He gives us a mission for our time, but he also gives us a history to prepare us for our present calling. Without critically and constructively examining this foundation we are ill equipped for building the church God wants today. This is true not only for the structures of church architecture, but also for the structures of church worship.

1. Geoffrey Barraclough, ed., "Calvinism: The Majesty of God," in *The Christian World: A Social and Cultural History* (New York: Harry N. Abrams, Inc., 1981): 178–79.

Designed to Communicate

Just as church leaders through the ages have structured their buildings to reflect their understanding of the gospel, they have also structured what happens inside those buildings to do the same. Already we have seen how the placement of pulpit, altar, and pew could convey a message. What was done in the pulpit, at the altar, and in the pew was also structured to communicate. For example, in the Roman Catholic Mass, the priest stood between the altar and the people when dispensing the elements to symbolize his intercessory role. By contrast, many Protestant Reformers intentionally stood behind the Communion Table when administering the Lord's Supper to demonstrate the people's immediate access to Christ.[2] The physical placement of the furniture, pastor, and people was designed to communicate a clear gospel message: "Nothing and no one comes between Christ and the believer."

We may think that "the medium is the message" is a modern insight, but the ancient church practiced such communication principles long before Marshall McLuhan coined the phrase. Church leaders understood that if the message was inconsistent with the means by which it was communicated, then the message could easily get lost. Thus, they painted the message of the gospel with every communication brush their structures would provide: building architecture, decoration, pulpit design, furniture placement, the position of worship leaders, and even the placement of participants in the worship service.

Never was there only one right structure for communicating the gospel for all regions, cultures, and times. Nor was adequate wisdom always applied. Sometimes the truth of the message got lost in embellishment; other times the beauty of the gospel was veiled in reactionary starkness. But in every age, including our own, those who build churches have been forced to consider how their understanding of the gospel gets communicated by the structures in which it is presented.

Gospel Worship

Gospel understanding is not only embedded in physical structures, but it is also communicated in the worship patterns of the church.[3] The structure

---

2. K. Deddens, "A Missing Link in Reformed Liturgy," *Clarion* 37, nos. 15–19 (1998): 6, http://www.spindleworks.com/library/deddens/missing.htm.

3. Robert E. Webber, *Ancient-Future Worship: Proclaiming and Enacting God's Narrative* (Grand Rapids: Baker Books, 2008), 110.

of a church's worship service is called its liturgy.[4] Many Protestants think "liturgy" only describes highly ceremonial worship in Catholic, Orthodox, or Anglican churches. We normally talk about our worship in terms of a "Sunday service" or the "worship time." The activities that surround the Sermon we may describe as the "song service," "the service of prayer," or simply as "the worship." However, the biblical word for all that's included in our worship is "liturgy" (*latreia*, see Rom. 12:1), and it simply describes the public way a church honors God in its times of gathered praise, prayer, instruction, and commitment.[5] All churches that gather to worship have a liturgy—even if it's a very simple liturgy.

The customary ways that a church arranges the aspects and components of its public worship form its liturgical tradition. Similar to church architecture, a church's traditional worship practices can be very elaborate (sometimes called liturgical, or high church) or simple (non-liturgical, or low church). The differences in worship services can be significant, leading many onlookers to think there is no rhyme or reason to the varying liturgical approaches. In this increasingly secularized era, even church leaders may not know why different elements of their worship services are present or sequenced as they are—and may think everything is up for grabs as long as people are not put off by the changes.

But, analogous to church architecture, the *order of worship* (another way of describing the liturgy) conveys an understanding of the gospel. Whether one intends it or not, our worship patterns always communicate something. Even if one simply goes along with what is either historically accepted or currently preferred, an understanding of the gospel inevitably unfolds. If a leader sets aside time for Confession of Sin[6] (whether by prayer, or by song, or by Scripture reading), then something about the gospel gets communicated. If there is no Confession in the course of the service, then something else is communicated—even though the message conveyed may not have been intended.

Similar to church architecture, differing church traditions and cultural contexts have resulted in great variation in the structure of Christian liturgy. But, also similar to the physical structures of the church, where the truths of the gospel are maintained there remain commonalities of worship structure that transcend culture. Despite having great architectural variety,

---

4. Peter Leithart, "For Whom Is Worship?" *New Horizons* 23, no. 4 (April 2002): 5.

5. John W. de Gruchy, "Aesthetic Creativity, Eucharistic Celebration and Liturgical Renewal: With Special Reference to the Reformed Tradition" (paper for the Buvton Conference, Stellenbosch, South Africa, September 1, 2003), 1.

6. Here and elsewhere in this book terms such as Confession of Sin that may have a common and generic meaning in Christian devotion are capitalized when they refer to a distinct or formal component of a worship service.

Christian churches still have common denominators: a place to proclaim the Word; a place to gather for prayer, praise, and receiving the Word; a place to administer and receive the sacraments; and others. No one has imposed these architectural features on all churches; rather, the way we dispense, receive, and respond to the gospel in a corporate setting has necessitated these familiar structures. For similar reasons, there are common liturgical structures that transcend individual contexts and traditions.

Gospel Continuity

Liturgy tells a story. We tell the gospel by the way we worship. Where a church maintains the truths of the gospel, it inevitably discovers aspects of worship that are in harmony with other faithful churches. In fact, worshiping with these aspects is one important way a church maintains fidelity with the gospel.

Because they understood the importance of our worship, early church fathers designed an architecture for worship that is still reflected in most churches today. As early as the second century,[7] records indicate that the church divided its worship into two major segments: the Liturgy of the Word (see chart 1.1 on page 23) and the Liturgy of the Upper Room (see chart 1.2 on page 24).[8] Today we think of the Liturgy of the Word as the portion of the worship service that culminates in preaching. We think of the Liturgy of the Upper Room as the part of the worship service that includes the Lord's Supper, or Communion. Even if our churches do not practice Communion every week, they still typically break the service into these two major segments on the occasions the ordinance is observed. By moving from Proclamation to Communion in the order of worship, churches through the ages retell the story that those who truly hear God's Word will share his love.[9]

My hope in writing this book is that readers who just had an "aha" moment in the preceding paragraph—discovering that their worship pattern unites them with multiple centuries of fellow Christians who have worshiped similarly—will also be delighted to find how their worship can unite them in mission with those fellow believers. In every age, we worship God to further the cause of his gospel. We know the "good news" of that gospel as we recognize the holiness of our Creator, confess our sin, seek his

7. De Gruchy, "Aesthetic Creativity," 278.

8. John M. Barkley, *Worship of the Reformed Church* (Richmond, VA: John Knox, 1967), 41.

9. Mark L. Dalbey, "A Biblical, Historical, and Contemporary Look at the Regulative Principle of Worship" (DMin diss., Covenant Theological Seminary, 1999), 37.

grace, are assured of his mercy, give him thanks, petition his aid, seek his instruction, and, in loving response to all his mercies, live for him. Charts 1.1 and 1.2 (see pages 23–24) show how different church traditions have tried to express these gospel truths through the architecture of their liturgy.

Liturgy Strategy

At first glance, what will be most apparent about these liturgies are their differences. Looking at them will be something like observing the skyline of a modern city. All we will see initially are the different shapes, sizes, and complexities of the structures. But the more we observe, and the more the architecture is explained, the more we will begin to understand that each of the architects built with the same basic materials and design principles. Form varies according to specific functions and design intentions, but every architect still had to make sure walls bore the proper weight, ceilings were the right height, and foundations were laid at sufficient depth. After further study, we may conclude that some did not design or build as well as others, but we will also see that the most successful still had to learn from those who preceded them. No one built without considering what others had learned.

Perhaps the simplest way to begin seeing common patterns among all the varying details of these charts is to note that even the two basic divisions of the liturgy have separate movements. The Liturgy of the Word, in each of the five traditions listed, has elements that lead to the preaching of the Word. Preaching is not the only thing done in the Liturgy of the Word. There is "Preparation" prior to "Proclamation." This "Preparation," as we will soon see, is not random or arbitrary. The components of the worship service prior to and after the Sermon lead the heart through various stages of awe, humility, assurance, and thanksgiving to make us receptive and responsive to the instruction of the Word. There is a strategy to the liturgy.

Opening "Stuff"

We will unfold the beauty and power of this strategy in later chapters. Essential now is the realization of how sad is the common misperception of what happens prior to the Sermon in many Protestant churches. I often hear that misperception when I am invited to preach during a regular pastor's absence from a local church. A lay leader will often orient me to the worship service with words similar to these: "I'll take care of the opening stuff, so that you can do the sermon."

That "opening stuff" is in most people's minds the requisite assortment of hymns and prayers that we need to chug through prior to the "real thing"—the Sermon. The "stuff" that fills the time early in the service is considered only the prelude to the Sermon, the opening act to the main event, or the pleasantries we need to get past so that we can get to the "meat of the matter." Typically no one thinks much about the "opening stuff," and no one is going to complain about it unless someone changes the traditional order, changes a familiar tune, or forgets the offering.

If a complaint comes, it is not likely to be based on a rationale rooted in gospel priorities. People will instead talk about their lack of comfort with what is personally unfamiliar or uninspiring, or about someone else's lack of respect for what is traditional. Because they have not been taught to think of the worship service as having gospel purposes, people instinctively think of its elements only in terms of personal preference: what makes me feel good, comfortable, or respectful.

Gospel Goals

One great advantage of looking at the specifics of the different worship liturgies below is seeing that their designers had loftier goals than satisfying personal preferences. Church leaders designed their orders of worship to communicate the truths of Scripture, touch the hearts of worshipers with the implications of those truths, and then equip believers to live faithfully in the world as witnesses to those truths. We may not agree with the way all of these liturgies frame the truths of the gospel, but it's hard to fault the missional impulse behind their designs. Our goal, therefore, should not be to mimic the liturgies that follow, but to learn how the church has used worship to fulfill gospel purposes through the ages so that we can intelligently design worship services that will fulfill gospel purposes today.

In order for us to think of worship in *gospel* terms, we need to be careful not to think only in *evangelistic* terms. While the gospel includes the good news of God's grace for those who would turn to him in faith, the gospel is not just for outsiders or unbelievers. Great power lies in the line popular among young Christians today: "We must preach the gospel to our own hearts every day."[10] This ethic is not just about repeating those portions of the gospel that lead to new conversions; it is about engaging the power of the good news that God has provided his grace to save, to sanctify, and

10. Bob Kauflin, *Worship Matters: Leading Others to Encounter the Greatness of God* (Wheaton, IL: Crossway, 2008), 135.

to equip his people for this day, every day, and forever. We need this gospel to enter Christ's kingdom, but we also need it to walk with him through our daily trials and demands. This is the gospel the ancient liturgies teach, and the best liturgies still echo. Examples are grouped together in charts 1.1 and 1.2, so that we can begin to see common patterns before analyzing important differences and, ultimately, discovering how they unite to inform our gospel purposes today:

Rome

The Roman Catholic liturgy had a pervasive and profound influence on later liturgies in Western culture. My depiction of that order of worship is intentionally sparse, reflecting Catholic worship prior to the sixteenth-century Council of Trent, when much additional complexity was added to aid the sacramental emphases of that tradition. The division of the Roman liturgy into two main movements relating to Word and sacrament (seen in all the liturgies above) becomes foundational for all subsequent liturgies. These divisions of worship are evident as early as the second century.[11] The Protestant Reformer John Calvin also specifies these two movements as the Liturgy of the Word and the Liturgy of the Upper Room in his worship book, *The Form of Ecclesiastical Prayers and Songs*.

These basic divisions in the order of worship are probably even older than the liturgies listed here. Barkley says these divisions were reflected in synagogue worship, where a declaration of the mighty acts of God was followed by a response of the people. He further subdivides the two major movements by saying that the Liturgy of the Word ". . . divides into two sections consisting of the Old Liturgy of the Word derived from the synagogue, basically the proclamation of the mighty acts of God, and the . . . introduction, consisting of preparation to receive the Word."[12] Thus, we follow an ancient practice when we sequence our worship services to flow from the Preparation for the Word to the Proclamation of the Word. As a result of centuries of continuity regarding these basic divisions of worship, there has been significant similarity among various traditions' general worship pattern despite great differences in individual elements of their liturgies.

Reformers

The liturgies of key Reformation influencers (Luther, Calvin, and the Westminster Assembly) are also schematized and are based on key docu-

11. Nicholas Wolterstorff, "The Reformed Liturgy," in *Major Themes in the Reformed Tradition*, ed. Donald K. McKim (Grand Rapids: Eerdmans, 1992), 278.
12. Barkley, *Worship of the Reformed Church*, 41.

Chart 1.1 General Structures of Historic Liturgies—Liturgy of the Word

Rome pre-1570	Luther ca. 1526	Calvin ca. 1542	Westminster ca. 1645	Rayburn ca. 1980
Liturgy of the Word	*Liturgy of the Word*	*Liturgy of the Word*	*Liturgy of the Word*	*Liturgy of the Word*
Choral Introit	Entrance Hymn / Introit	Scripture Sentence (e.g., Ps. 121:2)	Call to Worship / Opening Prayer:	Call to Worship / Hymn of Praise
			•Adoration	Invocation (or Adoration Prayer)
Kyrie ("Lord have mercy")	*Kyrie*	Confession of Sin (with pardon at Strasbourg)	•Supplication for Grace	Confession of Sin / Prayer for Pardon
Gloria	*Gloria*	Psalm Sung	•Supplication for Illumination	Assurance of Grace
Salutation ("The Lord be with you . . .")	Salutation			
				Thanksgiving Hymn / Offering
Collect(s)	Collect			Prayer of Intercession (with Lord's Prayer optional)
Old Testament Reading / Antiphonal Chant		Ten Commandments (sung with *Kyries* at Strasbourg)	Old Testament Reading / Psalm Sung	Old Testament Reading / Hymn or Anthem
Epistle Reading / Gradual (a psalm sung)	Epistle Reading / Gradual		New Testament Reading / Psalm Sung	New Testament Reading
			Confession and Intercession	
Alleluia				
		Prayer for Illumination (with Lord's Prayer)	Prayer for Illumination	Prayer for Illumination
Gospel Reading	Gospel Reading / Apostles' Creed / Sermon Hymn	Scripture Reading	Scripture Reading	Sermon Scripture
Sermon	Sermon	Sermon	Sermon	Sermon
			Thanksgiving and Service Prayer / Lord's Prayer	Service Prayer
Nicene Creed Sung (or *Gloria*)	Post-Sermon Hymn		Psalm Sung	Hymn of Response
Dismissal of Non-communicants	Exhortation		Dismissal (if no Communion)	Dismissal/ Benediction

Chart 1.2 General Structures of Historic Liturgies—Liturgy of the Upper Room

Rome pre-1570	Luther ca. 1526	Calvin ca. 1542	Westminster ca. 1645	Rayburn ca. 1980
Liturgy of the Upper Room [Always]	*Liturgy of the Upper Room [Always]*	*Liturgy of the Upper Room [Quarterly]*	*Liturgy of the Upper Room [Optional]*	*Liturgy of the Upper Room [Optional]*
Offertory		Collection of Alms	Offertory	
	Prayer for the Church	Intercessions Lord's Prayer		
			Invitation; Fencing	Invitation; Fencing
				Hymn
Preparation of Elements	Preparation Hymn	Apostles' Creed (sung as elements prepared)		Apostles' Creed (recited by all)
Salutation				
Sursum Corda	*Sursum Corda*			
Sanctus	*Sanctus*			
Benedictus				
Eucharistic Prayer: •Remembrance (*Anamnesis*) •Offering Elements for Holy Use (*Oblation*)	Preparation: •Call for Holy Spirit (*Epiclesis*) •Consecration of Elements •Remembrance (*Anamnesis*)			
			Preparation: •Exhortation	Preparation: •Exhortation
•Words of Institution (*Verba*) •Call for Holy Spirit to Change Elements (*Epiclesis*) •Amen	•Words of Institution (*Verba*)	Words of Institution Exhortation	•Words of Institution	•Words of Institution
Lord's Prayer	Lord's Prayer	Consecration Prayer	•Consecration Prayer (for participants and elements)	•Consecration Prayer
Kiss of Peace				
Fraction		Fraction	Fraction	Fraction
Agnus Dei	*Agnus Dei*			
Communion	Communion (with psalms sung)	Communion (with Scriptures read)	Communion	Communion
			Exhortation Prayer	
Collect	Collect	Psalm Sung	Psalm Sung	Praise Hymn
	Thanksgiving	Thanksgiving Prayer		
Dismissal Blessing	Aaronic Blessing Closing Hymn	Aaronic Blessing	Benediction	Benediction

ments that would set the stage for later developments in each tradition. For example, Luther gave initial liturgical instruction in his *German Mass and Order of God's Service* (1526); Calvin took ideas from Luther and added his own in what became known as the Geneva Liturgy, described in *The Form of Ecclesiastical Prayers and Songs* (1542); and the Westminster divines appended their thoughts to the Westminster Confession of Faith in their Directory for Publicke Worship (1645).

Rayburn

Robert G. Rayburn sought to describe a well-ordered service for evangelical congregations in late-twentieth-century North America in his book, *O Come, Let Us Worship* (1980). Rayburn's work has not been the most influential on later practice, but it astutely reflects, combines, and anticipates various traditions that are. His work is particularly helpful for examining modern liturgies because it allows us to reflect on adaptations that have both intentionally and unintentionally evolved into common practice. We will not assume that "common" means universal. Even within most denominations, what is common today is a great variety of worship practices and styles. Some churches seek to distance themselves from traditional worship, while others deliberately march toward the future with the goal of resurrecting ancient models. Rayburn's perspective will give us opportunity to examine each. However, what will become apparent as this book unfolds is that where the gospel is honored, it shapes worship. No church true to the gospel will fail to have echoes of these historic liturgies.

Notes on Charts

These liturgies represent major movements that have had significant influence in North America. The list of elements in each tradition is not meant to be exhaustive (specifics will be explained later) or to suggest that every worship service in each tradition contained all these elements. The elements are arranged in typical patterns so that those unfamiliar with the various traditions can see the "bones" of each liturgy, while recognizing that each could vary and be fleshed out more. Many more traditions could be shown, but my intention is to demonstrate patterns present in those liturgies most representative of or influential for evangelical Protestant worshipers in North America.

Horizontal lines are for visual clarity and do not necessarily indicate a break in the worship components.

2

The Roman Story

The Roman Catholic liturgy is foundational for most subsequent liturgies in Western culture. Thus, the first order of worship depicted below represents a Catholic liturgy prior to the Council of Trent. Before Trent, there were various strands of Catholic liturgy (associated with Justin Martyr, Augustine, Constantinople, etc.) too numerous to represent here in detail.[1] My goal is to present a *basic* picture of Western European practice in the period closest to the Protestant Reformation. For reasons explained below, this period was the most influential for later practice by both Catholics and Protestants.

The Council of Trent convened over a number of years as the Roman Catholic Church's official response to the challenges of the Protestant Reformation. Trent codified Catholic dogma and practice to make them more uniform. The council not only reaffirmed seven sacraments, transubstantiation, purgatory, the necessity of the priesthood, and justification through the church, but also regularized the liturgy to reinforce these particulars. In 1570, the council issued instructions for a universal format for celebration

1. Geoffrey Wainwright and Karen B. Westerfield, eds., *The Oxford History of Christian Worship* (Oxford: Oxford University Press, 2006), 97; Robert E. Webber, *Ancient-Future Worship: Proclaiming and Enacting God's Narrative* (Grand Rapids: Baker Books, 2008), 101; Peter J. Wallace, "Worship: The Heavenly Pattern (The Geneva Liturgy of John Calvin—Heaven on Earth?)," Michiana Covenant Church, May 4, 2006, http://www.freerepublic.com/focus/f-religion/1626924/posts, 7.

of the Mass. The rules lasted centuries. Mandated ritual and complexity underscored the sacramental emphases of a tradition that previously was simpler and easier to decipher in relation to the gospel story.

The Roman Liturgy of the Word

To help us see the gospel story in the liturgical structures of Roman Catholicism, the following chart describes the simpler, pre-Trent liturgy of the Catholic Church.[2] For clarity and brevity, not every detail is included. It is important to note that there are marked differences with present-day Catholicism's practices and terminology.[3] My goal in using this older liturgy is to identify key elements that would create continuity with later traditions, as well as to identify elements against which later traditions will react.

Chart 2.1 Rome's Liturgy of the Word Highlights

Rome pre-1570
Liturgy of the Word
Choral Introit
Kyrie ("Lord have mercy")
Gloria
Salutation ("The Lord be with you . . . ")
Collect(s)
Old Testament Reading
Antiphonal Chant
Epistle Reading
Gradual (a psalm sung)
Alleluia
Gospel Reading
Sermon
Nicene Creed Sung (or *Gloria*)
Dismissal of Non-communicants

---

2. Wainwright and Westerfield, *Oxford History of Christian Worship*, 97.
3. St. Agnes Cathedral, Rockville Centre, New York, "Understanding the Catholic Mass," http://www.stagnescathedral.org/Parish/mass/mass.htm, 1–2.

Adoration

This simpler version of the Catholic Liturgy of the Word begins with a Choral Introit. In early church history, the Introit began as a psalm sung by the priest and others in vocational ministry as they approached the altar at the beginning of the Mass. As the Roman service evolved, the Introit became a psalm of celebration, identifying the theme of worship and calling congregants to the celebration of the Mass. Singers were those involved in church vocation (including cantors) who sang from the "choir," a space between the congregation and the altar that was often separated from the laypeople by a screen. The congregation did not sing the Introit or any other portion of the service.

Confession and Assurance

In this early Catholic liturgy, the note of adoration struck in the Introit soon changes to penitence. The service proceeds to a prayer known as the *Kyrie* (short for *kyrie eleison*, translated "Lord have mercy"). The phrase includes the opening words of an ancient prayer for grace: "Lord have mercy; Christ have mercy; Lord have mercy" (reflecting Pss. 4:1; 6:2; 9:13, etc.). The prayer typically is said by the priest and repeated by the congregation. As this prayer unfolds, the priest may also say various lines of petition, and the congregation responds to each line with the words of the *Kyrie*. Through the *Kyrie*, the people both recognize the greatness of God and petition him for mercy.

Thanksgiving

In a number of older liturgies, the *Kyrie* is followed by the *Gloria*, a hymn of praise (see below) whose opening words reflect the angels' praise in the nativity account of Luke 2. The placement of the *Gloria* after the *Kyrie*'s plea for mercy is apt since the angels' song also reflects thanksgiving for God sending his Son into the world and, therefore, implicitly speaks of the pardon, comfort, and peace found in Him.

Gloria

Glory to God in the highest,
and peace to his people on earth.
Lord God, heavenly King, almighty God and Father,
we worship you, we give you thanks, we praise you for your glory.
Lord Jesus Christ, only Son of the Father,
Lord God, Lamb of God,
you take away the sin of the world; have mercy on us;

you are seated at the right hand of the Father; receive our prayer.
For you alone are the Holy One, you alone are the Lord,
You alone are the Most High, Jesus Christ,
with the Holy Spirit, in the glory of God the Father. Amen.

Having acknowledged God's glory and their need, the priest then greets
the people with a Salutation that acknowledges God's presence and care:
"The Lord be with you," and the people respond, "And also with you."

Petition

Next, the priest invites the people to act in accord with their confidence
in the presence of God by praying. This prayer of the gathered people of
God is traditionally known as a Collect (in "high church" Protestantism this
is sometimes identified as the "Prayer for the Day"). Originally the Collect
was a short prayer that followed a traditional form whereby a person of the
Godhead was addressed, an attribute of God was identified that related to the
petition to be made, the petition was made, the desired/expected result was
stated, and a statement of dependence on God was made with his praise.

Example of a Collect: Almighty God, to whom all hearts are open, by whom all
desires known, and from whom no secrets are hid; cleanse the thoughts of our
hearts by the inspiration of your Holy Spirit, that we may perfectly love you and
worthily magnify your holy name, through Jesus Christ our Lord. Amen.

Instruction

Scripture follows in Readings from the Old Testament and Epistles so
that the entire Word of God is honored. Between the readings, a psalm might
be chanted antiphonally, or a Gradual (a Scripture response arranged in
song) may be sung by the choir. In the early centuries of the Roman liturgy,
a Gradual was an entire psalm. A Gradual is also ordinarily sung after the
Epistle Reading. In response to challenges as to whether the God of the
Old Testament was the same as the God who had revealed himself in Jesus
Christ in the New Testament, the church as early as the fourth century also
sang the *Gloria Patri* as the conclusion to the Antiphonal Chant following
the Old Testament Reading. The words of the *Gloria Patri* affirmed the
unity of the testaments' witness to our Trinitarian God.

Gloria Patri
Glory be to the Father and to the Son and to the Holy Ghost,
As it was in the beginning, is now and ever shall be, world without
end. Amen.

The final reading of the Liturgy of the Word is from a New Testament Gospel. This Gospel Reading is meant to focus on Christ's unique ministry and is the culmination of all that has preceded. Thus, the Gospel Reading is preceded by the Alleluia, a chant with repeated alleluia (translated "Praise God!") phrases sung by the choir to acknowledge God's goodness and glory.

A Sermon or Homily follows the Gospel Reading. Prior to Trent, when the sacraments became so much more a focus of the liturgy, Roman Catholic sermons were more than the brief homilies common today. The Sermon was a means of congregational instruction, encouragement, and inspiration for a life of godliness.

Response

The Sermon was followed by an Affirmation of Faith, both to underscore the conformity of the Sermon with the truths of the gospel and to bolster the congregation with the foundations of faith for the challenges of life in the days to come. This Affirmation of Faith was made by the choir singing the Creed (Nicene or Apostles') or, possibly, the *Gloria*. By such profession of faith the church renewed its commitment to make God's reign present in the lives of God's people and in the world.

Following the profession of faith but prior to the Liturgy of the Upper Room, the ancient church announced the Dismissal. This Dismissal was *not* the parallel of the ending rite of the Catholic liturgy today, when the priest ends the entire Mass by saying to all: "Go in the peace of Christ" or "The Mass is ended, go in peace." In the ancient church, catechumens (children and others learning the gospel) and the unbaptized were dismissed at the end of the Liturgy of the Word so that only communicants participated in the Liturgy of the Upper Room.

The Roman Liturgy of the Upper Room

The Liturgy of the Upper Room, also known as the Liturgy of the Faithful, was for those who could profess their faith (see chart 2.2). The practice of distinguishing the faithful in the ancient church reminds us that congregations have always been composed of three groups: communicants (believers eligible for Communion), catechumens (those learning the gospel), and seekers (those seeking to know whether the truths of the Christian faith are for them). These categories will help us think through important worship issues in later chapters.

Chart 2.2 Rome's Liturgy of the Upper Room Highlights

Chart 2.2 Rome's Liturgy of the Upper Room Highlights

Rome pre-1570
Liturgy of the Upper Room *[Always]*
Offertory
Preparation of Elements
Salutation
Sursum Corda
Sanctus
Benedictus
Eucharistic Prayer:
•Remembrance (*Anamnesis*)
•Offering Elements for Holy Use (*Oblation*)
•Words of Institution (*Verba*)
•Call for Holy Spirit to Change Elements (*Epiclesis*)
•Amen
Lord's Prayer
Kiss of Peace
Fraction
Agnus Dei
Communion
Collect
Dismissal Blessing

Offertory

In the ancient church, the Liturgy of the Upper Room was always present in a formal order of worship. It begins with an Offertory that included presentations of bread and wine that would be used for the Eucharist (this word derived from the Greek for "gratitude" or "thanksgiving" identifies in a Roman Catholic service what Protestants call Communion or the Lord's

Supper). During the Offertory, congregants may also present material and monetary gifts for the church's ministry and provision. Depending on the era, these offerings might be made by the men of the church first coming forward, followed by women doing the same. The bread and wine elements are then prepared by the priest, who places each in its proper location and container on the altar.

Consecration

The priest next invites the people to the Eucharist with a Salutation, "The Lord be with you," reminding them of the Lord's presence, and they respond, "And with your spirit," in preparation for prayer that will consecrate the elements for the celebration of the Lord's Supper.

In the history of Catholicism, the Prayer of Consecration (or Eucharistic Prayer) has taken various forms. For many centuries this prayer has been prefaced with the *Sursum Corda* (Latin for "lift your hearts"), a responsive Call to Worship initiated by the priest presiding over the Mass.

Salutation and *Sursum Corda*

Presider: The Lord be with you.
People: And with your spirit.
Presider: Lift up your hearts.
People: We lift them up unto the Lord.
Presider: Let us give thanks to the Lord our God.
People: It is meet and right so to do.

The *Sursum Corda* unites all present in assurance of God's presence, along with prayer and thanksgiving for his blessing.

The preface to the Prayer of Consecration continues with the *Sanctus* (Latin for "holy" from Isa. 6:3 and Matt. 21:9), an ancient hymn incorporating prophetic Scriptures that are sung or said to remind congregants of the holiness of God and the sacrament he provides:

Sanctus

Holy, holy, holy, Lord God of Hosts:
Heaven and earth are full of your glory.
Hosanna in the highest.
Blessed is he that cometh in the name of the Lord.
Hosanna in the highest.

The *Sanctus* is followed immediately by the *Benedictus* (Latin for "blessed"), which is usually sung. Its text is taken from Matthew's account of the triumphal entry and anticipates the presence of Christ in the Eucharist in accord with Catholic theology of transubstantiation.

Benedictus

Blessed is he who comes in the name of the Lord.
Hosanna in the highest.

Following these features of preface, the Eucharistic Prayer includes components that have varied through the centuries. However, because these components reflect scriptural language used in many traditions' celebration of Communion, they remain familiar. These elements include: a call to remembrance of Christ's work through the Lord's Supper (*Anamnesis*); offering the bread and wine for God's purposes (*Oblation*); repeating Christ's words of institution from Gospel or Pauline accounts (*Verba*); and, unique for the Catholic celebration, calling for the Holy Spirit to perform the work of transubstantiation, i.e., turning the bread and wine into the body and blood of Christ (*Epiclesis*).

Communion

As the "Amen" for the Prayer of Consecration is said, this change is presumed. The priest elevates the bread and wine to honor Christ, now considered present in the elements, and then leads the people in the Lord's Prayer (this order has varied through the centuries, but the major features are consistently present). This prayer prepares all to partake of the Lord's Supper by honoring the memory of Christ, requesting the power of his presence, asking his forgiveness, and reminding all of their need to unite in mutual forgiveness. Thus, the Lord's Prayer also prepares the people for "communion" with one another, and naturally precedes the Kiss of Peace where members express their love for one another in forms of greeting appropriate for their culture.

The priest then breaks the bread (a process known as "Fraction"), both to symbolize Christ's suffering for his people and to show that all are united in partaking of his body that will be distributed to them. During Fraction, the *Agnus Dei* (translated "Lamb of God" from John 1:29) is sung or recited. This is repeated when the consecrated bread (or bread and wine) is displayed to the people before being distributed to them.

Agnus Dei

Lamb of God, who takes away the sins of the world, have mercy upon us.

Lamb of God, who takes away the sins of the world, have mercy
upon us.
Lamb of God, who takes away the sins of the world, grant us peace.

Typically, the people then process to receive the elements of the Lord's
Supper from the priest. When all have been served in this Communion,
another Collect is sung and the final Dismissal is announced.

Experts will know there are many variations and exceptions to the
sketch of the Roman Catholic liturgy outlined above. My goal has not
been to provide an exhaustive history or detailed description of Catholic traditions, but to acquaint readers with the foundational elements of
an ancient liturgy still reflected in the modern worship services of most
churches in Western culture.

Evangelical Protestants will feel appropriate queasiness about aspects of
this liturgical structure that are designed to express distinctives of Roman
Catholic theology. However, these same evangelicals are likely also to be
surprised that beneath all the foreign "smells and bells" of Catholic ceremony are remarkably familiar echoes of their own worship practices.
Understanding these continuities, while at the same time being wise about
underlying distinctives, will be our own key to designing worship that fulfills gospel purposes for this and future generations. Learning how others
in our history have echoed and reacted to this traditional Catholic liturgy
to lead the church in gospel-healthy worship in their day is the subject
of the next chapters. The paths of our predecessors can lead us to their
discoveries, guide us from their errors, and direct us toward paths we must
forge into the future.

3

LUTHER'S STORY

As the next chapters' comparisons will demonstrate, the Protestant Reformers' orders of worship were a reactive reflection of the Roman Catholic liturgy. They react against liturgical practices that support theological positions no longer affirmed but that continue to emulate familiar practices that reflect gospel principles still appreciated. There are many parallels with earlier Catholicism but there were also significant differences in the orders of worship that framed the gospel story the Reformers wanted to tell. They wanted their liturgies both to follow New Testament worship patterns and to reinforce the message of the gospel as it culminated in Christ's work of grace.

Luther's Liturgy of the Word

Luther did not want his worship to be interpreted as a propitiatory sacrifice offered to God by a priest on behalf of the people. Christ had been sacrificed once for all (Heb. 9:12, 24–28). Because the work of salvation was done, it was now only to be received and celebrated by faith. Jesus was not transubstantiated in the elements of the Mass to be sacrificed again. Instead of the service requiring a priest to offer Christ again in sacrifice, Luther understood worship as God's gift to the people. Through the liturgy, God's people could praise him for grace already completed in Christ's finished work of salvation. This concept of the liturgy being God's provision for the people to respond to grace, rather than for the priest to obtain their forgiveness, radically changed the way key worship elements were practiced. Still, their order continued to reflect the basic gospel story of older liturgies (see chart 3.1).

People as Priests

Luther wanted the worship service to be a participatory experience, in keeping with his understanding of church being a community of faithful people praising God for his salvation.[1] Two key changes resulted that are not obvious from only observing the order of the worship elements. First, the music was no longer the exclusive domain of those in sacred orders.[2] The choir could assist the congregation, but the congregation was to sing. Music was to be more than a decorative accompaniment to the Latin phrases of the Mass; music was an expression of the praise of the people. And for their praise to be sincere, it had to be understood. This meant that the hymns were in the language of the people, not in ecclesiastical Latin.

The commitment to worship in the vernacular of the people led to the second major change in liturgical practice. Not only were there new hymns in the language of the people, but Luther also expected the worship service to be in their vernacular. Educated clergy and laity could continue to worship in Latin, but Luther wanted everyone else to be able to learn God's ways and offer praise in their own tongue. Commitment to the "priesthood of believers" led not only to translation of the Bible into German but also to significant transitions in liturgical practice.

Adoration

Right from the beginning, the Lutheran service reflects the German monk's distinctive theology. The service begins not with a choir chant, but with a congregational Entrance Hymn of praise. The people are involved in or sing prior to the Introit (a Scripture spoken or sung that sets the theme of the service). Their praise counts just as much as the professional clergy's.

Confession and Assurance

The initial progression of the service remains familiar. The people recite the *Kyrie*, asking for mercy from the God they have just praised. The

1. Nicholas Wolterstorff, "The Reformed Liturgy," in *Major Themes in the Reformed Tradition*, ed. Donald K. McKim (Grand Rapids: Eerdmans, 1992), 280.
2. Lawrence Roff, *Let Us Sing* (Philadelphia: Great Commission Publications, 1991), 43.

Chart 3.1 Luther's Liturgy of the Word Highlights

Rome pre-1570	Luther ca. 1526
Liturgy of the Word	*Liturgy of the Word*
Choral Introit	Entrance Hymn
	Introit
Kyrie ("Lord have mercy")	*Kyrie*
Gloria	*Gloria*
Salutation ("The Lord be with you . . .")	Salutation
Collect(s)	Collect
Old Testament Reading	
Antiphonal Chant	
Epistle Reading	Epistle Reading
Gradual (a psalm sung)	Gradual
Alleluia	
Gospel Reading	Gospel Reading
	Apostles' Creed
	Sermon Hymn
Sermon	Sermon
Nicene Creed Sung (or *Gloria*)	Post-Sermon Hymn
Dismissal of Non-communicants	Exhortation

people are greeted and respond in a Salutation, and then are united in a Collect prayer.

The first notable difference in the order of worship is not signaled by an added innovation, but by the absence of a standard component. Luther omits the Old Testament Reading from his German Mass. The emphasis on the New Testament message affects what Luther wants regularized in his service. Psalms of praise still have a place in the liturgy (note the Gradual).

But the law's loud thunder that has been quenched by Calvary's melodies is not allowed to rumble again. The Lutheran order marches toward the gospel, plants its flag there, and wants no other banner to fly.

By Luther's design, the Old Testament Reading of the ancient liturgy loses its long-held position. Epistle Readings are allowed because the apostles' letters were reflections on the gospel. But Luther does not want the Old Testament with its emphasis on law and sacrifice to distract congregants from the freedoms they have in Christ, or to misdirect them back toward Roman ceremonies. The service, the readings, and the Sermon are about the gospel, and the Gospel Reading (from one of the four New Testament Gospels) is the culmination of that portion of the Lutheran service traditionally known as the Preparation for the Word (see chapter 1).

Instruction

Before the Sermon, the people help in the final preparation for the Word that will be preached by singing a Sermon Hymn. The Lutheran Sermon always concentrates on the gospel, the provision of Christ to save and equip his people. After the Sermon, the people sing again. They are presumed to be co-laborers in the gospel, not merely those who are passively represented by a priest. So, they respond in affirmation to the instruction from the Word with a Post-Sermon Hymn. For Luther, the church is God's "mouth house," and everyone inside participates in the proclamation of the gospel.

Response

The minister next charges the congregation to live in accord with the Word preached by an Exhortation. Less emphasis is placed on a Dismissal from the Liturgy of the Word because people are presumed to have gathered out of heart conviction rather than under the compulsion of receiving needed grace infused by a sacrament administered in words they cannot understand.

Luther's Liturgy of the Upper Room

We should remember that Luther initially wanted to reform the Roman Catholic Church, not to depart from it. The resolve to separate came later and with much regret. He did not believe that all he had learned in Catholicism was without value. There were basic patterns in the ancient liturgy he strove to maintain because he believed they were consistent with the gospel he wanted to communicate. Thus, while Luther rejected transubstantiation and its theology of infused grace, he still believed the sacrament of the

Lord's Supper was a means of grace whereby Christ was communicated to his people "in, with and under" the elements of Communion. Luther's treasuring of this means of grace was evident in his instruction to have it *always* celebrated in his weekly liturgy.

The Lutheran Communion service reflects the Catholic Mass, while making key distinctions (see chart 3.2 on page 40). Avoiding the sense of a "magical" order needed for grace, Luther offered various liturgical options for observing the Lord's Supper (only one of which is reflected below). These options were similar in basic outline but reflected Luther's appreciation for practices both old and new that would reflect the gospel story he wanted to tell.

Communion

The first distinguishing feature of Luther's Communion liturgy is the substitution of a Prayer for the Church in place of the Offertory that began the Roman Liturgy of the Upper Room.[3] The displacement of the Offertory prevented any miscommunication of the gospel message Luther wanted to tell. He had fought hard against indulgences. Now to encourage persons to bring material gifts to the altar just before they receive a sacrament would come dangerously close to echoing past abuses.[4] Luther would not allow the opportunity for misperception, and substituted prayer for the church's ministry in the place of material provision for it.

A Preparation Hymn followed the prayer. This too was a new practice that expressed gospel principles. Not only did the hymn involve people in worship, but their participation in this stage of the liturgy signaled their rediscovered access to God in the portion of the service considered most "priestly." By their singing, the people were celebrating not only their communion with Christ, but also the priesthood of believers of which they were now contributing members. This contribution was signaled also during the distribution of the elements, when additional hymns were corporately sung.

Consecration

Preparation continued with the "ordinary" features of the Mass's Eucharistic Prayer ceremony. However, these features were adjusted to reflect biblical thought and to prevent repetition of previous misconceptions. The call for the Holy Spirit's work (*Epiclesis*) was moved from the climactic

---

3. Howard L. Rice and James C. Huffstutler, *Reformed Worship* (Louisville: Geneva, 2001), 4.

4. Hughes Oliphant Old, *Leading in Prayer: A Workbook for Worship* (Grand Rapids: Eerdmans, 1995), 363.

Chart 3.2 Luther's Liturgy of the Upper Room Highlights

Rome pre-1570	Luther ca. 1526
Liturgy of the Upper Room [Always]	*Liturgy of the Upper Room [Always]*
Offertory	
	Prayer for the Church
Preparation of Elements	Preparation Hymn
Salutation	
Sursum Corda	*Sursum Corda*
Sanctus	*Sanctus*
Benedictus	
Eucharistic Prayer:	Preparation:
•Remembrance (*Anamnesis*)	•Call for Holy Spirit (*Epiclesis*)
	•Consecration of Elements
•Offering Elements for Holy Use (*Oblation*)	•Remembrance (*Anamnesis*)
•Words of Institution (*Verba*)	•Words of Institution (*Verba*)
•Call for Holy Spirit to Change Elements (*Epiclesis*)	
•Amen	
Lord's Prayer	Lord's Prayer
Kiss of Peace	
Fraction	
Agnus Dei	*Agnus Dei*
Communion	Communion (with psalms sung)
Collect	Collect
	Thanksgiving
Dismissal Blessing	Aaronic Blessing
	Closing Hymn

ending of the Roman Prayer of Consecration to the beginning of the sacrament's Preparation.[5] Luther was happy to call on the Spirit but did not want this to be misperceived as causing the transformation of the bread and wine into Christ's body and blood (i.e., transubstantiation). So, he

5. Ibid., 28.

put the *Epiclesis* first and, in so doing, called on the Holy Spirit to bless the entirety of the sacrament rather than to trigger its mysteries.

The Lord's Prayer and *Agnus Dei* remained in honored and familiar placement in Luther's service. After all, the Lord's Supper was appropriately celebrated with the Lord's Prayer and recognition of the work of the Lamb. Both bind participants to each other and to the Lord in appropriate assertions of congregational confession, mutual forgiveness, and need of Christ's grace. Symbolic of the mutual ministry that each had to one another in this priesthood of believers, hymns were sung during Communion as the bread and wine were distributed and consumed.

Celebration

Less apparent to most modern Protestants was Luther's use of familiar components of the Catholic liturgy in special ways. The celebration of the Lord's Supper truly became celebrative after the distribution and consumption of the bread and wine. A time of Thanksgiving followed the participants' communion with each other and the Lord. The thanksgiving chord is struck with another Collect, the *Nunc Dimittis* (from Simeon's song in Luke 2:21–35, typically saved for special occasions in the earlier Catholic tradition—see below), and a final Salutation ("The Lord be with you . . ."), reminding everyone of the Lord's continuing presence for the trials of the week ahead.

Nunc Dimittis

Now dismiss your servant, O Lord, in peace, according to your word: For mine own eyes hath seen your salvation, which you hast prepared in the sight of all the peoples, a light to reveal you to the nations and the glory of your people Israel.

Culminating these themes of blessing is the pronouncement of the Aaronic Benediction (from Num. 6:22–27, see below), so that no one could leave without the assurance that the God who had just provided his holy Word and sacrament was also granting his peace. To make sure that no minister could be interpreted as having the last word of priestly intercession or absolution, the *people* conclude the Lutheran liturgy with a Closing Hymn.

Aaronic Benediction

May the Lord bless you and keep you; may He make His face to shine on you and be gracious to you; may He lift up His countenance on you and give you peace.

4

CALVIN'S STORY

We can readily trace the lineage of key aspects of John Calvin's liturgy to Luther. While pastoring French Huguenot refugees in Strasbourg from 1538 to 1541, Calvin became acquainted with the liturgy of Martin Bucer, who was pastor of a large German congregation. Bucer had studied Luther, adopting much of the earlier Reformer's theology and worship perspectives.

Calvin was profoundly affected by the simple, biblical principles that guided Bucer. The French Reformer did not adopt all of Bucer's practices, but the German Reformer's imprint is clear (i.e., emphasis on the Sermon, reduction of ceremony, congregational involvement, and psalm singing without instruments). Also obvious is the further influence of Calvin on other French refugees, especially those who would join him later in Geneva before they dispersed across Europe. In addition, Calvin's liturgy became a model for a Scottish refugee named John Knox, who came to Geneva before adopting a similar worship pattern that would be taken up by Protestants in Scotland, across the British Isles, and into the Americas.[1]

Guiding Principles

Based on their study of Acts 2:42, Bucer and Calvin identified four elements essential for worship that should continue according to their understanding

---

1. Terry L. Johnson, ed., *Leading in Worship* (Oak Ridge, TN: Covenant Foundation, 1996), 121–30.

of apostolic patterns in the New Testament: the Word, prayer, the meal, and alms.[2] The two Reformers fleshed out these elements in the services of their respective German- and French-speaking congregations. Shortly before leaving Strasbourg and returning to Geneva, Calvin wrote a treatise on the Lord's Supper, and added more thoughts on worship in *The Form of Ecclesiastical Prayers and Songs* in 1542 and the *Geneva Catechism* in 1545.

Understanding

Before enumerating the particulars in Calvin's order, a few global observations about it are important. First, the service is in French. Calvin joined his fellow Reformers in wanting God's people to *understand* God's Word and worship. Faith is not merely slavish identification with a corporate church to avoid the horrors of hell; faith is real only through the devotion of one's heart to God. Such devotion is impossible without being able personally to understand God's will or to honor his name. Commitment to worship in the vernacular led the French Reformer—as it had Reformers before him—to Bible translation, prayer, and worship in the language of the people.

Participation

Second, commitment to the priesthood of believers is evident not only in the language Calvin used to involve the laity, but also in his encouragement of their participation in the worship service. The people sing in Calvin's liturgy. And, as we will see, Calvin fought for their right to do so. Additionally, the people have special access to the privileges of their faith. Before he faced undesired strictures at Geneva, Calvin stood in front of the altar—among the people of Strasbourg—for all of the service prior to the reading and proclamation of the Word. During his ministry in Geneva, Calvin's famous chair—common in size and style—was not used simply to carry him to the pulpit when he was feeble and old. The chair sat beneath the pulpit—among the people and on their level, as a statement of the preacher's identification with the congregation prior to his acting as God's representative in leading worship.

Singing was not the only participation of the people Calvin encouraged. His psalters included other written texts used in the worship service.[3]

2. Howard L. Rice and James C. Huffstutler, *Reformed Worship* (Louisville: Geneva, 2001), 3.

3. Michael A. Farley, "Reforming Reformed Worship: Theological Method and Liturgical Catholicity in American Presbyterianism, 1850–2005" (PhD diss., St. Louis University, 2007), 218.

People were encouraged to read along, grow familiar with the progress of the service, and participate in various portions of the liturgy. Responses in these "service books" were both spoken and sung as the people participated with the pastor in expressing metrical psalms, the Apostles' Creed, and other new or ancient readings.

Regulation

A third global observation is that Calvin believed devotion to God needed to be on God's terms. True devotion could not be found in human invention or ceremony—these were only subtle forms of idolatry—whereby humankind asserted its pride in its own provision. God establishes the way that he is to be worshiped in his Word, and this Regulative Principle of Christian worship meant that Calvin studied the Scriptures to find his liturgy.[4] Calvin believed that this study would not only prescribe what should be done in worship, but would free the church from "the basic principles of the world" (Col. 2:20–23) and "rules taught by men" (Isa. 29:13; Matt. 15:8–9).[5] Significant for our purposes is noting that such study yielded a liturgy that, though it differed in significant ways from earlier liturgies, still had contours that are quite recognizable. Formative gospel principles are embedded in all.

Calvin's Liturgy of the Word

As noted previously, Calvin divides his order of worship (later known as the Geneva Liturgy) into the standard two divisions: the Liturgy of the Word (see chart 4.1) and the Liturgy of the Upper Room (see chart 4.2 on page 52).

Adoration

The Liturgy of the Word starts not with a ceremonial Introit, but with a Scripture Sentence declaring the goodness and glory of God.[6] Though that simple sentence may vary, Calvin's standard is, "Our help is in the name of the Lord, the Maker of heaven and earth" (see Pss. 121:2; 124:8). With this simple sentence Calvin varies from Bucer (who began with a Confession of Sin), but echoes the ancient pattern of starting the gospel

---

4. R. J. Gore Jr., *Covenantal Worship: Reconsidering the Puritan Regulative Principle* (Phillipsburg, NJ: Presbyterian and Reformed, 2002), 89; Greg Perry, "Reforming Worship," *Reformed Theological Review* 61, no. 1 (April 2002): 34.

5. Ibid., 35.

6. Johnson, *Leading in Worship*, 122.

Chart 4.1 Calvin's Liturgy of the Word Highlights

Rome pre-1570	Luther ca. 1526	Calvin ca. 1542
Liturgy of the Word	*Liturgy of the Word*	*Liturgy of the Word*
Choral Introit	Entrance Hymn Introit	Scripture Sentence (e.g., Ps. 121:2)
Kyrie ("Lord have mercy")	*Kyrie*	Confession of Sin (with pardon at Strasbourg)
Gloria	*Gloria*	Psalm Sung
Salutation ("The Lord be with you . . .")	Salutation	
Collect(s)	Collect	
Old Testament Reading Antiphonal Chant		Ten Commandments (sung with *Kyries* at Strasbourg)
Epistle Reading	Epistle Reading	
Gradual (a psalm sung)	Gradual	
Alleluia		
		Prayer for Illumina- tion (with Lord's Prayer)
Gospel Reading	Gospel Reading Apostles' Creed Sermon Hymn	Scripture Reading
Sermon	Sermon	Sermon
Nicene Creed Sung (or *Gloria*)	Post-Sermon Hymn	
Dismissal of Non-communicants	Exhortation	

story of the liturgy with an assertion of the nature of God that both awes and humbles the worshiper.[7] Calvin's opening sentence does not match

7. K. Deddens, "A Missing Link in Reformed Liturgy," *Clarion* 37, nos. 15–19 (1998): 3, http://www.spindleworks.com/library/deddens/missing.htm.

the ceremony of the Roman Catholic Introit, but accomplishes the same purpose with scriptural simplicity.

Confession and Assurance

The Geneva Liturgy then moves directly into a Confession of Sin.[8] Again, the simplicity of Calvin's order is apparent, but so also is the sincerity of expression. A Confession of Sin from Calvin's days in Strasbourg demonstrates this genuineness:

Confession of Sin

Almighty, eternal God and Father, we confess and acknowledge that we, alas, were conceived and born in sin, and are therefore inclined to all evil and slow to all good; that we transgress thy holy commandments without ceasing, and ever more corrupt ourselves. But we are sorry for the same, and beseech Thy grace and help. Wherefore have mercy upon us, most gracious and merciful God and Father, through Thy Son our Lord Jesus Christ. Grant to us and increase in us Thy Holy Spirit, that we may recognize our sin and unrighteousness from the bottom of our hearts, attain true repentance and sorrow for them, die to them wholly, and please thee entirely by a new godly life. Amen.

Aware that the early placement of a Confession of Sin in his service may be a bit jarring to ordinary sensibilities as well as familiar traditions, Calvin explains this early placement in his *Institutes of the Christian Religion*:

For since in every sacred assembly we stand before the sight of God and the angels, what other beginning of our action will there be than the recognition of our own unworthiness? But that, you say, is done through every prayer; for whenever we pray for pardon, we confess our sin. Granted. But if you consider how great is our complacency, our drowsiness, or our sluggishness, you will agree with me that it would be a salutary regulation if the Christian people were to practice humbling themselves through some public rite of confession. For even though the ceremony that the Lord laid down for the Israelites was a part of the tutelage of the law, still the reality underlying it in some manner pertains also to us. And indeed, we see this custom observed with good result in well-regulated churches: that every Lord's Day the minister frames the formula of confession in his own and the people's name, and by it he accuses all of wickedness and implores pardon from the Lord. In short, with this key a gate to prayer is opened both to individuals in private and to all in public. (3.4.1)

---

8. D. G. Hart, "It May Be Refreshing, but Is It Reformed?" Review of *Worship in Spirit and Truth*, by John M. Frame, *Calvin Theological Journal* 32 (1997): 407.

Calvin goes on to defend the early placement of the Confession of Sin with both biblical and historical precedent, citing Nehemiah and Chrysostom. The arguments must have been convincing because the early Confession of Sin became standard and remains an identifying characteristic of the Geneva Liturgy when practiced today. (Note: the liturgy does not precisely "begin" with the Confession of Sin because it is preceded by the Scripture Sentence acknowledging God's help and power.)

Other arguments of Calvin were not as convincing. For instance, he wanted to follow the Confession of Sin with Words of Comfort, or an Assurance of Pardon and Absolution. For the church and city leaders at Geneva, who had endured the sometimes-violent tides of Catholic and Protestant power struggles, this was too much. Any hint of absolution was a reminder of priestly rule, a concession that could ignite a fickle populace into yet another church revolt. Calvin had used beautiful words of comfort and pardon following the Confession in his Strasbourg liturgy:

Assurance of Pardon

Let each of you confess that he is really a sinner who has to humble himself before God. He must believe that the heavenly Father will be gracious to him in Jesus Christ. To all who have repentance and who seek Jesus Christ for their salvation, I pronounce forgiveness in the name of the Father, the Son, and the Holy Spirit, Amen.

The beauty of these words did *not* convince the Genevan officials, nor did Calvin's argument that the Roman church did not possess sole right to comfort God's people with the assurance of his grace. Calvin never got his "Words of Pardon" inserted into the Geneva Liturgy. However, his opinions were well known (see *Institutes* 4.1.20–22), and those he trained put such words of assurance in their liturgies as they dispersed across Europe and into the Americas.

Calvin also did not get his preference regarding the frequency of Communion,[9] as he had practiced it in Strasbourg. When Calvin returned to Geneva, he inherited William Farel's liturgy. Farel's valiant efforts to bring the Reformation to Geneva lacked some of the refinement Calvin would bring. Farel's liturgy was more like Zwingli's, reacting to Catholicism by both the infrequency of Communion and the absence of singing.[10] Anti-Catholic sentiment remained so strong in Geneva that Calvin was never able to have the weekly (or even the monthly) Communion that he

---

9. John Calvin, *Institutes of the Christian Religion*, ed. John T. McNeill, trans. Ford Lewis Battles, Library of Christian Classics (Philadelphia: Westminster, 1960), 4.17.46.

10. Deddens, "Missing Link," 6.

preferred.[11] He spoke publicly about the infrequent celebration of the Lord's Supper, saying, "Our practice is abnormal," but officials continued to insist on the quarterly schedule.[12]

Thanksgiving and Response

Calvin did get his way regarding the inclusion of singing. Farel's liturgy had no congregational singing, but Bucer's influence on Calvin convinced the French Reformer that the people needed to participate in the service in this way. Calvin was initially unconvinced that singing was a biblical element of New Testament worship, but ultimately reasoned that song could be a form of prayer.[13] And, he knew that prayer was included in New Testament worship![14] Calvin's Regulative Principle also led him to the conclusion that songs in formal worship should be the Words of God, and thus he published psalters and largely limited the congregation to psalm singing.

In his Geneva Liturgy, Calvin regularly followed the Confession of Sin with a rhymed and sung Psalm, but also allowed the *Gloria* (reclaimed from Catholic uses because it was based on words of Scripture, as was the *Nunc Dimittis* used on Communion Sundays). The hymn "I Greet Thee, Who My Sure Redeemer Art" has origins in Calvin's time, although it is unlikely to have been penned by him or used in his Geneva Liturgy. The musicality of Calvin's psalter hymns is often a strain for modern tastes, but Calvin is wrongly typed as too austere in his approach to music. To satisfy critics and his own scruples, he wrote that music in the church should possess "gravity and majesty,"[15] but for a people unaccustomed to congregational music in worship, these so-called "Geneva jigs" were fresh air.[16]

More refreshing was the message Calvin could communicate in the music. While he was not able to include a formal Assurance of Pardon in the liturgy, the singing of a rhymed Psalm after the Confession of Sin gave the minister an opportunity to choose a Scripture with the message of God's grace. This lesson was not missed by John Knox, whose own book of liturgical advice was published as he was pastoring an English

11. John W. de Gruchy, "Aesthetic Creativity, Eucharistic Celebration and Liturgical Renewal: With Special Reference to the Reformed Tradition" (paper for the Buvton Conference, Stellenbosch, South Africa, September 1, 2003), 5–6.

12. Deddens, "Missing Link," 6.

13. Rice and Huffstutler, *Reformed Worship*, 3.

14. Charles Garside Jr., *The Origins of Calvin's Theology of Music*, Transactions of the American Philosophical Society 69, pt. 4 (Philadelphia: American Philosophical Society, 1979), 8–9, 15, 17.

15. Ibid., 18.

16. Lawrence Roff, *Let Us Sing* (Philadelphia: Great Commission Publications, 1991), 60.

congregation in Geneva. Knox followed Calvin's liturgy in advising that the English service progress with Confession of Sin, a Prayer for Forgiveness, and the singing of a rhymed Psalm. Further, Knox advised that the psalm deal with the subject of God's forgiveness. Knox's intention to echo Calvin's desires is indicated in the extended title of the Scot's worship handbook: *The Forme of Prayers and Administration of the Sacraments, etc., used in the Englishe Congregation at Geneva; and approved by the famous and godly learned man, John Calvin.* Calvin clearly communicated the need for an Assurance of Pardon, even if he could not list it as a formal element of his liturgy.

What follows in the Geneva Liturgy appears very simple and sparse compared with its predecessors. There is no complex sequence of Old Testament, Psalms, Epistle, and Gospel readings with interspersed chants, creedal recitations, and ceremonial rituals. Instead, Calvin includes only a reading of the Ten Commandments, Prayer for Illumination, and Lord's Prayer prior to his ascending the pulpit for the Scripture reading and Sermon.[17] Again, Calvin seeks to pare down to scriptural essentials, but he communicates much by doing so.

The reading of the Ten Commandments is more than a reminder of the requirements of the law, and more than a form of Old Testament Reading. While he was in Strasbourg, Calvin followed the Confession of Sin and Assurance of Pardon with the singing of the Decalogue by the congregation. Calvin wrote the rhymed version himself. However, he did not want the congregations merely to repeat the commands. His version began with the scriptural introduction to the Ten Commandments, "I am the LORD your God, who brought you out of Egypt, out of the land of slavery" (Exod. 20:2). The words are a reminder of the faithfulness of God to his covenant and to his people. True obedience for them and for us is a response to God's grace, not an attempt to earn it.

By singing God's law in the context of his faithfulness, the congregation is reminded that their own holiness is a response to the God who has already heard their confession and yet remains faithful to his covenant. The placement of the Decalogue after the Confession of Sin (and in the place of the *Gloria* of the Catholic tradition) indicates that Calvin understood our obedience to be a response of thanksgiving for grace, not a means to gain it.[18] The *Gloria* followed the *Kyrie* ("Lord have mercy") and echoed the angels' praise for God's mercy evident in the provision of his Son.

Underscoring the message that holiness is believers' response to mercy was the way Calvin interspersed the singing of the *Kyrie* with the singing

17. Deddens, "Missing Link," 6.
18. Ibid., 9.

of the Decalogue. In Strasbourg Calvin had the people sing the first table of the law with the *Kyrie* repeated after the prologue and each command. Then, Calvin paused for prayer. Next, the congregation sang the second table of the law, and again the *Kyrie* was included after each command and a conclusion.[19] Twelve times the people sang, "Lord have mercy." The words were not simply a prayer for mercy, but a petition for help from the God who had already promised mercy and pardon.

Calvin's zeal for the theology of grace in his liturgy was rightly motivated, but perhaps the arduousness of the multiple repetitions of the *Kyrie*—together with the need to be sensitive to the previously music-less liturgy of Farel—led Calvin to insist only on a read version of the Ten Commandments in Geneva.[20] Even the read version, however, was a notable substitution for the Old Testament readings of the Roman liturgy and a significant departure from the law-absent liturgy of Luther.

Instruction

Calvin's view of the unity of Scripture and the progressive nature of the covenant made the scriptural divisions of the Catholic liturgy inappropriate, and the law-gospel uneasiness of the Lutheran liturgy irrelevant. For Calvin, the whole of Scripture is the gospel. All needs to be understood in its christocentric context. The Bible does not need to be chopped into some portions considered merely preliminary with other portions still relevant. All is God's Word. For this reason the Scripture Reading (or Readings) prior to the Sermon may be from any portion of the Bible. Sermons are preached from any and all parts of Scripture.

Since the Sermon is God's Word preached, it demands reverence from God's people and God's aid for their understanding. Thus, prior to the Scripture reading, the Geneva Liturgy includes a Prayer for Illumination that typically folds into the Lord's Prayer. The Prayer for Illumination (a contribution to the historic liturgy originated by Calvin and other Reformers) petitions the Holy Spirit to equip preachers to understand and proclaim the Word inspired by him; the Lord's Prayer is uttered so that the Spirit will prepare the hearts of listeners to receive his Word.[21] The necessity of the Spirit's work was underscored by the continuing miracle that Calvin believed occurs with all faithful preaching:

19. Ibid., 5.
20. Ibid., 6.
21. Nicholas Wolterstorff, "The Reformed Liturgy," in *Major Themes in the Reformed Tradition*, ed. Donald K. McKim (Grand Rapids: Eerdmans, 1992), 290.

Among the many excellent gifts with which God has adorned the human race, it is a singular privilege that he deigns to consecrate to himself the mouths and tongues of men in order that his voice may resound in them. (*Institutes* 4.1.5)

"When the Bible speaks, God speaks," Augustine wrote. Calvin additionally believed that when the Word of God is faithfully preached, Jesus still speaks in his church by his Spirit in the hearts of his people. This is blessed work that requires the Spirit's presence and motivates the preacher's prayer.

Calvin's understanding of Christ speaking through his Word also explains why the Geneva Liturgy makes the reading and preaching of the Word the apex of the service. The unadorned liturgy and ceremony point without distraction to Christ's ministry in the pulpit. Others would criticize the French Reformer's services as being only "four white walls and a sermon," but Calvin would not necessarily consider this a fault. By his design, the hearts of the people are prepared in praise, confession, and pardon to receive the ministry of their Savior, but the preparation is for the primacy of the Word where Christ alone provides the glory of the worship service.

Calvin's Liturgy of the Upper Room

As indicated above, Calvin yielded to anti-Catholic pressure to remove an Assurance of Pardon from his Liturgy of the Word and to refrain from weekly observance of the Liturgy of the Upper Room.[22] He believed both these excisions were mistakes and later regretted that he had not been more insistent on their inclusion in the Geneva Liturgy (see *Institutes* 4.17.44–46).[23] The infrequency of the Lord's Supper, however, did not signal that Calvin would give any less care to the gospel messages he wanted to share in the Communion observance. Chart 4.2 (see page 52) maps the structure of his Communion communication.

Offering and Intercession

As indicated earlier, Calvin and Bucer believed that almsgiving is an essential component of New Testament worship. On the quarterly Sundays that the Lord's Supper was observed in the Geneva Liturgy, a collection

22. Gore, *Covenantal Worship*, 73.
23. Wolterstorff, "Reformed Liturgy," 293–94.

Chart 4.2 Calvin's Liturgy of the Upper Room Highlights

Rome pre-1570	Luther ca. 1526	Calvin ca. 1542
Liturgy of the *Upper Room* *[Always]*	*Liturgy of the* *Upper Room* *[Always]*	*Liturgy of the* *Upper Room* *[Quarterly]*
Offertory		Collection of Alms
	Prayer for the Church	Intercessions
		Lord's Prayer
Preparation of Elements	Preparation Hymn	Apostles' Creed (sung as elements prepared)
Salutation		
Sursum Corda	*Sursum Corda*	
Sanctus	*Sanctus*	
Benedictus		
Eucharistic Prayer:	Preparation:	
•Remembrance (*Anamnesis*)	•Call for Holy Spirit (*Epiclesis*)	
•Offering Elements for Holy Use (*Oblation*)	•Consecration of Elements	
	•Remembrance (*Anamnesis*)	
•Words of Institution (*Verba*)	•Words of Institution (*Verba*)	Words of Institution
•Call for Holy Spirit to Change Elements (*Epiclesis*)		Exhortation
•Amen		
Lord's Prayer	Lord's Prayer	Consecration Prayer
Kiss of Peace		
Fraction		Fraction
Agnus Dei	*Agnus Dei*	
Communion	Communion (with psalms sung)	Communion (with Scriptures read)
Collect	Collect	Psalm Sung
	Thanksgiving	Thanksgiving Prayer
Dismissal Blessing	Aaronic Blessing	Aaronic Blessing
	Closing Hymn	

served as the preface to Communion. We should not infer from this practice that Calvin was unsympathetic to Luther's concerns about an Offertory. The French Reformer also knew that having offerings at the beginning of the table service could easily stimulate indulgence-inspired perceptions about the need to "pay off" God before "gaining" his grace.

Calvin avoids such misperceptions by casting the Collection in terms of "almsgiving" rather than an Offertory. Alms are directed toward the care of the needy (an apt concern to express prior to the "communion" of mutual care indicated by the Lord's Supper), whereas an Offertory is more readily perceived as provision for the church (possibly implying the "payoff" Luther and Calvin wished to deny).

Almsgiving demonstrates that the Lord's Supper has both horizontal (believer-to-believer) and vertical (believer-to-Redeemer) dimensions in Calvin's theology. The horizontal dimension of the Lord's Supper is also reflected in Calvin's reminder that the sacrament is a shared meal. New Testament believers were to share nourishment and serve one another in their observance of Christ's ordinance (see 1 Cor. 11:33). So the church's meal (as well as baptisms) and Intercessions of prayer come after the Sermon. In this way congregational members can care for one another in light of the grace received from instruction in God's Word. The community also bound itself together in a mutual profession of its beliefs and dependence on God by singing together the Apostles' Creed as Calvin brought the bread and wine to the table.[24]

Consecration and Communion

The vertical aspect of the sacrament is its promotion of the "mystical union" of the believer with the risen Christ. The Geneva Liturgy removes all ritual that would imply a reappearing or material presence of Christ in the elements. By prayer and scriptural Words of Institution the elements are set aside for holy use. Calvin perceives it as important to have Scripture precede the Prayer of Consecration, so Christ's command rather than human prayer sets apart the elements.[25] They are made useful *not* by being transubstantiated into Christ (i.e., Catholicism) or by communicating his real presence into the body of the believer (i.e., Lutheranism), nor is the Lord's Supper a simple memorial service where believers are merely reminded what Jesus did (i.e., Zwinglianism). Calvin understands the New Testament to teach that the elements of Communion are rightly appropriated by faith into a spiritual meal (John 6:63) whereby the believer is lifted

24. Rice and Huffstutler, *Reformed Worship*, 35.
25. Ibid.

to union with Christ. Christ is not re-embodied on earth (1 Cor. 11:25–26), but the believer is lifted to a spiritual communion with the Savior that is the nourishment and strength of grace for living in loving obedience.

In order for this spiritual nourishment to occur, the believer needs to come in faithful dependence on Christ's grace. For the sacrament truly to be a means of grace one must not merely participate in the ceremony; rather, one must sincerely acknowledge and faithfully receive what the sacraments signify. The minister promotes this devotion in an Exhortation that urges confession of sin, reconciliation with neighbor, reliance on grace—and a warning not to partake if these are not genuine (a form of Fencing the table that will be formalized in later Puritan liturgies).[26]

The spiritual progeny of Calvin in Reformed churches across Europe would later formalize the Exhortation, not only promising grace for the penitent but also warning that sinners were "bound" (this was called the Formula of Retention) to sins unconfessed.[27] Such warning can be misunderstood as making God's forgiveness conditional upon the adequacy of our repentance rather than upon faith in the adequacy of his provision. Still, such words can stimulate profound changes in any church where Christians have been tempted to think of their faith only in personal terms ("it's all about me"). The Exhortation may be a needed reminder of the radical call to reconciliation with neighbor ("it's about us too") implicit in communion with the body of Christ.

The remaining aspects of the Geneva Liturgy are familiar. Noteworthy is how little they vary from the previous forms from which Calvin had learned, *except* in their spare expression. There is little adornment, ritual, or ceremony. Calvin's goal was to represent gospel truths in a manner consistent with New Testament principles and practice. He did not want to add to Scripture; he wanted to reflect it. However, in reflecting the gospel, the influential Frenchman obviously found significant aspects of previous liturgies not only instructive but eminently applicable.

Later generations of Reformed believers would find Calvin's unadorned services both attractive and severe.[28] Some responded by adding rules he did not use; others found his principles attractive but his applications too restrictive; and still others made him a rule he would never have approved. Those most faithful to his principles are the ones who seek to make the gospel most plain for their time, as he did in his.

---

26. Ibid., 33.
27. Deddens, "Missing Link," 7–9.
28. Rice and Huffstutler, *Reformed Worship*, 4.

5

WESTMINSTER'S STORY

The Westminster Assembly is a high-water mark of thought and practice for Protestant worship. The major renewal efforts of the Reformation had been in process for over a hundred years before the assembly convened. The thought and practice of Reformed worship had flourished, diversified, and matured. God had used time and opposition to blow away the chaff of novelty and craziness and to deepen biblically rooted ideas so that they could now flower.

A Great Confluence

Those who gathered at Westminster Abbey to hammer out the Westminster Confession of Faith, Larger and Shorter Catechisms, and Directory for Publicke Worship could glean the best from various traditions: Catholic, Anglican, Lutheran, Continental Reformed, Puritan, and Presbyterian—as well as old and new philosophical traditions. The divines had a long list of creeds and doctrinal summaries from which to draw: those of Greek, Latin, and Continental Reformed origins, as well as theological directories and confessions of English heritage that had evolved from the Thirty-Nine Articles and Lambeth Articles of Anglicanism, the Scots Confession of John Knox and others, and—most influential—the Irish Articles of James Ussher (1615).

Different kinds of churchmen were present: Episcopalian (Anglican), Independent, Erastian, and Presbyterian—with Presbyterians being the most numerous by far. Representatives were united in basic Calvinistic theology, but held differing perspectives on matters of church government and worship. England, Wales, and Scotland were represented in the discussion, though the Scots could not vote. The Irish luminary Ussher was chosen as a representative but for political reasons was forbidden to participate by the English king.

Overflowing Blessings

The consequence of the confluence of all these streams of influence on the Westminster Assembly's Directory for Publicke Worship was a river that overflowed its banks. In borrowing so many good ideas from their pasts, the divines structured an order of worship so full that it proved impractical and quickly fell into disuse. The beauty of the Westminster Assembly's liturgy is not its utility but its reflection of the gospel story in Reformed thought matured by experience, conviction, and persecution.

The Directory for Publicke Worship was appended to the Confession of Faith and published in 1645. Framers of the directory were committed to the Regulative Principle.[1] This principle said that only what is mandated by explicit instruction of Scripture or logically required as a good and necessary consequence of Scripture's statements was appropriate for the public worship of God. The directory reflects the worship of the Book of Common Order used in Scotland from 1564, which is derived from John Knox's *Forme of Prayers* used in the English congregation in Geneva.

Tensions and Traditions

The acceptance of the Westminster Liturgy (see chart 5.1 on page 57 and chart 5.2 on page 64) was hampered not only by its complexity but also by power struggles within the assembly. Many of the Episcopalians (and their congregants) continued to prefer the form and ceremony of the Book of Common Prayer. The Scots, who were not allowed to vote, also cherished certain worship traditions that the English did not. So, when the worship

1. R. J. Gore Jr., *Covenantal Worship: Reconsidering the Puritan Regulative Principle* (Phillipsburg, NJ: Presbyterian and Reformed, 2002), 25–40; David Lachman and Frank J. Smith, eds., *Worship in the Presence of God* (Greenville, SC: Greenville Seminary Press, 1992), 16–17, 75–79; Terry L. Johnson, ed., *Leading in Worship* (Oak Ridge, TN: Covenant Foundation, 1996), 4–5.

Chart 5.1 Westminster's Liturgy of the Word Highlights

Rome pre-1570	Luther ca. 1526	Calvin ca. 1542	Westminster ca. 1645
Liturgy of the Word	*Liturgy of the Word*	*Liturgy of the Word*	*Liturgy of the Word*
Choral Introit	Entrance Hymn / Introit	Scripture Sentence (e.g., Ps. 121:2)	Call to Worship / Opening Prayer:
			•Adoration
Kyrie ("Lord have mercy")	*Kyrie*	Confession of Sin (with pardon at Strasbourg)	•Supplication for Grace
Gloria	*Gloria*	Psalm Sung	•Supplication for Illumination
Salutation ("The Lord be with you. . .")	Salutation		
Collect(s)	Collect		
Old Testament Reading / Antiphonal Chant		Ten Commandments (sung with *Kyries* at Strasbourg)	Old Testament Reading / Psalm Sung
Epistle Reading / Gradual (a psalm sung)	Epistle Reading / Gradual		New Testament Reading / Psalm Sung
			Confession and Intercession
Alleluia			
		Prayer for Illumination (with Lord's Prayer)	Prayer for Illumination
Gospel Reading	Gospel Reading / Apostles' Creed / Sermon Hymn	Scripture Reading	Scripture Reading
Sermon	Sermon	Sermon	Sermon
			Thanksgiving and Service Prayer
			Lord's Prayer
Nicene Creed Sung (or *Gloria*)	Post-Sermon Hymn		Psalm Sung
Dismissal of Non-communicants	Exhortation		Dismissal (if no Communion)

directory omitted or redirected Scottish customs, the Scots were not pleased. For example, the Scots preferred to have an intercessory prayer ("the long prayer") after the Sermon. The English, who had the votes at the assembly, insisted this congregational prayer be included with the prayers prior to the Sermon. As a consequence, the Scottish Adopting Act for the Westminster Confession of Faith and Larger and Shorter Catechisms explicitly stated that Westminster's worship directory should "be no prejudice to the order and practice of this Kirk [i.e., church]."[2]

Mind-sets as well as particular differences kept tensions taut. Persecutions had encrusted the Scottish Covenanters' resistance to anything perceived as Catholic. So, when the English tried to change Scottish worship practice by restricting the reading of Scripture to the ordained minister, the Scots smelled sacerdotalism. The Scots had a long tradition of a "Reader's Service" in which a layman would read Scripture, give explanations, and lead the congregation in psalm singing prior to the minister's arrival for the formal service.[3] The Westminster Assembly's actions virtually outlawed this hour of "Sunday school." The Scots would themselves later curb the practice, but the apparent imposition of English will and the odor of "priestly" rights for ministers was not acceptable to many in the Scottish Kirk.

Lessons of the "Long Tables"

Other differences separated the English and Scottish traditions. None was dearer to the Scots than taking Communion at the "long tables." The Scots did not simply come to the front of the church to receive Communion from the minister. Their custom was to place long tables across the front of the sanctuary (and down the center aisle) where congregants would sit as families. Then the minister would distribute the elements to individuals closest to himself, so that those sitting at the table could serve one another. The New Testament significance of serving one another and sharing Communion was preserved by prohibitions on the minister reading Scripture during the table sharing.[4] A psalm could be sung as groups who had been served moved away from the table to make room for the next wave of communicants, but the communing itself was not to be interrupted. In addition, no one was to leave the service until all had been served. The bonds of Communion were not to be broken in any way.

2. William D. Maxwell, *An Outline of Christian Worship: Its Development and Forms* (London: Oxford University Press, 1952), 131.
3. Joel Garver, "Uniformity in This Kirk," http://www.joelgarver.com/writ/hist/uniform.htm, 4.
4. Ibid., 5.

The instructions of Westminster said communicants were to sit "about" or "at" the Communion Table. The wording was a begrudging compromise hammered out in two weeks of debate, allowing the Scots to continue their custom despite the common view in England that partaking in the pews was proper practice. Yet even this custom varied from the Continental Reformed practice of communicants gathering around a table at the front of the church to be served by the minister.[5]

The Communion practices unique to the Scots lasted for centuries. The author once pastored a church started by a Scottish missionary to the Americas. It was the first Presbyterian church in the Indiana Territory— before statehood. In that church, the Scottish custom of having a midweek "Preparation Service," where one would receive a token providing admission to the Communion Table on Sunday, was still treasured. We no longer sat at long tables for Communion, but they were stored in the attic just in case someone got interested in a Scottish revival.

I mention these uniquely Scottish traditions, and the Westminster Assembly's reticence to endorse them, not to advocate any particulars but to remind readers that even such honored divines were not uniform in their perspectives. The Protestant tradition values liberty of expression within more general principles of biblical faithfulness.[6] The church goes to war when these principles are extended to enforce someone's preferences over others' freedoms. Broad study of the church's history of worship should not merely inform us of differing practices but help us to see what is merely preference in a specific context and what are gospel principles needed for every context.

Westminster's Liturgy of the Word

Many previous Reformation distinctions are reflected in the Westminster Liturgy: the twofold division for Word and sacrament, worship in the vernacular, concern for the Regulative Principle, involvement of the people, and an order that emphasizes the primacy of the Word. In addition, there is enough distance from first experiments differentiating Reformed and Roman Catholic liturgy to have a more objective view rather than a reflexive revulsion to older liturgies.

There remains among the Westminster divines great concern to excise sacerdotal echoes, but they appreciate elements of the ancient liturgy that further the priorities of the gospel. Sadly, attempts to spell out every particular and claim every opportunity to affirm the best of biblical practice

5. Ibid., 4.
6. Johnson, *Leading in Worship*, 5–7, 17.

made the Westminster Liturgy burdensome. Yet, despite these practical limitations, the principles of the divines still teach us a great deal about how the gospel can be promoted in worship.

Adoration

The Westminster Liturgy of the Word begins with a Call to Worship. The divines are more explicit than Calvin in specifying why such an exhortation is important at the beginning of the service. The Call to Worship reminds the people of the nature of their God and compels them to gather for his praise in light of his greatness and goodness. The Call to Worship is followed by an Opening Prayer whose elements are specified: Adoration, Supplication for Grace, and Supplication for Illumination. These last elements are both reflections of and reactions to the divines' Calvinistic heritage.

Confession

Similar to Calvin, the Westminster divines put Confession of Sin toward the beginning of the worship service as a Supplication for Grace. In this they echo the French Reformer's concern to do nothing before God without recognizing our need of him. However, the divines differ from Calvin in their greater willingness to stimulate this humility by praise that recognizes the greatness and goodness of God. The Supplication for Grace is preceded by Adoration because facing the greatness of God causes believers to fall on their faces before him (Deut. 5:23–27; Isa. 6:5; Luke 5:8).

Such humility leads us to call for his grace, and in order to apprehend God's mercy there is need to understand the truths of his Word. Thus, the Opening Prayer includes a Supplication for Illumination in which the minister petitions God to open the hearts and minds of all to understand his Word. This Prayer for Illumination naturally precedes Scripture Reading. Important for liturgical development is the resurrection of all the elements of Scripture Reading found in the Roman service centuries before.

Desire to elevate the Word over ceremony, and to honor understanding of the Word over mere ritual, led the divines to advocate readings from every portion of Scripture in every service. The Old Testament Reading resurfaces as a specific component of the liturgy. So also does a separate New Testament Reading. And each is followed with the singing of a Psalm. Adding to the weight being given to Scripture (and to the length of the service) is the expectation that Scripture readings are to be chapter-long and read in their entirety.

Understanding the requirements of God in his Word naturally leads to apprehension of human failing, and the need for a Prayer of Confession, as well as the minister's Intercession on behalf of God's people (in the English tradition). This "Pastoral Prayer" becomes standard in later liturgical traditions both in its content and placement in the order of worship. This Prayer of Intercession (known in some churches as "The Great Prayer") is perceived as the church's continuation of Christ's ministry in behalf of his people and participation in his work of furthering the kingdom. The Reformers understood such prayer to include petitions for: governing authorities and the welfare of society (Jer. 29:7; 1 Tim. 2:1–4); the welfare of the church—especially hurting individuals within it (2 Cor. 13:7; Phil. 4:6; James 5:14–16); and the progress of the gospel (Matt. 5:44; 6:9–10; Eph. 6:18–20; Col. 4:3).[7]

Assurance

Still reacting to concerns about being too Catholic, but also being sensitive to Calvin's desire to allow words of comfort after confession, the Westminster Directory is silent on the subject of an Assurance of Pardon after Confession. Ministers could speak or pray as they felt was most appropriate in this regard. This allowance reflected an ethic that runs pastorally throughout the Westminster Confession and Directory. Because so many views were being considered by the assembly, care was taken to allow godly discretion whenever possible. Certain matters were intentionally not addressed or were stated with ambiguity to create unity where distinctions did not have to be made. For example, beyond some basic guidelines the Directory does not mandate words for prayers, use of the Lord's Prayer, recitation of the Apostles' Creed, words or actions for sacrament administration, forms for weddings or funerals, body postures for minister or congregant, placement of worship articles, or ministerial garb. The goal was to provide a uniform structure that ensured the clarity of the gospel but not to provide uniformity of words or ritual that would bind a sincere conscience.

Instruction

The ethic of freedom within guidelines is evident in the Prayer for Illumination preceding the reading of the Sermon Scripture. The divines thought it best that all be reminded of needed dependence on the Holy Spirit for the proclamation and understanding of the Word. Thus, the liturgy includes instructions for a prayer prior to the Scripture Reading

---

7. Hughes Oliphant Old, *Leading in Prayer: A Workbook for Worship* (Grand Rapids: Eerdmans, 1995), 176–79.

and Sermon. However, the divines do not try to prescribe how that prayer should be uttered every week.

The Sermon itself is to expound Scripture by explaining, illustrating, and applying what it says. These homiletic categories (advocated by Stephen Marshall, the English Puritan who drafted the preaching instructions in the Directory) are more remarkable because they differ from the simple "doctrines and uses" divisions so typical of the Puritan method much practiced in that period. The goal of the Westminster Sermon was twofold: the exposition of the Word and the edification of the hearer. Neither was to be sacrificed, and Marshall went so far as to encourage illustrations that "convey the truth to the hearers' heart with spiritual delight."[8]

Continuing commitment to the Word was evident both in the structure of the Preparation for the Word in the Westminster Liturgy and in the content of the Proclamation of the Word. The Preparation for the Word prior to the Sermon was (except for prayer) more reading and singing of the Word. For the actual Proclamation of the Word, the divines also advocated an expository method that focused on the Scriptures themselves. The Directory says, "Ordinarily, the subject of the sermon is to be some text of Scripture. . . ." Additionally, the preacher is to focus on "raising doctrines from the text," to make sure that doctrines were "grounded in the text" and to cover "the scope of the text."

This concern for the primacy of the Word, however, did not negate concern for the "necessities and capacities" of listeners. Out of concern for hearers' necessities, the divines prescribed that the Scripture text be studied in the original languages; but out of concern for hearers' capacities, the divines also advised "abstaining from an unprofitable use of unknown tongues" in the Sermon. With wonderful pastoral prudence, the divines also advised that the preacher "needeth not always to prosecute every doctrine in his text, so is he wisely to make choice. . . ." The goal is the hearers' understanding of, and growth in, the Word of God, not the display of the preacher's eloquence or erudition.

At least a dozen times, the Directory urges plainness or clarity of expression in preaching in order that "the meanest [humblest] may understand." By these statements the Westminster Reformers press away from both medieval extravagances and Puritan rigor. The Westminster Sermon was neither ornate oratory driven by allegorical methods (medieval homiletics) nor intricate doctrinal exploration topically launched from isolated verses (Puritan homiletics). The pastor is to concentrate his message on "those doctrines

---

8. From "The Directory for the Publicke Worship of God," in *The Confession of Faith* (Glasgow: Free Presbyterian Publications, 1973), 380.

chiefly intended [by the biblical writer], and make most for the edification of hearers."

Thanksgiving and Response

The Sermon that is so designed calls for a response. The preacher offers such in a post-sermon Thanksgiving and Service Prayer in which he thanks God for the blessings of his Word and petitions God to help his people apply them in service to Christ's kingdom. In Scottish practice, the Service Prayer would flow into the Intercessions of the "long prayer." For both the English and Scottish traditions, this final prayer then folds into the Lord's Prayer that the people repeat with the minister (except on Communion Sundays, when the Lord's Prayer was used in the Liturgy of the Upper Room). The Liturgy of the Word closes with the singing of a Psalm by all and a Dismissal given by the minister.

Westminster's Liturgy of the Upper Room

The Westminster divines added few innovations to Calvin's Communion service (see discussions in previous chapters for descriptions of most of the elements listed below in the Westminster Liturgy of the Upper Room; see chart 5.2 on page 64). The goal of Westminster was not to innovate but to represent best practices and right theology.[9] The sacramental doctrine of the Confession and Catechisms is clearly Presbyterian, with enough ambiguity at key points to satisfy Scots, Independents, and Episcopalians (see page 58 on "long tables" at Communion). The Communion liturgy in the Directory reflects both the precision and discretion the divines wanted to communicate.

Communion

The beginning Offertory represents another aspect of discretion allowed in the Westminster Directory. This order was not mandated, but common practice in the English and Scottish churches reflects the liturgy of Calvin with the Offertory put in the place of almsgiving on a day of Communion. The symbolism of uniting in care for one another and the church by such a collection again overrides possible misunderstanding of making "payment" prior to partaking of the sacramental means of grace.

9. Gore, *Covenantal Worship*, 78; D. G. Hart, "It May Be Refreshing, but Is It Reformed?" Review of *Worship in Spirit and Truth*, by John M. Frame, *Calvin Theological Journal* 32 (1997): 413; Charles W. Baird, *Eutaxia*; reprinted 1855 as *The Presbyterian Liturgies* (Grand Rapids: Baker Academic, 1960), 5.

Chart 5.2 Westminster's Liturgy of the Upper Room Highlights

Rome pre-1570	Luther ca. 1526	Calvin ca. 1542	Westminster ca. 1645
Liturgy of the Upper Room [Always]	*Liturgy of the Upper Room [Always]*	*Liturgy of the Upper Room [Quarterly]*	*Liturgy of the Upper Room [Optional]*
Offertory		Collection of Alms	Offertory
	Prayer for the Church	Intercessions	
		Lord's Prayer	
			Invitation; Fencing
Preparation of Elements	Preparation Hymn	Apostles' Creed (sung as elements prepared)	
Salutation			
Sursum Corda	*Sursum Corda*		
Sanctus	*Sanctus*		
Benedictus			
Eucharistic Prayer:	Preparation:		
•Remembrance (*Anamnesis*)	•Call for Holy Spirit (*Epiclesis*)		
•Offering Elements for Holy Use (*Oblation*)	•Consecration of Elements		
	•Remembrance (*Anamnesis*)		
			Preparation:
			•Exhortation
•Words of Institution (*Verba*)	•Words of Institution (*Verba*)	Words of Institution	•Words of Institution
•Call for Holy Spirit to Change Elements (*Epiclesis*)		Exhortation	
•Amen			
Lord's Prayer	Lord's Prayer	Consecration Prayer	•Consecration Prayer (for participants and elements)
Kiss of Peace			
Fraction		Fraction	Fraction
Agnus Dei	*Agnus Dei*		
Communion	Communion (with psalms sung)	Communion (with Scriptures read)	Communion
			Exhortation Prayer
Collect	Collect	Psalm Sung	Psalm Sung
	Thanksgiving	Thanksgiving Prayer	
Dismissal Blessing	Aaronic Blessing	Aaronic Blessing	Benediction
	Closing Hymn		

Consecration of Participants

A significant specific in the Westminster Liturgy of the Upper Room is Fencing the table with the Invitation to Communion. The Invitation is a call to duty, not simply celebration. Believers are charged to partake as an expression of contrition and dependence on Christ. By words of warning, however, the unbeliever and the impenitent are "fenced" from the table and charged *not* to partake of the Lord's Supper until they have repented of their sins. In those churches where Preparation Services (see Scottish "long table" discussion above) are the norm, Communion is closed to those who have not properly prepared. In most other churches, Communion is closed to those who are not members of the church or who have not been examined by the minister or elders regarding their adequate understanding of the gospel.

The reason for such sober-mindedness regarding the "celebration" of the Lord's Supper is revealed in the words by which the minister fences the table. He reminds potential partakers that, according to Scripture, those who partake in an "unworthy manner" (being unreconciled to God or neighbor) eat and drink damnation to themselves (see 1 Cor. 11:27–32). Those who perceive themselves as unworthy in light of personal examination should exempt themselves from immediate participation in the Lord's Supper, but should hasten to take care of matters in order to be able to fulfill the duty of Communion at its next offering. Those who are unworthy in light of being unexamined by the church or under the discipline of the church are denied the elements by the minister or elders. By such denial the church's leaders protect the spiritually negligent from the judgment of God.[10]

Consecration of Elements

Although the doctrine expressed in the Westminster celebration of the Lord's Supper was undeniably Calvinistic, one feature of the assembly's worship direction was clearly more Zwinglian: infrequent Communion. Generations following the Westminster Liturgy typically celebrate the Lord's Supper quarterly or monthly. Because frequency was not specified in the Directory, however, there were other approaches.[11] Some of the Scottish churches observed Communion every half-year, but many Anglican congregations communed only once a year.

In recent decades, there has there been a resurgence of weekly observance among Presbyterian congregations in North America. Reflecting today's discussions, church leaders at the time of the assembly debated whether

10. See also Hughes Oliphant Old's discussion of "fencing" with an eye toward evangelism in *Leading in Prayer*, 233.
11. Gore, *Covenantal Worship*, 74–75.

weekly Communion was more likely to create appreciation for or apathy toward the Lord's Supper. But the Zwinglian allowance (if not zeal) to separate the preaching service from the sacrament prevailed.

There are clear historical reasons why the Zwinglian view took root.[12] The goal of most Reformers was to renew the church though understanding of and faithfulness to Scripture. Passive worship, nominal faith, presumed salvation by mere church association, and superstitious reliance on ceremonial observance were the enemies. Thus, reclaiming the centrality of the Word dominated Reformed liturgical concerns. People were to be consecrated by the Word. Understanding what was read and preached from the Bible was the Spirit's primary instrument for a needed revolution in the church and in the soul. Thus, even when Communion was observed, the service (from the time of Calvin) was still rich with instructions, readings, explanations, and mini-sermons that tended to make the sacrament more sermonic than celebrative. The Scots actually had to tell preachers to limit the instructions that accompanied the distribution of bread and wine to keep Communion from becoming another preaching service.[13]

Why was there so much emphasis on the spoken Word even in the Liturgy of the Upper Room? For most Reformers, true worship was the Word understood, not simply observed. All mind-numbing, superstition-tempting, false-hope-arousing routines were eschewed, even those potentially caused by frequent observance of the Lord's Supper. Thus, leaders attempted to protect the sacredness of the sacrament by making its ceremonial features less prominent and its verbalization preeminent.

No abiding consensus about the wisdom of this approach to the Lord's Supper has been reached in subsequent centuries, and none is likely. As long as the church can be tempted to superstition, some voices will urge her to deemphasize symbols and ceremonies to protect the gospel. And, as long as Christ's instruction to honor him and to feast on his grace by a sacred meal echoes in the church, voices will call us to regular faithfulness in this demonstration of the gospel. True faithfulness will allow us to ignore neither the commands of Scripture nor the realities of our culture. The Reformers clearly returned the church to its New Testament faithfulness by focusing on the primacy of the Word. For them the preaching of the gospel was sacramental—Christ was present in his Word. The goal of worship leaders was to make the Word known; this was true of the Liturgy of the Word, as well as of the Liturgy of the Upper Room.[14]

12. Ibid., 74–76.
13. Garver, "Uniformity in This Kirk," 6.
14. For more discussion on this subject, see chapter 23 "Communion Services" among the resources in part 2 of this book.

Worship Consequences

The consequences of making worship primarily about knowledge are both positive and negative in post-Reformation Protestantism. On the positive side, believers are consistently urged to worship in spirit and *in truth*. Ideally, they are led to heart engagement with their God not by sentiment nor by superstition, but by right understanding of his Word. Such worship protects the church from error and the believer from idolatry.

The negative impact of turning the sanctuary into the lecture hall is training believers to become merely reflective about the gospel in worship and tempting them to believe that right worship is simply about right thought. As a consequence, the worship focus becomes study, accumulating doctrinal knowledge, evaluating the Sermon, and critiquing the doctrinally imprecise. Congregational participation, mutual encouragement, heart engagement, expressions of grief for sin, and joyous thanksgiving may increasingly seem superfluous, or even demeaning. Celebration is dismissed as "charismatic," awe is lost, and sacrament is reduced to remembrance instead of encounter with the presence of the risen Lord. As another has written, even the praise can become more about "exhortation to thanksgiving than giving thanks."[15] When this happens, then those whose hearts yearn to respond to God in all the ways his Word describes (and all the ways he has made us to worship) will seek him elsewhere—including those places where truth has been sacrificed to experience.

The effects of these positive and negative influences are still being felt. The children and grandchildren of the Westminster tradition are far-flung—more so than most of them realize. The English Baptists later adopted a London Confession that (except for matters of polity and baptism) was largely a reflection of the Westminster Confession. Even when power was wrested from the Presbyterians, and Anglo-Catholicism was restored as the ruling voice in the Church of England, the Puritan influences of Westminster continued to affect doctrine, preaching, piety, and worship preferences. The revival movements that touched the English churches (Independent, Methodist, and evangelical) inevitably were seasoned with Westminster. And, as English Colonialism and the nineteenth-century missionary movement took British influences first to the Americas and then to Africa and Asia, Westminster patterns became the default style of worship for much of the Protestant world.[16]

15. Nicholas Wolterstorff, "The Reformed Liturgy," in *Major Themes in the Reformed Tradition*, ed. Donald K. McKim (Grand Rapids: Eerdmans, 1992), 296.

16. Robert E. Webber, *Ancient-Future Worship: Proclaiming and Enacting God's Narrative* (Grand Rapids: Baker Books, 2008), 79.

Gospel Expression

The reason this liturgy became so common, however, cannot simply be explained by cultural currents. The liturgy did not merely form the patterns for gospel worship; the gospel formed the liturgy. Where the gospel was truly understood and rightly held, this pattern of worship naturally unfolded—not simply because English culture held sway, but because the gospel forms the best container for its expression. A milk carton differs from an egg carton because the contents determine the structure of their container. So also the content of the gospel forms the worship that best expresses it. The commonality of the Westminster tradition is more attributable to its conformity to the contours of the gospel than to the power of any culture or church to determine a universal style of worship.

But it is this very irrepressibility of the gospel that has urged subsequent generations to press beyond some of the Westminster contours. The biblical need to give thanks, as well as to be exhorted to give thanks; the rightness of being awed by the sacraments, as well as being instructed in them; the appropriateness of being lost in wonder, love, and grace, as well as acquiring sound doctrine—all are good and right. Seeking such totality of worship expression has sometimes led to excess, abuse, and neglect. Innovators have sometimes been naïve, and sometimes heretical. Others, such as those discussed in following chapters, have faithfully sought to honor the biblical principles Westminster so beautifully reflects while also honoring additional dimensions of appropriate gospel expression.

6

The Modern Story

The search for worship that is gospel-true, heart-resonant, and culturally relevant has taken several turns over the last half century. Some movements have sought release from formalism and traditionalism; others have found renewed appreciation for ancient forms of worship that link the contemporary church to its primitive roots. Each has sought to unchain the church from cultural norms that keep the worshiper from experiencing the reality of Christ. The norms that some want to escape are what they consider anachronistic traditions that have deadened church culture. The norms that others want to escape are the secular consumer values that they think have invaded church culture.

Praise Worship Movements

The charismatic renewals—whose worship had roots in older revival movements—brought greater freedom of expression to the organized church. In this renewed worship many found a sense of release from formalism and relief from daily pressures. North American parallels existed in African American traditions and previous revival movements. However, the African

American traditions were more likely to have developed worship structures to shape the expected expressiveness.

By contrast, the worship of the charismatic renewal movements lost some of its gospel shape and became more distinguished by the emotional flow of the service. In this modern tradition, contemporary praise music has been the prime instrument to lead worshipers from celebration to contemplation to preparation for preaching.[1] In fact, what many think of as "contemporary worship" is defined only by the style of music.

Skilled worship leaders may select music with the intention of leading worshipers from adoration to confession to assurance to thanksgiving and preparation for instruction, but this is not the norm. The more likely mindset is that worship leaders will select and sequence music that will wake people up, then get them fired up, then settle them down for the Sermon, and send them home afterward feeling good. Perhaps this is a crass way of explaining it, but such an approach is instinctive and understandable if one has little sense for the history and purposes of the church's worship.

The great blessing of the contemporary worship music that was sparked by, and then fueled, the charismatic renewal movements is its ability to connect with people. The worship music echoes secular trends, making the church seem less odd for the unchurched and less remote from everyday life for those who have found their churches' music traditions stale. For many people who have felt that they cannot authentically participate in traditional worship because it is not resonant with their lives outside church, contemporary worship styles have been a blessed path into (or back to) corporate worship. Various churches (or church movements) have recognized these dynamics and used contemporary worship music to support or revise traditional church services. Noteworthy among these are: Willow Creek, Calvary Chapel, Vineyard, Saddleback, and the Church Growth Movement—together with the thousands of local churches that have in some measure copied these larger efforts to revitalize congregational worship and reach out to local communities.[2]

Within these church contexts, contemporary worship services may have a more traditional flow, but few in the congregation are likely to connect what worship leaders are doing with historical liturgical goals. Most people and many church leaders simply assume we need to do the "opening stuff" well in order to get people ready for the "real thing," the Sermon (which is typically narrative in form and therapeutic in content). As a consequence,

1. Duane Kelderman et al., *Authentic Worship in a Changing Culture* (Grand Rapids: CRC Publications, 1997), 16.
2. Thomas G. Long, *Beyond the Worship Wars: Building Vital and Faithful Worship* (Herndon, VA: Alban Institute, 2001), 7; Kelderman et al., *Authentic Worship*, 17, 88–89.

the Preparation for the Word is evaluated only for its ability to hold attention, build emotion, and attract people. The Liturgy of the Upper Room is not a priority—perhaps performed in a separate service for those mature in doctrine or years—and rarely observed by the vast majority of the congregation. The service gets refined by what will make the Sermon or the experience attractive to the most people.[3]

There have been various reactions to this "consumer" approach to worship. Traditionalists and cynics may complain that the contemporary services have sold out to secular tastes. The most cynical simply presume that any church growth is an automatic sign of doctrinal compromise; the more pragmatic will say that it's just sad the way the church has to adjust to changing times. These reflex criticisms of what is personally unfamiliar can easily cause many to ignore the gospel motivations, evangelistic successes, and generational resurgence typical of many contemporary churches. These achievements are particularly significant in the context of an increasingly secularized culture where churches chained to familiar traditions have lost numbers, influence, and their own children.

Contemporary Classical Movements

But the criticisms have not simply come from "old fogies." A new generation of church leaders recognizes that while one segment of church culture is trying to "connect" with secular culture, another segment is looking for anchors in the sweeping tide of secularism. Instead of letting contemporary trends set the agenda for the church, these leaders have tried to discern how the traditions of the church can become an integrating grid for helping believers understand and transform their world. Such a grid does not morph the church to the shape of the world, but rather becomes a means for examining the world through traditions that have helped God's people maintain gospel priorities across the centuries.

Innovators have dipped into different eras of church history to identify helpful traditions, and the "convergent" results have been quite varied.[4] The Ancient-Future Church movement of Robert Webber has experimented with ancient liturgies, celebration of the church calendar, clerical garb, incense, and icons.[5] The Center-City Model of Redeemer Church in New York City reaches for young professionals and artists with traditional

---

3. Kelderman et al., *Authentic Worship*, 53.

4. Michael A. Farley, "Reforming Reformed Worship: Theological Method and Liturgical Catholicity in American Presbyterianism, 1850–2005" (PhD diss., St. Louis University, 2007), 346–47.

5. Kelderman et al., *Authentic Worship*, 19.

liturgy, culturally sensitive preaching, and musical excellence in a variety of worship styles. The Emerging Churches use contemporary music in the context of community life, mercy ministries, and in-your-face preaching. The Neo-Catholic movement continues to gain momentum inside and outside Roman Catholicism as evangelicals and ex-Catholics tire of both mainline and evangelical churches without historical continuity or unity.

Modern Vanguard

Reacting to formless consumerism and reaching for the best of church tradition, Robert G. Rayburn became the vanguard of these modern integrative liturgies. His 1980 *O Come, Let Us Worship* sought to re-introduce evangelicalism to its history and liturgy. His order of service was a perceptive summary of North American traditions birthed in frontier revivalism combined with a respectful reiteration of Westminster Puritanism. The effect was an intentional honoring of Calvinistic roots and an instinctive echoing of more distant patristic (i.e., ancient Catholic) practices in a worship context dominated by forms of evangelicalism that venerated spontaneity over form.

Distinctive Puritan influences include: non-liturgical use of the Lord's Prayer, non-insistence on "frequent" Communion, "dialogical" participation of the congregation in the progress of the service, and a distaste for "uncommented" Scripture reading.[6] The Catholic strains remain evident in the obvious reflections of the ancient liturgy—from the standard division of the service into a Liturgy of the Word and a Liturgy of the Upper Room to the use of multiple Scripture readings in the Preparation for the Word. But there are also features reflective of North America's frontier and populist church movements that do not have deep roots in the traditional liturgies (e.g., the weighted significance of opening aspects, an Offertory prior to the Sermon, dominant use of extemporaneous prayer, a service structure that does not require a closing sacrament, and, most significantly, encouragement to vary the order and components of worship to keep the experience of the gospel authentic).[7]

With his resurrection of traditional liturgy concerns, Rayburn anticipated the more influential movements of Robert Webber, Thomas Oden,

6. Robert G. Rayburn, *O Come, Let Us Worship: Corporate Worship in the Evangelical Church* (Grand Rapids: Baker Academic, 1980), 118, 259.
7. D. G. Hart, "It May Be Refreshing, but Is It Reformed?" Review of *Worship in Spirit and Truth*, by John M. Frame, *Calvin Theological Journal* 32 (1997): 409.

and Hughes Oliphant Old. These reintroduced the wisdom of ancient liturgies to a generation seeking continuity with the church ancient and universal. At the same time, Rayburn also provided rationale and order for features of the "frontier" liturgy that is more common and familiar among most North American Protestants. This is the liturgy whose underlying assumptions had previously been flexible enough (or obscure enough) to allow the massive stylistic variations of Willow Creek, Calvary Chapel, Saddleback, and the larger contemporary worship movement.

The confluence of streams is made more interesting with the personal note that Rayburn (brother to Jim Rayburn, founder of Young Life) was himself the admixture of the movements he represented. Though formal in bearing, he once was the piano player for his traveling evangelist father. Yet, despite being weaned on the popular worship of the revival tent, Rayburn became a senior professor of worship, teaching traditional liturgy at the school where Robert Webber earned his first advanced degree *and* began his teaching career. Rayburn would not have fully supported the later developments of either the populist or liturgical worship streams that shaped him, but his position at their intersection makes his order of worship a helpful vantage point from which to examine the wide river of modern worship practice.

Rayburn's Liturgy of the Word

Adoration

The Rayburn Liturgy of the Word begins with a Call to Worship (see chart 6.1 on page 74). Rayburn's Call is more explicit than Calvin's and more emphatic than Westminster's. The people are *charged* to worship in light of God's nature (see "Call to Worship" article in the appendix). Rayburn was clear that the Call was not simply the reading of a favorite text to set a holy "aura" for the service. The content of the selected text(s) specifically calls God's people to respond in worship to his goodness and greatness. The Call to Worship should *call* the people to "do" something: praise, adore, gather, give thanks, etc. If the words of Scripture do not expressly include this Charge, then the minister should add words that make the text a *Call* to Worship (e.g., "Since God has declared his glory in this way, let us respond by offering him praise").[8]

---

8. Rayburn, *O Come, Let Us Worship*, 176–77.

Chart 6.1 Rayburn's Liturgy of the Word Highlights

Rome pre-1570	Luther ca. 1526	Calvin ca. 1542	Westminster ca. 1645	Rayburn ca. 1980
Liturgy of the Word	*Liturgy of the Word*	*Liturgy of the Word*	*Liturgy of the Word*	*Liturgy of the Word*
Choral Introit	Entrance Hymn Introit	Scripture Sentence (e.g., Ps. 121:2)	Call to Worship Opening Prayer:	Call to Worship Hymn of Praise
			•Adoration	Invocation (or Adoration Prayer)
Kyrie ("Lord have mercy")	*Kyrie*	Confession of Sin (with pardon at Strasbourg)	•Supplication for Grace	Confession of Sin Prayer for Pardon
Gloria	*Gloria*	Psalm Sung	•Supplication for Illumination	Assurance of Grace
Salutation ("The Lord be with you . . .")	Salutation			
				Thanksgiving Hymn
				Offering
Collect(s)	Collect			Prayer of Intercession (with Lord's Prayer optional)
Old Testament Reading Antiphonal Chant		Ten Commandments (sung with *Kyries* at Strasbourg)	Old Testament Reading Psalm Sung	Old Testament Reading Hymn or Anthem
Epistle Reading Gradual (a psalm sung)	Epistle Reading Gradual		New Testament Reading Psalm Sung	New Testament Reading
			Confession and Intercession	
Alleluia				
		Prayer for Illumination (with Lord's Prayer)	Prayer for Illumination	Prayer for Illumination
Gospel Reading	Gospel Reading Apostles' Creed Sermon Hymn	Scripture Reading	Scripture Reading	Sermon Scripture
Sermon	Sermon	Sermon	Sermon	Sermon
			Thanksgiving and Service Prayer Lord's Prayer	Service Prayer
Nicene Creed Sung (or *Gloria*)	Post-Sermon Hymn		Psalm Sung	Hymn of Response
Dismissal of Non-communicants	Exhortation		Dismissal (if no Communion)	Dismissal/ Benediction

Call to Worship Examples

Sing to the LORD, you saints of his; praise his holy name. (Ps. 30:4)

I will extol the LORD at all times; his praise will always be on my lips. My soul will boast in the LORD; let the afflicted hear and rejoice. Glorify the LORD with me; let us exalt his name together. (Ps. 34:1–3)

Sing to the LORD, for he has done glorious things; let this be known to all the world. Shout aloud and sing for joy, people of Zion, for great is the Holy One of Israel among you. (Isa. 12:5–6)

Therefore, brothers, since we have confidence to enter the Most Holy Place by the blood of Jesus, by a new and living way opened for us through the curtain, that is, his body, and since we have a great priest over the house of God, let us draw near to God with a sincere heart in full assurance of faith, having our hearts sprinkled to cleanse us from a guilty conscience and having our bodies washed with pure water. (Heb. 10:19–22)

This call to biblical responsibility may be made by minister (as a Scripture reading) or choir (as an Introit). Rayburn chiefly directs his instructions for the call to the minister, and the examples he provides are for ministerial use. But the absence of a requirement that the minister make the call will be significant for our future discussion.

The opening of the service also includes a Hymn of Praise. This practice not only echoes earlier Protestant convictions about the importance of the participation of the priesthood of believers, but it also reflects a worship pattern Rayburn wanted to unfold throughout the service. In the Hymn of Praise, the people respond to the initial call from the worship leader. This dialogue of worship involves the people in responding to God and in ministering to one another.[9]

Response

For Rayburn, worship is definitely not passive observance or robotic ritual. God speaks to his people in the presentation of his Word, and they respond to him in their congregational roles. An understanding of this dialogue with heaven is key for renewing appreciation for historical liturgical practices and for involving the heart in worship. God speaks to us and we speak back to him—the concept is simultaneously inspiring and humbling. God condescends to speak to us and grants us the privilege of

9. Ibid., 165, 174; Kelderman et al., *Authentic Worship*, 39.

addressing him. Our minds receive his Word and our hearts revel in the knowledge that he delights in ours.

But the importance of the worship dialogue is not exhausted in its vertical expression toward God; a horizontal, earthly dialogue also occurs. The people dialogue with God in biblical worship, and they also "speak with one another in psalms, hymns and spiritual songs" (Eph. 5:19)—and in the prayers, responsive readings, unison prayers, and congregational "Amens" that are encouraged in the Rayburn liturgy.[10] Enthusiasm for worship is to be stimulated not simply by how well the music pleases one's sensibilities but by the awe-inspiring recognition that *my worship engages my heart in dialogue with the Creator of the Universe and the eternal soul of my neighbor.*

Understanding of the vertical dialogue with God makes Rayburn a fresh advocate for offering the Lord praise in his own words (singing the psalms and using multiple Scripture readings in worship).[11] The worthiness of the words of Scripture makes them ideal for addressing the heavenly audience of our worship. But understanding of the horizontal dialogue that ministers to fellow believers also makes Rayburn an advocate for singing hymns of human origin, differentiating him from his Puritan predecessors.[12]

The concern to minister to neighbor, however, does not erase awareness that all of the worship is in God's presence and for his glory. Thus, Rayburn is concerned for the orderliness of the service, as well as the general order of the worship. He gives many instructions for what he considers the proper deportment and posture of minister and congregants. These instructions reflect not only fastidiousness but concern to help churches understand the significance and meaning of the elements of worship in an era when lack of knowledge had led to either liturgical formlessness or weekly "plugging and chugging" through tired routines.[13]

Regarding the hymns used, Rayburn also advocates a commitment to musical excellence with lyrics that are doctrinally sound and doxological (i.e., more about God's glory than the experience of human feelings). The line between what is doxological and experiential is fuzzy, however, and sometimes leads Rayburn to a more curmudgeonly stance toward contemporary hymnody than is necessary. Still his ethic remains sound and has been important for maturing and deepening the content of the best contemporary worship music.

10. Rayburn, *O Come, Let Us Worship*, 151.
11. Ibid., 228.
12. Ibid., 231.
13. Ibid., 162–63.

Confession

After the congregation praises God in the opening Hymn of Praise, the minister offers an Invocation for God's present care for his people. This leads to a Confession of Sin followed by a Prayer for Pardon. Then the minister offers an Assurance of Grace. This sequence provides numerous insights into the story Rayburn wants the liturgy to tell.

Putting the Confession of Sin toward the beginning of the worship service echoes Calvin's desire that we humble ourselves before approaching God. However, Rayburn follows Westminster with a greater willingness to stimulate this humility by praise. We do not fully recognize our need of God without the light of his glory. Thus, both the Call to Worship and the opening hymn proclaim God's great glory to prepare the heart to confess its great need.

The Confession of Sin is so important for right apprehension of the gospel that Rayburn offers numerous examples for churches to use (see below). But, again, the engagement of the heart is more important than correctness of routine. Rather than dull the conscience with repetition, Rayburn advises keeping hearts attentive to their confession by varying the way confession is offered.[14] The Confession of Sin can be offered in silent individual prayer, unison reading of a historical or scriptural confession, responsive reading of a psalm, respectful attention to an appropriate choral piece, the singing of a penitential hymn, or other means that enable believers humbly and sincerely to confess their need of God's grace.

Confession of Sin Examples

Have mercy on me, O God, according to your unfailing love; according to your great compassion blot out my transgressions. Wash away all my iniquity and cleanse me from my sin. For I know my transgressions, and my sin is always before me. Against you, you only, have I sinned and done what is evil in your sight, so that you are proved right when you speak and justified when you judge. (Psalm 51:1–4)

> Almighty God, our heavenly Father,
> we have sinned against you and against our neighbor,
> in thought and word and deed,
> in the evil we have done
> and in the good we have not done,
> through ignorance, through weakness,
> through our own deliberate fault.
> We are truly sorry and repent of all our sins.
> For the sake of your Son, Jesus Christ, who died for us,
> forgive us all that is past;

14. Ibid., 188–89.

and grant that we may serve You in newness of life
To the glory of Your Name. Amen.[15]

Pardon and Assurance

With confession comes perception of the need for pardon, and so the
Prayer for Pardon naturally follows. Rayburn then differed from the Westminster Liturgy and followed Calvin's desire (rather than his practice) by
specifying the offer of a scriptural Assurance of Grace. Rayburn is careful
to say that the assurance is not "Absolution," since only God forgives.[16]
However, like Calvin, Rayburn has the pastoral sensitivity to know that
God's people need the comfort of his grace. Thus, he says, "it is perfectly
right and proper for worshipers to be assured of the special forgiving grace
of God which is based on the full atonement of Christ and confirmed by
the promises of the Word of God."[17]

So that the Assurance may *really* be heard, it, too, needs to be rescued
from routines. It may be offered in a pulpit prayer, in words of Scripture
said by the minister (see below), in a hymn sung by the congregation, or
in a choral anthem. Again, the goal is not to tie the congregation to liturgical propriety but, rather, truly to minister the gospel with the elements
of the worship service.

Assurance of Grace Examples

The LORD is compassionate and gracious, slow to anger, abounding in
love. He will not always accuse, nor will he harbor his anger forever; he
does not treat us as our sins deserve or repay us according to our iniquities.
For as high as the heavens are above the earth, so great is his love for those
who fear him; as far as the east is from the west, so far has he removed our
transgressions from us. (Ps. 103:8–12)

Surely he took up our infirmities and carried our sorrows, yet we considered
him stricken by God, smitten by him, and afflicted. But he was pierced for
our transgressions, he was crushed for our iniquities; the punishment that
brought us peace was upon him, and by his wounds we are healed. We all,
like sheep, have gone astray, each of us has turned to his own way; and the
LORD has laid on him the iniquity of us all. (Isa. 53:4–6)

If we confess our sins, he is faithful and just and will forgive us our sins and
purify us from all unrighteousness. (1 John 1:9)

15. Adapted from ibid., 307–9.
16. Ibid., 192.
17. Ibid.

Gospel Considerations

Sensitivity to the message of liturgy is reflected not only in Rayburn's advice to let the elements of the order be expressed in differing ways, but also in his willingness to vary the order of the elements. He wants variety that allows the congregation to "experience" the gospel as the liturgy proceeds. There is a logical order to the gospel dialogue of the liturgy, but Rayburn knows relationships can get lost in routine.[18] So, he is willing to advise the minister to make adjustments appropriate for the themes of the service, the purposes of the Sermon, and the human dynamics of the congregation. So that people do not get lost in these adjustments or jaded to the routine of the liturgy, Rayburn encourages the minister to use "rubrics" that briefly explain how the elements of the liturgy represent the flow of grace through the service.[19]

Not only do the rubrics knit the service into a gospel theme, but they also explain to the congregation how the elements relate to one another. For example, we do not confess sin simply because the bulletin lists Confession as next in the order; rather, the minister says, "The glory of God we have just praised makes us realize that we have not lived to his glory. Let us, therefore, confess our sin to him." We do not sing a Doxology after the Offering simply because we have always done so; rather, the minister encourages the Doxology to praise God for his provision for the ministry of the church and the needs of his people.

Rayburn does not want us to press mindlessly through the liturgy like lemmings marching to the sea. We need opportunities to consider why we are doing what we are doing, and we may need time to let the significance of aspects of worship weigh in our hearts. Meditation, reflection, and silence can be as important to worship as simply taking the next traditional step in the service. Scripture can add to our reflection as an appropriate text is read prior to a Prayer of Confession, or a Hymn of Praise, or an Offering.

Examples of Rubrics before Confession

The LORD is in his holy temple; the LORD is on his heavenly throne. He observes the sons of men; his eyes examine them. The LORD examines the righteous, but the wicked and those who love violence his soul hates. . . . For the LORD is righteous, he loves justice; upright men will see his face (Ps. 11:4–5, 7). Let us confess our sins. . . .

18. Ibid., 162, 174.
19. Ibid., 163–64. Explanations and examples of rubrics are offered in part 2 of this book.

O LORD, you have searched me and you know me. You know when I sit and when I rise; you perceive my thoughts from afar. You discern my going out and my lying down; you are familiar with all my ways. Before a word is on my tongue you know it completely, O LORD (Ps. 139:1–4). In light of God's complete knowledge of our thoughts and actions, let us confess our sins. . . .

"Even now," declares the LORD, "return to me with all your heart, with fasting and weeping and mourning." Rend your heart and not your garments. Return to the LORD your God, for he is gracious and compassionate, slow to anger and abounding in love. . . . (Joel 2:12–13)

The worship leader can show additional understanding of the liturgy's gospel message by planning for the emotions, as well as the truth, of each element to be expressed. For example, it makes doctrinal sense for a Prayer of Confession immediately to follow a Hymn of Praise at the opening of the service, but this may make little "human" sense.

The heart does not jolt through its gears like a motorcycle hurtling from a stop. Going from joyous praise to abject confession is not a two-second process. The heart that has soared in praise needs sequence, segue, and transition before it can sincerely bow in humble confession. Thus, following the lead of the emotive Irish, who further refined the Westminster Liturgy, Rayburn adds a Prayer of Adoration after the Hymn of Praise to allow a transition for emotion as well as thought.[20] The Irish similarly added scriptural "sentences" (e.g., Gen. 1:1; John 1:1–3, or affirmations appropriate for the season of the Christian calendar) after the Call to Worship. These Affirmations of Faith acted as rubrics affirming God's greatness and goodness, preparing the heart for confession.

Thanksgiving

The expected response to an Assurance of Grace is thanksgiving. Rayburn's liturgy takes advantage of this anticipated dialogue by placement of an Offering. This Offering is out of sequence with most traditional liturgies, which put the Offering with the Liturgy of the Upper Room.[21] But non-insistence on weekly Communion in the profoundly influential liturgies of Geneva and Westminster has made infrequent Communion the norm among North American Protestants (except for the high church minorities). Thus, Rayburn reflects the norm by placing the Offering with

20. Ibid., 180.
21. Ibid., 194.

the Preparation for the Word. Still, he provides a rationale and sequence that make great gospel sense.

The Offering follows the Assurance of Grace as an expression of gratitude for mercy. In preparation for the Offering, a Thanksgiving Hymn provides the emotional segue from the contrition of the confession sequence. Rayburn advises that the Thanksgiving Hymn be carefully chosen to express the believers' appreciation for the cross of Christ and the provision of his grace.[22]

Petition and Intercession

The Offering is followed by a Prayer of Intercession (and occasional recitation of the Lord's Prayer), which is the natural response of a heart that has honored God's provision with the Offering. When we have thanked God for his goodness, we rightly and naturally seek more of his grace for others and ourselves.

The gospel rhythm of the Rayburn liturgy next moves into the instruction sequence. Having honored God for his greatness and grace, the heart wants and needs instruction to further mature in grace. In an age of diminishing scriptural literacy, Rayburn takes the advice of the ancient liturgies and recommends both Old Testament and New Testament readings.[23] However, even these familiar elements are not ritualized. He advises they be introduced with other rubrics (see below) and interspersed with hymns or choral anthems.

Instruction and Charge

The instruction sequence climaxes with a Sermon in an expository style that is preceded by a Prayer for Illumination and a Sermon Scripture, which may be taken from either testament. Following the Sermon are the equally familiar elements of a Service Prayer that seeks God's aid for his people's application of the Word, and a Hymn of Response (again the congregation responds to God's Word in the dialogue of the liturgy). All is concluded with a scriptural Benediction that follows a brief Dismissal worded in the form of a Charge for the congregation to live in accord with the worship in which they have just participated.

Dismissal Example
Go in peace and serve the living God who has called you to be ambassadors of his mercy and glory in a world of sin and strife.

22. Ibid., 193.
23. Ibid., 204, 208.

Rayburn's Liturgy of the Upper Room

A glance at Rayburn's Liturgy of the Upper Room indicates that it varies little from the Westminster and Calvinistic traditions except in its increasing simplicity (see chart 6.2).[24] Rayburn's main commentary on Communion relates to a Calvinist explanation of its significance, and instructions regarding his preferences on frequency (he preferred but did not insist on weekly) and administration procedures (cover the elements with a white cloth, break the bread in sight of the congregation, distribute the elements without music, partake individually rather than collectively after all have been served, etc.).[25]

Chief variances with the particulars of the Westminster Liturgy are the absence of the Offertory and insistence on the recitation of a creed (Apostles' or Nicene).[26] With characteristic concern for sincerity, Rayburn does not want the creed repeated every Sunday lest it become rote. Still, he wants this Affirmation of Faith and continuity with the ancient church to have an honored place in the regular celebration of the Lord's Supper.

Gospel Continuity

Significant for the purposes of this book is not the plainness of Rayburn's Liturgy of the Upper Room, nor the characteristics of some of his administration preferences. What is most remarkable about this liturgy with its Puritan roots and North American adaptations is how unremarkable it is. Its core structure echoes the earliest liturgies of the church universal. Despite 2,000 years of church innovation, doctrinal disputes, personality clashes, external attack, ecclesiastical wars, persecution of enemies, superstitious deception, cultural transition, political upheaval, continental relocation, and generational transfer, this Lord's Supper pattern maintains unmistakable contours. We have no trouble recognizing its elements because of their consistency with sacramental practice maintained throughout the history of the church.

Even more remarkable is the recognition we are now ready to explore in the remainder of part 1 of this book: what is true of the Liturgy of the Upper Room is also true of the Liturgy of the Word. That portion of the worship service often considered formless "opening stuff" also has familiar contours that have appeared throughout the history of the church. This is not simply because one church has control over all others—all would

24. Ibid., 219, 260.
25. Ibid., 262–69.
26. Ibid., 219.

Chart 6.2 Rayburn's Liturgy of the Upper Room Highlights

Rome pre-1570	Luther ca. 1526	Calvin ca. 1542	Westminster ca. 1645	Rayburn ca. 1980
Liturgy of the Upper Room [Always]	*Liturgy of the Upper Room [Always]*	*Liturgy of the Upper Room [Quarterly]*	*Liturgy of the Upper Room [Optional]*	*Liturgy of the Upper Room [Optional]*
Offertory		Collection of Alms	Offertory	
	Prayer for the Church	Intercessions Lord's Prayer		
			Invitation; Fencing	Invitation; Fencing Hymn
Preparation of Elements	Preparation Hymn	Apostles' Creed (sung as elements prepared)		Apostles' Creed (recited by all)
Salutation				
Sursum Corda	*Sursum Corda*			
Sanctus	*Sanctus*			
Benedictus				
Eucharistic Prayer: •Remembrance (*Anamnesis*) •Offering Elements for Holy Use (*Oblation*)	Preparation: •Call for Holy Spirit (*Epiclesis*) •Consecration of Elements •Remembrance (*Anamnesis*)			
			Preparation: •Exhortation	Preparation: •Exhortation
•Words of Institution (*Verba*) •Call for Holy Spirit to Change Elements (*Epiclesis*) •Amen	•Words of Institution (*Verba*)	Words of Institution Exhortation	•Words of Institution	•Words of Institution
Lord's Prayer	Lord's Prayer	Consecration Prayer	•Consecration Prayer (for participants and elements)	•Consecration Prayer
Kiss of Peace				
Fraction		Fraction	Fraction	Fraction
Agnus Dei	*Agnus Dei*			
Communion	Communion (with psalms sung)	Communion (with Scriptures read)	Communion	Communion
			Exhortation Prayer	
Collect	Collect	Psalm Sung	Psalm Sung	Praise Hymn
	Thanksgiving	Thanksgiving Prayer		
Dismissal Blessing	Aaronic Blessing Closing Hymn	Aaronic Blessing	Benediction	Benediction

deny that. Nor is the contour consistency explained through the church's unwillingness to innovate—history denies that. As has already been expressed, the consistent patterns of the Liturgy of the Word are formed by the gospel message they communicate. The gospel necessarily shapes the container that carries it. To the extent that the purposes of the gospel are maintained in worship, the basic shape of worship expression will also be maintained.

Just as the gospel is expressed symbolically in the sacrament, it is expressed structurally in the liturgy. The liturgy has a gospel purpose. This is as true of the Liturgy of the Word as it is of the Liturgy of the Upper Room. The implications of this realization are significant both for gauging what degree of consistency we need in our worship patterns in order to maintain the truth of the gospel, and for discovering what degree of innovation we need to seek in order to maintain the mission of the gospel.

7

THE GOSPEL STORY

When the gospel is embraced, it controls. It controls lives, affecting hearts, values, and commitments. The stories of those lives are reflected in the structures of their endeavors and achievements. Thus, structures tell life stories, revealing the principles and priorities of the people who formed them. The structure of a church's liturgy also inevitably tells its understanding of the gospel story.[1] This means the worship structures that communicate the gospel are themselves shaped by the gospel. "The medium is the message" because the message shapes the medium.[2]

Seeing how the gospel controls the structures that communicate it not only makes the continuity of church worship through the ages remarkable; such understanding also compels us to ask whether our worship structures truly reflect the gospel story in our time.[3] Worship cannot simply be a matter of arbitrary choice, church tradition, personal preference, or cultural appeal. There are foundational truths in the gospel of Christ's redeeming work that do not change if the gospel is to remain the gospel. So, if our worship structures are to tell this story consistently, then there must be certain aspects of our worship that remain consistent.

In order to discern how the gospel can be communicated in our worship, we should consider how God has kept the gospel message echoing in

1. Robert E. Webber, *Worship Is a Verb* (Dallas: Word, 1985), 29.
2. Mark A. Noll, "We Are What We Sing," *Christianity Today*, July 1999, 39.
3. Thomas G. Long, *Beyond the Worship Wars: Building Vital and Faithful Worship* (Herndon, VA: Alban Institute, 2001), 43.

his church through the ages.[4] This will require us to examine the various church traditions in a manner different than we have thus far. So far we have examined various liturgical traditions to highlight their differences. Now we need to look for continuity. The charts we have used to compare differences will still be helpful. But to gain perspective about how we can make our worship structure gospel-consistent, we will not look down the order of service in the different liturgical traditions; we will look across them. The worship components that are common across the traditions should tell the story of how God has used the church's liturgy over the ages to communicate his gospel. The commonalities should also reveal ways the gospel has shaped the church's worship in the past, and should now shape worship structures that continue to communicate gospel themes.

Adoration

Each of the traditions begins worship with recognition of the greatness and goodness of God (see chart 7.1). The ancient Roman Catholic liturgy starts with a praise Introit sung by the choir. Luther expands this praise into the congregation with an entrance Hymn. Calvin's more austere service emphasizes the importance of entering God's presence with humility. Thus, the Geneva Liturgy emphasizes confession toward the beginning of the service. But even Calvin begins with a Sentence of Praise, using Scripture that ascribes greatness to God and declares his willingness to help us (e.g., Ps. 121:2). This Geneva pattern reminds us that we cannot properly confess our sin, if we do not first recognize the nature of the One who deserves to hear our confession. The Westminster Liturgy reflects similar priorities. It also opens with praise, starting with a Call to Worship that moves into a Prayer of Adoration.

The modern tradition exemplified in Rayburn's worship service has the most obvious emphasis on opening praise. It is important to remember, however, that this liturgy is a reflection of North American practices that have continued to develop. Music and instrument availability, the institutionalization of church choirs and praise bands, the advantages of modern technology, and the consumer demands of modern culture have only heightened the inclination of church worship to "begin with a bang." This is not necessarily a demerit. While some may have unconsciously tripped into an entertainment mode, the desire to begin worship with God's praise is noble

4. John H. Armstrong, "Thinking Out Loud (Again) on Worship," *Reformation and Revival Weekly Newsletter*, May 21, 2002, 2–3.

Chart 7.1 Adoration Continuity Highlighted

Rome pre-1570	Luther ca. 1526	Calvin ca. 1542	Westminster ca. 1645	Rayburn ca. 1980
Liturgy of the Word	*Liturgy of the Word*	*Liturgy of the Word*	*Liturgy of the Word*	*Liturgy of the Word*
Choral Introit	Entrance Hymn Introit	Scripture Sentence (e.g., Ps. 121:2)	Call to Worship Opening Prayer: •Adoration	Call to Worship Hymn of Praise Invocation (or Adoration Prayer)
Kyrie ("Lord have mercy")	Kyrie	Confession of Sin (with pardon at Strasbourg)	•Supplication for Grace	Confession of Sin Prayer for Pardon
Gloria Salutation ("The Lord be with you . . .")	Gloria Salutation	Psalm Sung	•Supplication for Illumination	Assurance of Grace
				Thanksgiving Hymn Offering
Collect(s)	Collect			Prayer of Intercession (with Lord's Prayer optional)
Old Testament Reading Antiphonal Chant		Ten Commandments (sung with *Kyries* at Strasbourg)	Old Testament Reading Psalm Sung	Old Testament Reading Hymn or Anthem
Epistle Reading Gradual (a psalm sung)	Epistle Reading Gradual		New Testament Reading Psalm Sung	New Testament Reading
			Confession and Intercession	
Alleluia				
		Prayer for Illumination (with Lord's Prayer)	Prayer for Illumination	Prayer for Illumination
Gospel Reading	Gospel Reading Apostles' Creed Sermon Hymn	Scripture Reading	Scripture Reading	Sermon Scripture
Sermon	Sermon	Sermon	Sermon	Sermon
			Thanksgiving and Service Prayer Lord's Prayer	Service Prayer
Nicene Creed Sung (or *Gloria*)	Post-Sermon Hymn		Psalm Sung	Hymn of Response
Dismissal of Non-communicants	Exhortation		Dismissal (if no Communion)	Dismissal/ Benediction

and right. Just as idolatry begins with improper recognition of God, true worship begins with right recognition of his nature and attributes. Worship by definition ascribes to God his "worth." We praise him because he is worthy of praise. Beginning worship with recognition of the greatness and goodness of God is not necessarily capitulation to consumerism. Rather, praise has always been the appropriate beginning of worship because in such praise we recognize our God's true nature. Were we to get this understanding wrong, all the rest of our worship would be superfluous. Opening praise also makes God's honor the first "item of business" on the worship agenda. This is a proper priority, not simply because it makes logical sense but also because it makes gospel sense. We honor, bow before, love, seek, and obey God in response to comprehending his greatness and goodness. Recognition of God's true nature begins the flow of the gospel story not just in the progress of worship, but also in our heart. Seeing this pattern helps us understand how the gospel forms the worship structures that communicate it.

Confession

What is our automatic response when we truly recognize the greatness of God's glory? We bow down. When God reveals the glory of his holiness to Isaiah, the prophet immediately responds, "Woe to me! . . . I am ruined! For I am a man of unclean lips, and I live among a people of unclean lips, and my eyes have seen the King, the LORD Almighty" (Isa. 6:5). The light of the glory of God not only reveals his holiness; it simultaneously reveals the ungodliness of all that is human. Thus, in response to seeing God's glory, Isaiah confesses his sinfulness and the sinfulness of all he knows. Recognition of who God truly is leads to awareness of who we really are.

Some have questioned whether confession of sin has a place in contemporary worship. Such acknowledgment of our shortcomings may be perceived as a "downer" or "turnoff" to congregants who have little background in church. However, it is reasonable to question whether worship is Christian worship at all if there is no opportunity for confession. Human confession is the reflex response of divine encounter. If there really has been no confession in a worship service, then there has been no real apprehension of God. His praise necessitates our humility. We cannot truly honor his worth without sensing our unworthiness. We cannot really see who he is and fail to bow.

This gospel reflex is reflected across the liturgical traditions of the church (see chart 7.2).[5] In the Roman Catholic liturgy, the *Kyrie* ("Lord

5. John M. Barkley, *Worship of the Reformed Church* (Richmond, VA: John Knox, 1967), 43.

Chart 7.2 Confession Continuity Highlighted

Rome pre-1570	Luther ca. 1526	Calvin ca. 1542	Westminster ca. 1645	Rayburn ca. 1980
Liturgy of the Word	*Liturgy of the Word*	*Liturgy of the Word*	*Liturgy of the Word*	*Liturgy of the Word*
Choral Introit	Entrance Hymn Introit	Scripture Sentence (e.g., Ps. 121:2)	Call to Worship Opening Prayer:	Call to Worship Hymn of Praise
			•Adoration	Invocation (or Adoration Prayer)
Kyrie ("Lord have mercy")	*Kyrie*	Confession of Sin (with pardon at Strasbourg)	•Supplication for Grace	Confession of Sin Prayer for Pardon
Gloria Salutation ("The Lord be with you . . .")	*Gloria* Salutation	Psalm Sung	•Supplication for Illumination	Assurance of Grace
				Thanksgiving Hymn Offering
Collect(s)	Collect			Prayer of Intercession (with Lord's Prayer optional)
Old Testament Reading Antiphonal Chant		Ten Commandments (sung with *Kyries* at Strasbourg)	Old Testament Reading Psalm Sung	Old Testament Reading Hymn or Anthem
Epistle Reading Gradual (a psalm sung)	Epistle Reading Gradual		New Testament Reading Psalm Sung	New Testament Reading
			Confession and Intercession	
Alleluia				
		Prayer for Illumination (with Lord's Prayer)	Prayer for Illumination	Prayer for Illumination
Gospel Reading	Gospel Reading Apostles' Creed Sermon Hymn	Scripture Reading	Scripture Reading	Sermon Scripture
Sermon	Sermon	Sermon	Sermon	Sermon
			Thanksgiving and Service Prayer Lord's Prayer	Service Prayer
Nicene Creed Sung (or *Gloria*)	Post-Sermon Hymn		Psalm Sung	Hymn of Response
Dismissal of Noncommunicants	Exhortation		Dismissal (if no Communion)	Dismissal/ Benediction

have mercy") follows the introit of praise. Luther keeps the *Kyrie* in his service. Calvin expands the time of confession and makes its cause more explicit, especially in the Strasbourg service. There the Ten Command-ments are read with the *Kyrie* repeated after each (see chapter 4). In the Westminster service, the Opening Prayer includes a Supplication for Grace that immediately follows Adoration; and a later, fuller confession follows the Scripture readings. In the Rayburn liturgy, both a corporate Confession of Sin and a Prayer for Pardon follow the opening Hymn of Praise.

Assurance

The heart that cries out to God for mercy needs the assurance of his grace, or else there is no "good news" in the gospel. Such a gospel pattern is reflected in the account of Isaiah, whose cleansing from sin is followed by Assurance of Pardon:

> Then one of the seraphs flew to me with a live coal in his hand, which he had taken with tongs from the altar. With it he touched my mouth and said, "See, this has touched your lips; your guilt is taken away and your sin atoned for." (Isa. 6:6–7)

All the traditional Christian liturgies have similar elements—in some form—that assure the believer of God's pardon (see chart 7.3).

The Catholic liturgy follows the *Kyrie* with the *Gloria*, whose words in-clude, "Lord Jesus Christ, only Son of the Father, Lord God, Lamb of God, you take away the sin of the world." Then, the priest offers the Salutation, which includes a statement of God's presence with his people: "The Lord be with you . . ." People may have wandered from God, but God remains with them.[6] They have the assurance of Immanuel, God with us, despite their previous confession of need for mercy in the *Kyrie*.

Luther's service repeats the good news of God's provision for mercy and promise of his presence in a repetition of the *Gloria* and Salutation. As noted previously (see chapter 4), anti-Catholic concerns regarding "Abso-lution" forced Calvin to minimize the Assurance of Pardon in the Geneva Liturgy, but he offered an explicit assurance in his Strasbourg service. Additionally, Calvin provided for words of assurance in the Psalm that fol-lowed Confession. The opening prayer of the Westminster Liturgy includes a Supplication for Illumination following the Supplication for Grace. The illumination requested includes understanding of God's grace revealed in his Word. Finally, the Rayburn liturgy maintains its gospel pattern by fol-lowing the Prayer for Pardon with an explicit Assurance of Grace.

6. James A. De Jong, *Into His Presence* (Grand Rapids: Board of Publications of the Chris-tian Reformed Church, 1985), 62.

Chart 7.3 Assurance Continuity Highlighted

Rome pre-1570	Luther ca. 1526	Calvin ca. 1542	Westminster ca. 1645	Rayburn ca. 1980
Liturgy of the Word	*Liturgy of the Word*	*Liturgy of the Word*	*Liturgy of the Word*	*Liturgy of the Word*
Choral Introit	Entrance Hymn Introit	Scripture Sentence (e.g., Ps. 121:2)	Call to Worship Opening Prayer:	Call to Worship Hymn of Praise
			•Adoration	Invocation (or Adoration Prayer)
Kyrie ("Lord have mercy")	*Kyrie*	Confession of Sin (with pardon at Strasbourg)	•Supplication for Grace	Confession of Sin Prayer for Pardon
Gloria Salutation ("The Lord be with you . . .")	*Gloria* Salutation	Psalm Sung	•Supplication for Illumination	Assurance of Grace
				Thanksgiving Hymn Offering
Collect(s)	Collect			Prayer of Intercession (with Lord's Prayer optional)
Old Testament Reading Antiphonal Chant		Ten Commandments (sung with *Kyries* at Strasbourg)	Old Testament Reading Psalm Sung	Old Testament Reading Hymn or Anthem
Epistle Reading Gradual (a psalm sung)	Epistle Reading Gradual		New Testament Reading Psalm Sung	New Testament Reading
			Confession and Intercession	
Alleluia				
		Prayer for Illumination (with Lord's Prayer)	Prayer for Illumination	Prayer for Illumination
Gospel Reading	Gospel Reading Apostles' Creed Sermon Hymn	Scripture Reading	Scripture Reading	Sermon Scripture
Sermon	Sermon	Sermon	Sermon	Sermon
			Thanksgiving and Service Prayer	Service Prayer
			Lord's Prayer	
Nicene Creed Sung (or *Gloria*)	Post-Sermon Hymn		Psalm Sung	Hymn of Response
Dismissal of Non-communicants	Exhortation		Dismissal (if no Communion)	Dismissal/Benediction

Thanksgiving

The heart that knows grace longs to thank God for his mercy. Again, this is not an imposed pattern; it is the reflex response of the heart that has grasped the gospel. We see this pattern reflected in the account of Isaiah's encounter with God. Having received the assurance of pardon, the prophet immediately expresses his gratitude in renewed devotion:

> Then I heard the voice of the Lord saying, "Whom shall I send? And who will go for us?" And I said, "Here am I. Send me." (Isa. 6:8)

The liturgies reflect this heart flow by following assurance with some form of thanksgiving (see chart 7.4).

The Roman Catholic and Lutheran liturgies follow their assurance features with a Collect that includes a request for God to enable believers to express their devotion to God: ". . . cleanse the thoughts of our hearts by the inspiration of your Holy Spirit, that we may perfectly love you and worthily magnify your holy name, through Jesus Christ our Lord."

Calvin intends for the Psalm Sung after the Confession of Sin to include elements of thanksgiving for his grace that prepare the believer for devotion to God. The Supplication for Illumination in the Westminster Liturgy also includes petition for God to reveal what will enable believers to express proper devotion to him.

In all of the liturgies prior to Rayburn, thanksgiving is expressed by requesting God to enable believers to give themselves in proper devotion to him. However, the movement of the Offering from the Liturgy of the Upper Room to the Liturgy of the Word in the Rayburn order of worship allows for additional expressions of thanksgiving. Following long-established North American custom, Rayburn follows the Assurance of Grace with a Thanksgiving Hymn and an Offering. In both, believers are able to give immediate expression to their thanksgiving with the devotion of their voices and gifts.

Petition

Having thanked God for his grace, we naturally desire to see more of his grace in our lives and in the lives of others. The gospel has a progressive flow inward and outward; the same occurs in the story of the liturgy (see chart 7.5 on page 94). But we cannot expect this progress and flow without God's aid. Thus, in the Roman Catholic and Lutheran liturgies the initial Collect includes corporate petition for the progress of our devotion to God in our hearts and before others: ". . . cleanse the thoughts of our hearts by the inspiration of your Holy Spirit, that we may perfectly

Chart 7.4 Thanksgiving Continuity Highlighted

Rome pre-1570	Luther ca. 1526	Calvin ca. 1542	Westminster ca. 1645	Rayburn ca. 1980
Liturgy of the Word	*Liturgy of the Word*	*Liturgy of the Word*	*Liturgy of the Word*	*Liturgy of the Word*
Choral Introit	Entrance Hymn Introit	Scripture Sentence (e.g., Ps. 121:2)	Call to Worship Opening Prayer:	Call to Worship Hymn of Praise
			•Adoration	Invocation (or Adoration Prayer)
Kyrie ("Lord have mercy")	*Kyrie*	Confession of Sin (with pardon at Strasbourg)	•Supplication for Grace	Confession of Sin Prayer for Pardon
Gloria Salutation ("The Lord be with you . . .")	*Gloria* Salutation	Psalm Sung	•Supplication for Illumination	Assurance of Grace
				Thanksgiving Hymn Offering
Collect(s)	Collect			Prayer of Intercession (with Lord's Prayer optional)
Old Testament Reading Antiphonal Chant		Ten Commandments (sung with *Kyries* at Strasbourg)	Old Testament Reading Psalm Sung	Old Testament Reading Hymn or Anthem
Epistle Reading Gradual (a psalm sung)	Epistle Reading Gradual		New Testament Reading Psalm Sung	New Testament Reading
			Confession and Intercession	
Alleluia				
		Prayer for Illumination (with Lord's Prayer)	Prayer for Illumination	Prayer for Illumination
Gospel Reading	Gospel Reading Apostles' Creed Sermon Hymn	Scripture Reading	Scripture Reading	Sermon Scripture
Sermon	Sermon	Sermon	Sermon	Sermon
			Thanksgiving and Service Prayer	Service Prayer
			Lord's Prayer	
Nicene Creed Sung (or *Gloria*)	Post-Sermon Hymn		Psalm Sung	Hymn of Response
Dismissal of Non-communicants	Exhortation		Dismissal (if no Communion)	Dismissal/Benediction

Chart 7.5 Petition Continuity Highlighted

Rome pre-1570	Luther ca. 1526	Calvin ca. 1542	Westminster ca. 1645	Rayburn ca. 1980
Liturgy of the Word	*Liturgy of the Word*	*Liturgy of the Word*	*Liturgy of the Word*	*Liturgy of the Word*
Choral Introit	Entrance Hymn Introit	Scripture Sentence (e.g., Ps. 121:2)	Call to Worship Opening Prayer:	Call to Worship Hymn of Praise
			•Adoration	Invocation (or Adoration Prayer)
Kyrie ("Lord have mercy")	*Kyrie*	Confession of Sin (with pardon at Strasbourg)	•Supplication for Grace	Confession of Sin Prayer for Pardon
Gloria Salutation ("The Lord be with you . . .")	*Gloria* Salutation	Psalm Sung	•Supplication for Illumination	Assurance of Grace
				Thanksgiving Hymn
				Offering
Collect(s)	Collect			Prayer of Intercession (with Lord's Prayer optional)
Old Testament Reading Antiphonal Chant		Ten Commandments (sung with *Kyries* at Strasbourg)	Old Testament Reading Psalm Sung	Old Testament Reading Hymn or Anthem
Epistle Reading Gradual (a psalm sung)	Epistle Reading Gradual		New Testament Reading Psalm Sung	New Testament Reading
			Confession and Intercession	
Alleluia				
		Prayer for Illumination (with Lord's Prayer)	Prayer for Illumination	Prayer for Illumination
Gospel Reading	Gospel Reading Apostles' Creed Sermon Hymn	Scripture Reading	Scripture Reading	Sermon Scripture
Sermon	Sermon	Sermon	Sermon	Sermon
			Thanksgiving and Service Prayer	Service Prayer
			Lord's Prayer	
Nicene Creed Sung (or *Gloria*)	Post-Sermon Hymn		Psalm Sung	Hymn of Response
Dismissal of Non-communicants	Exhortation		Dismissal (if no Communion)	Dismissal/ Benediction

love you and worthily magnify your holy name." In his Strasbourg liturgy, Calvin divides the singing of the law into its two tables (honoring God and neighbor) as a means of reminding believers of the need to petition their Lord for aid in obligations to him and to neighbor. Then, the Lord's Prayer follows with such specific petitions.

Both the Westminster and Rayburn liturgies include specific prayers of petition and intercession prior to the Sermon (this also implicitly occurs in the Lord's Prayer offered in both liturgies). By the intercessions, these liturgies implicitly express the ethic that one's personal experience of grace should progress to outward expression of care for others. Intercession is petition in outward expression. Such concern for others is certainly not exclusive to these liturgies. The ethic simply appears later in each of the other liturgies as part of the Communion service through intercessory prayer, almsgiving, and the Lord's Prayer (see descriptions of the Liturgy of the Upper Room in previous chapters).

Instruction

Having praised God, received his grace, and petitioned for the increase of his blessing, God's people desire to know how to express more love for him, his creation, and his creatures (1 John 5:1–4). Desire for such instruction is addressed by all the liturgies' emphasis on instruction from God's Word. Though it appears in various forms, lengths, and styles, scriptural instruction is an obvious common thread in the worship of all the ages (see chart 7.6 on page 96).

The readings from Scripture, the Sermons that expound Scripture, and the other aspects of worship that quote the assurances and petitions of Scripture focus our worship on God's Word. The appropriateness of such a focus is evident when we remember that Scripture is God's "voice incarnate" (see further explanation of this terminology in chapter 19). By his Word, God yet is present to minister to his people, to express his love for them, and to guide them through life's challenges.[7] The primacy of the Word in these historic liturgies rightly honors the Word that represents God himself (see John 1:1; 1 Peter 1:23).

Charge and Blessing

The apex of spiritual experience in the life of the believer is not simply hearing the Word but living it (1 John 3:18). This truth also shapes the common liturgy of the church. Through the ages, the Liturgy of the Word

---

7. William H. Willimon, *The Service of God: How Worship and Ethics Are Related* (Nashville: Abingdon, 1983), 80.

Chart 7.6 Instruction Continuity Highlighted

Rome pre-1570	Luther ca. 1526	Calvin ca. 1542	Westminster ca. 1645	Rayburn ca. 1980
Liturgy of the Word	*Liturgy of the Word*	*Liturgy of the Word*	*Liturgy of the Word*	*Liturgy of the Word*
Choral Introit	Entrance Hymn Introit	Scripture Sentence (e.g., Ps. 121:2)	Call to Worship Opening Prayer:	Call to Worship Hymn of Praise
			•Adoration	Invocation (or Adoration Prayer)
Kyrie ("Lord have mercy")	*Kyrie*	Confession of Sin (with pardon at Strasbourg)	•Supplication for Grace	Confession of Sin Prayer for Pardon
Gloria Salutation ("The Lord be with you . . .")	*Gloria* Salutation	Psalm Sung	•Supplication for Illumination	Assurance of Grace
				Thanksgiving Hymn Offering
Collect(s)	Collect			Prayer of Intercession (with Lord's Prayer optional)
Old Testament Reading Antiphonal Chant		Ten Commandments (sung with *Kyries* at Strasbourg)	Old Testament Reading Psalm Sung	Old Testament Reading Hymn or Anthem
Epistle Reading Gradual (a psalm sung)	Epistle Reading Gradual		New Testament Reading Psalm Sung	New Testament Reading
			Confession and Intercession	
Alleluia				
		Prayer for Illumination (with Lord's Prayer)	Prayer for Illumination	Prayer for Illumination
Gospel Reading	Gospel Reading Apostles' Creed Sermon Hymn	Scripture Reading	Scripture Reading	Sermon Scripture
Sermon	Sermon	Sermon	Sermon	Sermon
			Thanksgiving and Service Prayer	Service Prayer
			Lord's Prayer	
Nicene Creed Sung (or *Gloria*)	Post-Sermon Hymn		Psalm Sung	Hymn of Response
Dismissal of Non-communicants	Exhortation		Dismissal (if no Communion)	Dismissal/ Benediction

ends with some form of a Charge and Benediction (see chart 7.7 on page 98). The Charge calls God's people to live the truths they have heard; the Benediction reminds them of the goodness of God extolled in the worship—needed grace that will accompany and enable them to fulfill the charge.

The Catholic Liturgy of the Word ends with the singing of the Nicene Creed to remind God's people of the truths on which their hope of blessing is based. Then those who are not partaking of the Lord's Supper are dismissed with the encouragement rightly to seek the Lord. Communicants are charged to continue with the obligations of the Lord's Supper.

The Lutheran Liturgy of the Word ends with a Post-Sermon Hymn that encourages the people to apply the truths that have been preached, as well as an Exhortation from the minister for the same purpose. Calvin is less explicit about the ending of his liturgy, but the Westminster divines, who sought to reflect his principles, conclude with a Service Prayer, recitation of the Lord's Prayer, a final Psalm, and a Dismissal—all intended to encourage application of the truths expounded. Rayburn places similar elements at the conclusion of his liturgy. He also commends a final Charge to the congregation, but acknowledges that such an ending exhortation has largely disappeared from use in North America.

The common absence of a Charge and Benediction is particularly regrettable, when we recognize that these function as emblems of hope for the believer. The gospel is not complete with our present fellowship and obedience.[8] Our ultimate blessings are eschatological, culminating in the consummation of all things. The Benediction (similar to the Lord's Prayer for the coming kingdom) reminds us that the best days are not behind us and the present does not contain all the goodness God provides. He blesses beyond our present experience.[9] We respond to God's Charge, moving outward and forward with the faith that he ultimately will accomplish his good will according to his promise to bless us, to keep us, and to give us the peace of his grace.[10]

Gospel Sequence

Despite their obvious differences, all these Liturgies of the Word have a sequence in common: Adoration, Confession, Assurance, Thanksgiving,

8. Robert E. Webber, *Ancient-Future Worship: Proclaiming and Enacting God's Narrative* (Grand Rapids: Baker Books, 2008), 23, 60–66.
9. Michael Horton, *A Better Way: Rediscovering the Drama of God-Centered Worship* (Grand Rapids: Baker Books, 2002), 135.
10. Duane Kelderman et al., *Authentic Worship in a Changing Culture* (Grand Rapids: CRC Publications, 1997), 48, 61.

Chart 7.7 Charge and Blessing Continuity Highlighted

Rome pre-1570	Luther ca. 1526	Calvin ca. 1542	Westminster ca. 1645	Rayburn ca. 1980
Liturgy of the Word	*Liturgy of the Word*	*Liturgy of the Word*	*Liturgy of the Word*	*Liturgy of the Word*
Choral Introit	Entrance Hymn Introit	Scripture Sentence (e.g., Ps. 121:2)	Call to Worship Opening Prayer:	Call to Worship Hymn of Praise
			•Adoration	Invocation (or Adoration Prayer)
Kyrie ("Lord have mercy")	*Kyrie*	Confession of Sin (with pardon at Strasbourg)	•Supplication for Grace	Confession of Sin Prayer for Pardon
Gloria Salutation ("The Lord be with you . . .")	*Gloria* Salutation	Psalm Sung	•Supplication for Illumination	Assurance of Grace
				Thanksgiving Hymn Offering
Collect(s)	Collect			Prayer of Intercession (with Lord's Prayer optional)
Old Testament Reading Antiphonal Chant		Ten Commandments (sung with *Kyries* at Strasbourg)	Old Testament Reading Psalm Sung	Old Testament Reading Hymn or Anthem
Epistle Reading Gradual (a psalm sung)	Epistle Reading Gradual		New Testament Reading Psalm Sung	New Testament Reading
			Confession and Intercession	
Alleluia				
		Prayer for Illumination (with Lord's Prayer)	Prayer for Illumination	Prayer for Illumination
Gospel Reading	Gospel Reading Apostles' Creed Sermon Hymn	Scripture Reading	Scripture Reading	Sermon Scripture
Sermon	Sermon	Sermon	Sermon	Sermon
			Thanksgiving and Service Prayer	Service Prayer
			Lord's Prayer	
Nicene Creed Sung (or *Gloria*)	Post-Sermon Hymn		Psalm Sung	Hymn of Response
Dismissal of Non-communicants	Exhortation		Dismissal (if no Communion)	Dismissal/ Benediction

Petition, Instruction, Charge, and Blessing. But, if we did not know this sequence was describing a liturgical pattern, we would probably think it was describing something else: the progress of the gospel in the life of an individual. This is a key observation.

Through the ages, the common pattern of the order of worship in the church reflects the pattern of the progress of the gospel in the heart. The gospel first affects the heart by enabling us to recognize who God is. When we truly understand the glory of his holiness, then we also recognize who we really are and confess our need of him. The gospel then assures us of the grace that he provides, and our hearts respond in both thanksgiving and humble petition for his aid so that we can give proper devotion to him. In response to our desire for his aid, God provides his Word. We heed his instruction, knowing that we are both charged to do so and have the promise of his blessing as we live for him. The common liturgy of the church through the ages reflects this sequential flow of the gospel in our hearts.

Gospel "Re-presentation"

The order of worship in the Liturgy of the Word is actually a "re-presentation" of the gospel. When the Liturgy of the Upper Room follows the Liturgy of the Word, this gospel message gets reinforced. By celebrating the Lord's Supper, congregations are reminded of God's holy nature and glorious provision for their sin; they are nourished for his service by the grace made manifest through partaking of the Lord's Supper; and they are encouraged in faithfulness by observing the Lord's Supper "until he comes" to culminate his purposes and fulfill his promises. The Liturgy of the Word and the Liturgy of the Upper Room tell the same gospel story—the latter tells the story by its symbols, while the former tells the story by its structure. While it is obvious to most that the Liturgy of the Upper Room is a "reenactment" of the gospel, the focus of the following chapters is enriching our understanding of how the Liturgy of the Word (the weekly worship of most Protestant churches) fulfills its purposes as a re-presentation of the gospel.[11]

The gospel is always present in faithful worship. The aspects of the liturgy join with the proclamation of God's Word to unite his people in consistent love, honor, and service of their Savior. Symbol, structure, and word support and reinforce one another for a consistent and coherent

---

11. In part 2 of this book, I will discuss weekly Communion for churches with that practice.

gospel message.[12] Again, we need to be reminded that this gospel is not simply an evangelism plan; it is the message of how the good news of God's provision affects our whole lives every day.[13] Not only is the gospel the narrative of God's past saving acts; it is the story of how those actions give us confidence for today and hope for tomorrow.

Consistent Elements of Historic Liturgies

The Common Flow: Looking across the Worship Structures
    Recognition of God's Character (Adoration)
    Acknowledgment of Our Character (Confession)
    Affirmation of Grace (Assurance)
    Expression of Devotion (Thanksgiving)
    Desire for Aid in Living for God (Petition and Intercession)
    Acquiring Knowledge for Pleasing God (Instruction from God's Word)
    Living unto God with His Blessing (Charge and Benediction)

The Consistent Message: The Gospel Re-presented

The worship of the church honors the gospel. The worship of the church communicates the gospel. And, the gospel shapes the worship of the church. We do not have a common liturgical thread through 2,000 years of church history because any church or tradition controls the way all churches should worship. This would be impossible and wrong. Yet, despite varying emphases and features that sometimes have to be stretched a bit to see their commonalities, the Christian church has a consistent worship pattern. We have this common pattern because the gospel that stimulates our worship also affects our worship.

We cannot honor the gospel and, at the same time, worship in ways that distort it. This would necessarily be the case if we praised God for his holiness but did not acknowledge our sin, or if we acknowledged our sin but did not mention his mercy. To ignore essential elements of the gospel necessarily damages it. Of course, different aspects of the gospel can receive different emphases on different worship occasions, and the sequence may vary just as it does in the heart. Sometimes we have to be brought to the end of ourselves before we can see the goodness of God, and sometimes we have to be overwhelmed by his greatness before we will humble ourselves. The point is not that the church can never vary the sequence or emphases of the liturgy, but

---

12. See Timothy J. Keller's similar comments in "Reformed Worship in the Global City" in *Worship by the Book*, ed. D. A. Carson (Grand Rapids: Zondervan, 2002), 215.

13. Bob Kauflin, *Worship Matters: Leading Others to Encounter the Greatness of God* (Wheaton, IL: Crossway, 2008), 130.

rather that the liturgy has necessary components that the heart longs (and needs) to express in order to be consistent with the gospel it claims.

Where the church remains true to the gospel, her worship reflects the truths she holds most dear. Where the gospel is lost, worship becomes reflective of a dead tradition or an evolving heresy. There are two immediate implications: (1) when the gospel is distorted, then the worship of the church will be distorted; and (2) when the worship of the church does not reflect the gospel, then the gospel itself is in danger. The goal for our worship should not simply be to honor tradition, or naïvely to assume there are no abiding truths to guide us, but rather to recognize that God has set an agenda for our worship that takes precedence over human tradition or preference. That agenda can have many variations, but it cannot vary from re-presenting the gospel without ultimately doing damage to the church.

The most important implication of these truths is the blessing made apparent by the consistency of the church liturgy traditions: Where the worship of the church continues to re-present the gospel, God maintains the testimony of his truth in his church despite all her weaknesses, frailties, and sin. Through gospel-consistent worship, God communicates his grace through the ages and beyond human limitations.

8

CHRIST'S STORY

We do not need to rely on church traditions alone to determine that our worship should re-present the gospel. Scripture also provides examples of this structure. This does not mean that everywhere we see worship in the Scriptures a mature gospel message will also appear, or even be implied. Worship in the Bible, as in the church, can be infant, truncated, or misdirected. But, where God intentionally provides models, they consistently echo the gospel pattern the church will later practice.

Old Testament Patterns

Individual

In the previous chapter, we considered how the effects of gospel truths were reflected in the experience of Isaiah. When he recognized the glory of the holiness of God, the prophet confessed his own lack of holiness. And when God cleansed Isaiah of sin and assured him of mercy, the prophet responded with grateful devotion that culminated in ministering God's Word to his people. The ministry would occur in a time of rebellion, and Isaiah would see little fruit from his service, but his devotion was based on God's renewed promise of covenant blessing. The following charts the progress of the gospel in the experience of the prophet:

Isaiah's Gospel Worship
(from Isaiah 6)

God's character recognized (vv. 1–4)
Human character confessed (v. 5)
God's grace exhibited (vv. 6–7)
God's grace assured (v. 7)
Response of thankful devotion (v. 8)
Instruction for obedience (vv. 9–12)
Promise of covenant blessing (v. 13)

By outlining Isaiah's experience this way I do not mean to imply that Scripture intends for these specific verses to establish the worship pattern of the church forever. That would press the text beyond its immediate purpose. My goal is simply to indicate that when faithful persons encounter God's glory, there are common responses. Isaiah's pattern of response also is not unique. Similar outlines could be drawn from the individual experiences of Jeremiah and Ezekiel (see Jer. 1:4–19; Ezek. 1:26–3:15). Thus, we should expect similar patterns will be reflected in the worship of others who encounter the glory of God in the testimony of his Word.

Corporate

The corporate pattern of Old Testament worship also reflects the pattern of individual responses to God's glory. When Moses summons the people of Israel to hear their covenant obligations, he rehearses the circumstances that led to their devotion (Deut. 5:1–33). The people face the glory of God in the fire on Mount Sinai (vv. 4, 22–24). In response, they perceive their unworthiness to confront him and send Moses to receive God's Word (vv. 5, 25–27). Moses reminds the people of the grace that released them from slavery (v. 6) and assures them that it still applies because God is maintaining the covenant he made prior to their obedience (vv. 2–3). In this context, God gives Israel the instruction of his Word (vv. 6–21). The people then promise their devotion (v. 27). Finally, Moses calls the people to covenantal response, charging them to obey God (vv. 32–33a) and promising his blessing (v. 33b).

Sinai Worship
(from Deuteronomy 5)

God's character recognized (vv. 4, 22–24)
Human character confessed (vv. 5, 25–27)
God's grace exhibited (vv. 2–3, 6)
God's grace assured (vv. 2–3)
Instruction for obedience (vv. 6–21, 32–33a)

Response of thankful devotion (v. 27)
Promise of covenant blessing (v. 33b)

The details of Israel's experience at Sinai vary greatly from Isaiah's temple vision but the pattern of response to God's glory and goodness is remarkably similar. By such patterns God makes his people familiar with the grace that will be ultimately manifest in the gospel of Jesus Christ. Through both individual and corporate worship, the people learn the nature of God's grace and the nature of a life that has apprehended it. In this way their worship prepares them to understand the gospel ministry of the One who will make it available.

The fullest Old Testament explication of the nature of the gospel comes in Israel's temple worship. We have to look at a wider swath of Scripture to gain a full perspective of how temple worship revealed the gospel and prepared God's people for worship of the Savior. The tabernacle and temple were furnished and adorned to represent the glory of God, and the Shekinah glory of the Lord descended upon both to remind the people that God was present among them (see Exod. 35–40; 2 Chron. 7; cf. John 1:14). Thus, as the people approached the place of worship, they were made to recognize the glory of God and praised him (e.g., Pss. 24; 100:4; 120–134).

At the sole entrance to the sanctuary stood the altar, a reminder that entry into true worship of such a glorious God also required recognition of human sin (Lev. 16:1–3). Between the altar and the sanctuary was the laver of cleansing that enabled the sacrifices to be cleansed and made acceptable to God. The priests who conducted the sacrifices and entered the sanctuary to make atonement for the people also declared the people's forgiveness (Lev. 4:26, 35), received their offerings and thanksgiving sacrifices (2 Chron. 31:2–10), made petitions for them (2 Chron. 30:27), instructed them in the law (Deut. 33:10), and charged them to live for God with his blessing (Lev. 9:22–23; Num. 6:22–26).

While this worship pattern has to be assembled by comparing various Scriptures that describe regular temple worship, the pattern is not conjecture. The single worship service most fully described in the Old Testament is Solomon's temple dedication, and it reflects similar contours. Though Solomon's temple dedication is more glorious than the weekly worship of Israel, its features and sequence are familiar enough for the people to appreciate.

Solomon's Worship
(from Temple Dedication of 2 Chronicles 5–7)

(*Adoration*)
Solomon gathers the people with the glories of the temple. (5:1–5)

(*Confession*)
The people acknowledge sin with sacrifice, and priests reassemble the place of atonement. (5:6–10)

(*Assurance*)
The priests praise God and assure the people of God's goodness. (5:11–13)
God shows that he is with his people. (5:13–14)

(*Thanksgiving*)
Solomon offers God praise and thanks for his deliverance and provision. (6:1–11)

(*Petition*)
Solomon petitions God to care for his people. (6:12–21)

(*Instruction*)
Solomon instructs the people from God's Word while praying. (6:22–42)

(*Benediction and Praise*)
God blesses his people with evidence of his presence and acceptance of their sacrifice as the people praise his goodness. (7:1–3)

(*Communion*)
Priests offer praise for God's love, and all Israel partakes of the peace offering. (7:4–9)

(*Dismissal*)
Solomon sends the people home. (7:10)

I do not mean by outlining Solomon's worship this way to imply that he consciously set out to establish a gospel message by the structure of his worship. Neither do I want to insist that every detail of his worship fits as neatly into this pattern as my categories may suggest. My intention is not to press every detail into this mold, but rather to indicate that there are regular and recognizable features to God's worship because there is continuity in his nature and the way he deals with his people. Not all occasions call for the same details of worship, but worship of God will necessarily echo basic truths about him. In Scripture these truths always have a redemptive context, so it is natural that these truths will assume redemptive features as they are communicated in worship.

The order of service in the regular temple (or tabernacle) worship further presages gospel truths.[1] Worshipers who had apprehended the glory of God

---

1. Jeffrey J. Myers, *The Lord's Service: The Grace of Covenantal Renewal Worship* (Moscow, ID: Canon, 2003), 78–81; Hughes Oliphant Old, *Themes and Variations for a Christian Doxology* (Grand Rapids: Eerdmans, 1992), 111–37; Allen P. Ross, *Recalling the Hope of Glory:*

in their ascent to the temple would next observe three types of sacrifice. These were always performed in the same order (see Lev. 9). First came the Purification Offering (emphasizing sacrifice for sin); next, the Ascension Offering (emphasizing cleansing and consecration to God); and then, the Peace Offering (symbolizing communion with God and fellowship with his people). In the first sacrifice, the worshiper confesses sin and the need of atoning sacrifice. In the second, the worshiper is assured of God's cleansing that allows one to "ascend" to his presence and live for his purposes. The final offering is presented as a means both of thanksgiving and celebration. The consecrated worshiper is allowed not only to present a gift of sacrifice, but also to eat and drink with God, his priests, and his people. Thus, the worship culminates in a remarkable Benediction of fellowship and peace between God and his people.

Temple Worship

Recognition of who God is
(*Temple Entrance*)

Acknowledgment of who we are
(*Purification Offering*)

Assurance of pardon
Thanksgiving and Charge to live unto God
(*Ascension Offering*)

Communion/Benediction
(*Peace Offering*)

Again, we need to take care not to press the details too tightly into our own liturgical pattern. Each of the sacrifices has some element of atonement, cleansing, thanksgiving, and so forth.[2] My goal in highlighting the sequence of the regular sacrifices is to show how the *emphasis* of each establishes a recognizable gospel pattern. Still, we should be able to recognize that various gospel elements exist in each sacrifice—the New Testament writers will mine this fact for much profit. For instance, it is important to recognize that each Old Testament sacrifice involves . . . sacrifice![3]

Biblical Worship from the Garden to the New Creation (Grand Rapids: Kregel, 2006), 173–208, 269–89; John Witvliet, "The Former Prophets and the Practice of Christian Worship," *Calvin Theological Journal* 37 (2002), 82–94.

2. Ibid., 89–92.
3. Ibid., 56.

Essential to full understanding of the Old Testament ceremonies is realizing that they are not primarily about communicating a theological system or a standard liturgy. They are primarily about revealing the person and work of Jesus Christ. We can see many important theological truths embedded in Old Testament worship, and we can glean important principles to guide our worship. But we can easily misuse these insights by making them the object of our worship rather than the ministry of the One they are meant to reveal.

We tug at texts and wrestle with obscure verses to get them to cough up the mysteries of Old Testament worship. Readers may already have raised an eyebrow at the way I parsed the passages above to construe gospel patterns in the worship the Bible describes. I don't object. We rightly question those who want to press the details of our worship into schemes they can "prove" are biblical in every detail. The fact is the Bible has remarkably few details about the intricacies of Old Testament liturgy. Yes, there are wonderful hints of glories to come and beautiful reflections of heavenly patterns in the biblical record, but the New Testament refers to these as shadows that were destined for obsolescence (Heb. 8:5, 13). If we were to try to re-stage a regular temple service based on what we actually know from the biblical record, we would appear as befuddled and wrong as ambulance drivers trying to do heart surgery.

The Bible provides enough information about Old Testament worship to prepare God's people for what will come but not enough for us to copy what was. We should not long wonder why. Humans have an almost infinite capacity for idolatry. If we knew the length of the latch on a priest's sandal, then someone would mandate it for modern clergy wear. If we knew the precise angle of the priest's hand when he pronounced the benediction, seminarians would practice that stance. If we could actually find the Ark of the Covenant or the staff of Moses, we would do more than make movies about them. The Bible mercifully denies us the worship detail we may desire, keeping our worship focused on heavenly themes rather than earthly proprieties.

New Testament Patterns

New Testament liturgy descriptions are even more spare than the Old Testament ceremony details. The New Testament does not provide us with even one bulletin from a worship service in the time of Jesus or Paul. The apostolic writers are more content to describe what most traditions call the "elements" of worship rather than their precise order or content. *Elements* are the practices the Bible records that were included in the corporate worship of the New Testament. These typically include prayer, reading and preaching God's Word, singing, and administering sacraments.[4] Many churches also consider worship practices such as commissioning, ordaining, giving testimonies, observing fasts, and taking vows to have New Testament precedent.

Yet, while there are many references to such worship elements in the New Testament, nowhere is a precise order or style mandated. And while we have examples of some of these elements, we never receive directives regarding the precise content or length for our expressions of them. Though these absent details may seem like oversights, they actually disclose great wisdom and mercy.[5] If the Bible even hinted that a Doxology followed the Offering in a New Testament service, then the tradition already concretized in many Protestant churches could never be altered. If the length of a Sermon had been suggested (and had the Bible not so graciously recorded that Paul preached long enough to put someone to sleep), then stopwatches would rule Sermons—more than they already do.

The scarcity of liturgical mandates in the New Testament cannot reflect the writers' lack of concern for rightly worshiping God. Too many give their lives for his glory. Instead, the lack of explicit detail must reflect an intention to guide us by transcendent principles rather than by specific worship forms that could become culture-bound, time-locked, and superstition-invoking.

The New Testament writers provide enough description of the transcendent principles to form the contours of our liturgy without providing details that would limit the authenticity and significance of our worship. The contours are consistent with the gospel principles revealed in Old Testament worship, but replace the focus on providing sacrifices with focus on the One sacrificed. The message of his full provision and finished work on our behalf would be damaged if a detailed liturgy implied that we make his worship acceptable by our perfection of it. Thus, the New Testament worship instruction lacks precise mechanics or intricate details. The biblical writers seem more concerned to have our hearts respond to the message

---

4. See such an understanding of elements (worship components with biblical precedent), as distinguished from "circumstances" (pragmatic considerations of human convention or convenience), in the Westminster Confession of Faith 1.6; 21.1,4,5. Extensive and historic debates on the nature and extent of these two (and similar) categorizations continue in almost every historical branch of the church. E.g., John Frame, *Worship in Spirit and Truth* (Phillipsburg, NJ: Presbyterian and Reformed, 1996), 37–66; R. J. Gore Jr., *Covenantal Worship: Reconsidering the Puritan Regulative Principle* (Phillipsburg, NJ: Presbyterian and Reformed, 2002); and Terry L. Johnson, ed., *Leading in Worship* (Oak Ridge, TN: Covenant Foundation, 1996), 4–14.

5. Ronald E. Man, "Including Worship in the Seminary Curriculum" (unpublished manuscript), 13.

of grace, rather than to compel us to honor it with scrupulous attention to some prescribed ceremony, wording, posture, music, decoration, and so on.

The New Testament priority on message over mechanics suggests that our worship should be framed more to communicate the gospel than to imply we ensure its blessings by our performance. Rather than mandating liturgical specifics that could stimulate anxiety or pride, the New Testament frames its worship standards in a gospel pattern that is now very recognizable. Because the Old Testament sacrificial system was intended to presage New Testament truths, we should expect these reflections. However, because the New Testament intends to focus our worship on the One sacrificed once for all, there is greater emphasis on the finishedness and completeness of his ministry (Heb. 8:25–27; 9:25–28). Ceremonial details dissolve into consistent gospel structures that communicate the effects of grace fully provided.

Individual

In an extended analogy, the apostle Paul urges us to engage in "spiritual worship" by offering our bodies as "living sacrifices" to God (Rom. 12:1). He then describes this worship, not in ceremonial detail, but as obedience to God in our corporate (12:3–8), individual (12:9–21), civil (13:1–7), and moral (13:8–14) responsibilities lived in mutual care for one another (14:1–15:13). These extended instructions could be interpreted as describing acts that will make us acceptable to God, except for the worship analogy that guides Paul's thought.

He does *not* say that we should offer our bodies to God so that we will become acceptable "living sacrifices." Paul says that we should offer our "bodies as living sacrifices, holy and pleasing to God" (12:1). "Holy and pleasing" are not descriptions of what we will *become*; they are declarations of what we *are*. Before we have performed our religious duties, God makes us holy and pleasing to himself.

How does God makes us holy apart from our obedience? Paul has already explained that righteousness for the Jews does not come from their obedience but from faith in the righteousness God provides for them (10:1–3). Now, the apostle says, this merciful covenant that God established to bless his chosen people has been extended to all nations (11:25–32). Because God embraces us in this mercy, he also declares us "holy and pleasing" to himself. Our obedience does not make our worship acceptable; our worship is acceptable because God has made us holy. He accepts our obedience as spiritual worship (and we delight to give it) "in view of God's mercy" that has made fallible people's praise pleasing to him (12:1).

By the apostle's gospel explanation we again learn that the imperatives God gives are based on the indicatives grace provides. We *are* holy and pleasing to God (the indicatives) by his mercy so that we can offer ourselves as living sacrifices (the imperatives) in worship. Awareness of God's mercy prepares the heart for a life of worship. Extending the analogy further, Paul begins this living order of worship with recognition of the greatness of such a merciful God: "Oh, the depth of the riches of the wisdom and knowledge of God! . . . For from him and through him and to him are all things. To him be the glory forever!" (11:33–36). Paul also ends this order of worship with a Charge and Benediction: "May the God of hope fill you with all joy and peace as you trust in him, so that you may overflow with hope by the power of the Holy Spirit" (15:13).

Spiritual Worship
(from Romans 11–15)

Recognition of God's Character (Rom. 11:33–36)
Acknowledgment of Our Need of Mercy (Rom. 12:1)
Assurance of Mercy (Rom. 12:1)
Thankful Response (Rom. 12:2)
Instruction in New Obedience (Rom. 12:3–13:14)
Communal Care for One Another (Rom. 14:1–15:12)
Charge and Benediction (Rom. 15:13)

The familiar pattern that glistens in Paul's "spiritual worship" analogy should not be construed as a liturgical model that he intends to mandate for the church. I would be wrong to imply this was his primary intent. My purpose in framing his instruction as a worship pattern is simply to demonstrate again that the gospel forms its own container. Whenever we try to frame the gospel, a familiar pattern of essential truths will emerge. Thus, when Paul frames the gospel in worship terms, his pattern of expression is familiar because certain principles are always essential when communicating a complete gospel story. Worship that intends to communicate this gospel story will also have this general pattern, even if particulars vary.

Corporate

The apostles' epistles were read in the corporate worship of the first churches so that congregations would understand the gospel and its implications for their lives. Since these epistles contain the gospel, they also typically reflect its pattern. For example, the Epistle to the Ephesians unfolds this way: God's character (chapter 1), human need (2:1–3), God's gracious provision (2:4–10), instruction in godliness (2:11–6:18), communal care and encouragement (6:19–22), and a benediction (6:23–24). I am not contending this epistle pattern was intended to establish the liturgy of the church, nor that this is the only way to organize the material of the epistle. The purpose of highlighting this familiar pattern in the epistles is simply to demonstrate again that the gospel shapes its own container.

Many writers see a gospel pattern etched in the eschatological worship described in the book of Revelation. The aptness of this observation is based on two dominant image sets that permeate the book: reflections of Old Testament temple worship and descriptions of Christ's ultimate triumph. The contrasting images of the Lamb who was slain and who also sits on the throne make sense together because they represent familiar gospel themes. Despite their seeming dissonance, the themes gloriously converge and tell the gospel as they assume familiar places in the narrative woven into the worship that unfolds through the book (see below).

Eschatological Worship
(Revelation 4–21)

Recognition of God's Glory (Rev. 4:1–11)
Acknowledgment of Human Sin (Rev. 5:1–7)
Prayer for and Assurance of God's Provision (Rev. 5:8–10)
Thanksgiving Praise (Rev. 5:11–14)
Cycles of God's Word Opened with Reactions in Heaven and Earth (Rev. 6:1–19:5)
    The Seven Seals (6:1–8:5)
    The Seven Trumpets (8:6–11:19)
    The Seven Signs (12:1–15:8)
    The Seven Bowls (16:1–21)
    Babylon Announcements (17:1–19:5)
Communion in Wedding and Royal Suppers (Rev. 19:6–10 and 11–21)
Charge Regarding Judgment and Benediction and the New Creation (Rev. 20–22)

Gospel Sensitivity

The gospel pattern is not precisely mirrored in each of the Scriptures discussed in this chapter. The Bible consistently shows that its worship is shaped by gospel themes, but not every component of the gospel is equally emphasized in every text or era. As indicated in the eschatological pattern above, there seems to be less cause for petition than for praise in the Eschaton. The prayers in Revelation seem to be requests for God's vindicating judgments more so than intercessions (see 5:8; 6:9–10; 8:3–4). Thus, suggesting that the gospel shapes worship into a consistent pattern need not force us to conclude the pattern never varies in emphasis, accent, or tone.

The aspects of the gospel pattern that remain consistent—and make it "gospel"—are its redemptive features. Right worship of God requires recognition of the glories of his nature; and true recognition of God's glory always causes awareness of human need that can only be met by God's provision. True recognition of God's character and ours creates an interplay of doxology and dependence—of honor and humility—which are the defining marks of Christian worship.

We do not have to insist on a particular order of worship elements or a particular style of expression to create authentic Christian worship. But what we cannot avoid, if we are to worship God rightly, are the dynamics of the gospel. The gospel that we are prepared to understand in the Old Testament and that we observe in the New Testament always confronts the believer with the greatness and goodness of God. This *good news* humbles believers so that their worship naturally and necessarily includes acknowledgment of their need for his mercy. When God's people receive assurance of his provision, they respond with thanksgiving and such desire to please him that they long for the instruction of his Word and communion with his people. In short, because they have experienced his love, God's people love what and whom he loves—and their worship of him naturally includes expression of such love.

Understanding worship as a love response to the truths of the gospel does not merely shape the contours of the worship service; it also shifts the focus of our hearts in worship. Worship becomes less about earning God's approval by correct observance of traditions and more about delighting to express our love for him in the ways that most please him.[6] Because we want to please him, we will study the worship instructions in his Word and we will long to learn how he has taught faithful people in other generations to honor him. Still, only the assurances of his grace will keep these concerns to rightly express our love from degenerating into rituals designed to legalistically merit his approval.

Christian liturgy has a gospel pattern, not because someone's rulebook demands it, but because believers express their love to God by responding to the way that he has expressed his for them. He expresses his love for us not by mandating rituals to constrain us, but by sending his Son to redeem us. Worship is a response to our Redeemer. The heart of Christian worship is love for Christ. We cannot love him without extolling his greatness,

6. See the particular emphasis of John Calvin well summarized by Timothy J. Keller in "Reformed Worship in the Global City" in *Worship by the Book*, ed. D. A. Carson (Grand Rapids: Zondervan, 2002), 203, 208.

confessing our weakness, seeking his goodness, thanking him for his grace, and living for his glory. So, out of love for him, we worship him in these ways. Our worship has a gospel pattern not because we are coerced into such ritual but because our hearts are so compelled to love Jesus.

Redemptive Priority

The redemptive flow of biblical worship inevitably makes our liturgy Christ-centered. This does not mean that Christian worship diminishes the honor of any other member of the Trinity. God the Father makes our worship Christ-centered by redeeming us through the work of his Son, and giving the Spirit to testify of him.[7] Because worship is a response to this witness of redemption, the grace God provides through his Son is the thread that sews the service together.[8] We do not gather simply to extol some attribute of God or to reflect the relationships of the Trinity. Heaven's glories would only devastate us, if God's grace did not shelter us. We do not gather merely to confess our sin. Our shame would destroy us, if his grace did not provide our pardon. We also do not worship only to learn our obligations. God's law would be our death, if the Lamb had not been slain for us. Christian worship inevitably makes Christ's work its central theme.[9]

The redemptive focus of worship means that the Redeemer is the focus of our worship.[10] In his face, we see the glory of the Father (2 Cor. 4:6).[11] By his Spirit, we have the testimony of the Son and learn the obligations of our love (John 15:26–27; 16:14–15). Neither the Father nor the Spirit takes a backseat in Christian worship; rather, they are presented to us in the ministry of Christ. Jesus represents the Father's power and love (John 14:9). Jesus is the object of the Spirit's ministry (John 15:26). Each person of the Godhead participates in our redemption, but because redemption is the theme of our worship, the ministry of the One who accomplishes our salvation shapes our liturgy. Ultimately, our worship has a gospel pattern because it is Christ-centered.

7. James B. Torrance, *Worship, Community and the Triune God of Grace* (Downers Grove, IL: InterVarsity Academic, 1996), 24, 36; Michael Horton, *A Better Way: Rediscovering the Drama of God-Centered Worship* (Grand Rapids: Baker Books, 2002), 149.

8. Bob Kauflin, *Worship Matters: Leading Others to Encounter the Greatness of God* (Wheaton, IL: Crossway, 2008), 72.

9. Torrance, *Worship, Community and the Triune God*, 23; Paul Waitman Hoon, *The Integrity of Worship: Ecumenical and Pastoral Studies in Liturgical Theology* (Nashville and New York: Abingdon, 1971), 116.

10. John Murray, "Christ Himself in the Assemblies of His People," *New Horizons* 23, no. 4 (April 2002): 4.

11. Ronald E. Man, "Proclamation and Praise: Hebrews 2:12 and the Role of Christ in Worship," *Viewpoint*, July–August 2000, 6.

The Christo-centrality of our worship should not imply that we make no mention of other members of the Godhead, or fail to give them great honor.[12] Rather, Christo-centrality commits us to honor Father, Son, and Holy Spirit by worshiping them in the context of the redeeming work that culminates in Christ. In doing so, we follow Scripture's own redemptive priorities.[13]

The Bible establishes its redemptive themes from the very beginning. God creates the world and declares all good. Then, when humankind corrupts the created order, God declares the gospel (Gen. 3:15). He says that One will come who, though wounded, will crush the source of evil. In this first gospel declaration (known as the Protoevangelium), we learn that the Creator will save his creatures through the suffering of his Son. The rest of Scripture unfolds the details of this great gospel theme. Every person, every battle, every betrayal, every king's reign, every prophet's word, every disciple's testimony—all are part of the great drama revealing how God will save an undeserving people by a divine Deliverer. The Father wills it all and the Spirit is the power behind it all, but the Son is at the center of the story. The great theme of redemption revolves around him, and its many dimensions are designed to help us understand what he accomplishes.[14]

Son Centrality

Keeping the ministry of the Son at the center of our worship is not abandonment of the glory of the Father or the Spirit, but is rather faithfulness to the gospel they make Scripture's focus.[15] We make our worship Christ-centered not by failing to mention Father or Spirit, but by honoring them with the gospel pattern that reflects their will and purpose. We honor the Father when we sing of his greatness to humble hearts and prepare them to receive the grace that Christ provides. And were we not to mention the provision of Christ, then we would have demeaned the God who sent him no matter how much more praise we heaped upon the Father. Similarly, we honor the Spirit when we call on him to help us understand Scripture's testimony of Christ's work. And we would grieve the Spirit if we were to make him, whose ministry is testifying of Christ, the chief object of our worship. In short, we don't need to worry that the Father will get his feel-

---

12. Torrance, *Worship, Community and the Triune God*, 31.
13. Ibid., 34.
14. Ibid., 9.
15. Hughes Oliphant Old, *The Reading and Preaching of the Scriptures in the Worship of the Christian Church*, vol. 1, *The Biblical Period* (Grand Rapids: Eerdmans, 1998), 351.

ings hurt if we glorify his Son, or that the Spirit will sulk in a corner if we magnify the Christ of his anointing.[16]

We make our worship Christ-centered not by simply mentioning the name of Jesus, and definitely not by failing to honor the Father and the Spirit; we make our worship Christ-centered by shaping it to help God's people understand and appreciate the grace in all Scripture that culminates in their Savior's ministry. Worship designed to foster appreciation for his love will reflect the message that all heaven gave him to provide and that he gave his all to share. That message of a great and gracious God who provides for our need despite our being undeserving is built into the structure of the liturgy that reflects the progress of redemption in the believer's life. Worship that is Christ-centered will re-present these gospel principles whether it is drawn from the Old Testament, New Testament, or a combination of both.

Even aspects of worship that do not directly reference Jesus will honor his purposes when the service is shaped by the contours of redemption that find their ultimate meaning in him. Worship does not have to be drawn from a New Testament account, echo a messianic prophecy, or quote Jesus in order to be Christ-centered. Worship that is Christ-centered leads the heart down the path it must follow to appreciate Christ's ministry. This gospel-formed path always puts us in contact with God's glory, our sin, his provision, our response, and his peace. By walking a worship path in step with this redemptive rhythm we simultaneously discover the pattern of our liturgy and the grace of our Savior.

16. Kauflin, *Worship Matters*, 76–77.

9

"RE-PRESENTING" CHRIST'S STORY

The liturgies of the church through the ages and the consistent message of Scripture combine to reveal a pattern for corporate worship that is both historical and helpful for our time. Christian worship is a "re-presentation" of the gospel. By our worship we extol, embrace, and share the story of the progress of the gospel in our lives.[1] We begin with adoration so that all will recognize the greatness and goodness of God. In the light of his glory, we also recognize our sin and confess our need of his grace. Assurance of his pardon produces thanksgiving. With sincere thanksgiving, we also become aware that all we have is from him and that we depend on his goodness for everything precious in our lives. Thus, we are compelled to seek him in prayer for our needs and his kingdom's advance. His loving intercession makes us desire to walk with him and further his purposes, so our hearts are open to his instruction and long to commune with him and those he loves. This progress of the gospel in our lives is the cause of our worship and the natural course of it. We conclude a service of such worship with a Charge and Benediction because the progress of the gospel is God's benediction on our lives.

Why This Gospel Again?

We worship God according to this gospel pattern not because of arbitrary worship rules, but because the content of the gospel shapes our response

---

1. Greg Perry, "Reforming Worship," *Reformed Theological Review* 61, no. 1 (April 2002): 48.

to it.[2] We love God because he has revealed the gospel to us, so it is natural that our expressions of love would be framed by the contours of his
redemptive work. Worship is our love response to his loving provision, so
nothing is more honoring of his grace than making its themes our own.
We honor God, confess the need of his Son, claim his pardon, bolster our
obedience, bless our neighbor, and testify of our Savior when our worship
echoes the gospel that saves and sustains us.

This gospel re-presentation will sound inadequate as a consistent pattern for worship if we assume that our hearts will tire of its expression
or that there can only be one mold for its formation. The first assumption could make sense, if we presumed that the human heart functioned
like an assembly line. If learning the gospel were like building a car, then
we could expect that once a truth was acquired we could move to new
stations of Christian maturity without returning to earlier stages of our
development. But the heart is not like an assembly line; we too easily forget the gospel, doubt its power, or get distracted from its purposes. New
spiritual problems always require responses based on our hearts' return
to foundational truths.

The corruption and weakness of our natures make it vital that we preach
the gospel to our own hearts every day.[3] Reminders of grace are not dry
cereal for the soul; they are daily bread, blessed manna, and needed meat.
For those in whom the Spirit dwells, grace is the fuel of obedience and
the foundation of hope. Without its regular support, we quickly resort to
self-dependence or private despair. The maturest believers most appreciate
regular nourishment from the truths of God's love. The old gospel song is
true: those who know "the old, old story" best are "hungering and thirst-
ing to hear it, like the rest." While the gospel's power can become lost
in canned and stale recitations, its sincere and authentic expression is a
never-ceasing source of the joy that is strength for God's people. Worship
that keeps the gospel before God's people serves their deepest needs and
highest aspirations, enabling them to feed on God's grace while praising
him for it.

Transcending the Traditions

As we never tire of love notes from our spouses, believers are never dis-
gusted by worship testifying of God's love—we need it! Apart from this

---

2. Thomas G. Long, *Beyond the Worship Wars: Building Vital and Faithful Worship* (Herndon, VA: Alban Institute, 2001), 10.
3. See discussion in chapter 1.

gospel we live in darkness. We are always longing for the light of God's "good news" to give us guidance through trials, joy at the end of the day, and hope for tomorrow. Worship that consistently shapes our understanding and appreciation of Christ's redeeming work supplies such light and draws God's people to it.

Because we want to supply "good" light, we naturally ask questions about what is proper for worship. The various worship traditions discussed earlier in this book may initially seem to confuse the answer. Awareness of the differences and disputes in the traditions naturally leads us to question, "Who's right, who's wrong, and what's out of bounds?" We have also discovered, however, that we cannot answer these questions simply by analyzing the traditions' differences. To discern what is proper for Christian worship we also need to identify elements of consistency in the worship traditions that echo worship principles revealed in Scripture. By doing this, we have discovered a gospel pattern for worship that transcends tradition, culture, time, and personal preference. This pattern reflects Scripture's own redemptive themes that culminate in Christ's ministry.

Worship that conforms to this redemptive pattern re-presents the gospel by moving worshipers down a path structured to parallel the progress of grace in the life of the believer. In previous chapters we have examined various ways that churches and the Scriptures have expressed worship distinctions, but we also have seen a basic pattern emerge with remarkable consistency across the Christian liturgies.

Christ-Centered Worship

Recognition of God's Character (Adoration)
Acknowledgment of Our Character (Confession)
Affirmation of Grace (Assurance)
Expression of Devotion (Thanksgiving)
Desire for Aid in Living for God (Petition and Intercession)
Acquiring Knowledge for Pleasing God (Instruction from God's Word)
Communing with God and His People (Communion)
Living unto God with His Blessing (Charge and Benediction)

This schematic way of looking at the Christian worship tradition makes it startlingly obvious that the liturgy of the church—the structure of our worship—does more than simply alert people what hymn or prayer should come next.[4] Just as preaching represents the gospel in word, and as the

4. Robert G. Rayburn, *O Come, Let Us Worship: Corporate Worship in the Evangelical Church* (Grand Rapids: Baker Academic, 1980), 259.

sacraments represent the gospel in symbol, so also the liturgy represents the gospel in structure.[5]

Glory and Good

The structure of the liturgy tells the story of the gospel. This means that our corporate worship reflects the purposes of the gospel that are present in our individual lives. The Shorter Catechism produced by the Westminster divines says our "chief end is to glorify God, and to enjoy him for ever." By his presence in our lives God intends to bring himself glory *and* to bring us his goodness (Pss. 16:11; 144:15). The gospel is God's means of conquering the effects of sin for precisely these purposes. Through our apprehension and appropriation of the gospel, God receives glory and we partake of his goodness. Worship that represents the gospel must have these same goals.

Worship is not only for God's glory, and it is not only for our good. In order for the gospel to be good news for God's people it must have both goals, and worship that is reflective of the gospel must also have both goals.[6] Well-intentioned, but overzealous, worship leaders sometimes argue that we should not take people's concerns into account when designing our worship. These leaders say that God is the true audience of our worship, so we must direct all our efforts toward his glory.

Making God's glory the exclusive goal of worship sounds very reverent but actually fails to respect Scripture's own gospel priorities. Certainly it is true that God is the most important audience member for our worship.[7] But if God were not concerned for the good of his people, his glory would be diminished. He expects us not only to praise his name (Ps. 30:4), but also to teach, admonish, and encourage one another in worship (Col. 3:16; Heb. 10:24). God is not only the chief audience of our worship; by his Word and Spirit, he is also the true speaker, singer, and prayer.[8]

Not only does he call us to worship in the voice of the minister, but God also speaks through and among us in our praise in order to minister to us (Heb. 2:11–12). God uses our worship to strengthen us as well as to glorify

---

5. James B. Torrance, *Worship, Community and the Triune God of Grace* (Downers Grove, IL: InterVarsity Academic, 1996), 77.

6. Rayburn, *O Come, Let Us Worship*, 159.

7. Mark L. Dalbey, "A Biblical, Historical, and Contemporary Look at the Regulative Principle of Worship" (DMin diss., Covenant Theological Seminary, 1999), 67–69.

8. Jeffrey J. Myers, *The Lord's Service: The Grace of Covenantal Renewal Worship* (Moscow, ID: Canon, 2003), 169; Robert W. Godfrey, "Worship: Evangelical or Reformed," *New Horizons* 23, no. 4 (April 2002): 11; Edmund Clowney, "The Singing Savior," *Moody Monthly*, July–August 1979, 40–41.

himself.[9] We need not exempt concern for ministering to one another from
our worship priorities. The gospel pattern of biblical worship indicates
that it is meant to minister God's goodness as well as to proclaim his glory
to his people.[10] In our worship we do not merely "point back" to God's
mighty acts, but we also "make present" his saving reality.[11] The gospel represented in the structures of our worship pictures the story of redemption
while also enabling us to re-enter that narrative and to live its truths with
the Savior they make present to each new generation's experience.[12]

Gospel Perspective

Corporate worship is nothing more, and nothing less, than a re-presentation
of the gospel in the presence of God and his people for his glory and their
good. The glorification of God requires us to honor his divine attributes
and his mighty acts (Ps. 150:2). God's people also rightly rejoice that these
have been directed toward their salvation, knowing God directs them to offer
thanksgiving in response (Deut. 12:12). The vertical, heaven-directed aspects
of worship do not require us to ignore human concerns. In fact, praising
God without acknowledging his love for his people would make our worship incomplete. The apostle Paul says in 1 Corinthians 14 that God desires
worship that promotes his people's love (1 Cor. 14:1), encouragement (14:3),
instruction (14:3–6), mutual edification (14:12, 26–28), thanksgiving (14:16),
witness (14:16, 23), and conviction (14:24–25). Worship should awe us with
glorification of God's transcendent character, but we cannot truly know him
if our worship has no horizontal dimension to reflect his goodness.

In order for our worship to minister God's goodness to his people, we
must have means to reflect his love in our liturgy. Sharing our praise, praying for one another, corporately confessing sin, encouraging one another
in song, collecting alms, receiving instruction together, demonstrating
concern for the lost, and communing together are obvious ways that we
express love for one another in the context of our worship. These horizontal

---

9. Torrance, *Worship, Community and the Triune God*, 10, 23, 44; Ronald E. Man, "Proclamation and Praise: Hebrews 2:12 and the Role of Christ in Worship," *Viewpoint*, July–August
2000, 6.

10. Gary A. Parrett, "9.5 Theses on Worship: A Disputation on the Role of Music," *Christianity Today*, February 2005, 42.

11. Duane Kelderman et al., *Authentic Worship in a Changing Culture* (Grand Rapids:
CRC Publications, 1997), 41.

12. Howard Vanderwall, ed., *The Church of All Ages* (Herndon, VA: Alban Institute,
2008), 95–96; Bryan Chapell, *Using Illustrations to Preach with Power*, rev. ed. (Wheaton, IL:
Crossway, 2001), 71–73, 186–90.

(person-to-person) aspects of the liturgy are not less important than the vertical (person-to-God) aspects of prayer and praise.

The horizontal and vertical dimensions of worship actually cannot be isolated in any aspect of worship. *Prayer* is directed to God (recognizing his glory) but offers petitions for his people (expressing human love). *Preaching* that fails to show love for God's Word fails to bring him glory, but preaching that fails to express love for God's people also fails to glorify him. *Praise* glorifies the greatness of God, and simultaneously encourages God's people with the implicit message that such a great God still delights to hear them. Worship must be offered with concern for God's glory *and* the good of his people. Worship cannot be a reflection of the gospel without both concerns.

Gospel Choices

This same gospel perspective, which will not allow us to segregate concerns about God's glory and his people's good, grants us much aid in making decisions about worship choices that sometimes seem to be in tension. The practical realities of planning worship will require church leaders to balance many concerns: reverence and relevance (e.g., musical styles), transcendence and transparency (e.g., biblical or personal illustrations in preaching), liberty and law (e.g., dress standards), elevation and engagement (e.g., choosing between traditional or modern translations), sobriety and joy (e.g., encouraging respectful silence or appreciative clapping after a moving testimony), classical or common expression (e.g., using seminary terms or street terms to describe sin). The choices are not between aspects of worship that are either good or bad, but between concerns that can all be legitimate in appropriate contexts.

One way to determine what choices to make when weighing these concerns is simply to fall back on local church tradition—do what has always been done. Another approach would be to choose according to personal preference—do what I want to do. A final alternative would be simply to do what most people in the church want to do—let's take a poll. Of course, none of these approaches guarantees that our worship will reflect Scripture's priorities.

Gospel Necessities

When our question is, "How can we balance valid but competing concerns in our worship choices?" our best approach is to consider what the gospel requires. Gospel priorities will force us to consider both God's glory and his people's good. We cannot simply fall back on what the church did in the past, especially if that no longer brings glory to God or ministers to his people. We cannot simply impose personal preference without idolizing our glory and good. We cannot simply respond to what a poll says without being more concerned for the people's present preferences than for God's ultimate glory and our neighbor's eternal soul. Since our worship should have a gospel pattern and purpose, the only biblical way of prioritizing legitimate, but competing, worship concerns is to consider how our worship practices are consistent with our understanding of how we would present the gospel in our context.

If I were given the task of presenting the gospel to a highly educated minister who had lost confidence in his faith, I would not hesitate to use every sophisticated theological term that would make sense in his life circumstance. But if I were to have the same opportunity with my daughter's high school friend, I would make very different word choices without believing I had compromised the gospel in any way. Similarly, if we were to determine that the best way to plant a church in a poor, urban neighborhood was to start worship services with music drawn exclusively from seventeenth-century England, then we should proceed in just that way. But if we came to believe that such music choices were a barrier to effective gospel witness, then our worship practice should change—even if we personally preferred seventeenth-century English hymnody. Regard for Christ's purposes and love for his people must trump personal preferences. Gospel priorities require us to try to understand the culture in which we minister, so that our worship will glorify God and minister his goodness in that context.

These comments should *not* be read as suggesting that we change the gospel pattern of our worship according to the secular preferences of our culture. For example, eliminating recognition of God's holiness or human sinfulness from worship may be more appealing to the culture, but such subtractions will not reach the culture with the gospel. Purging our worship of vital gospel truths damages our witness as well as our worship.

Biblical worship has a consistent gospel pattern through the ages because the gospel's truths transcend cultural trends or generational preferences. Removing the gospel pattern of our worship is as destructive to the church's ministry as imposing personal style preferences on worship. Concerns for relevance, connection, and understanding should affect the means we use to express the pattern of Christian worship, but should not encourage elimination of the gospel pattern of our worship. As we have already discussed, without a gospel structure for our worship we lose the gospel in our worship.

The Face of Jesus

The apostle Paul concludes his instruction to those who have experienced the love of Christ with an appeal to share it with others. He calls those in the church to be his partners in a "ministry of reconciliation" by which more and more will know how Christ has reconciled sinful people to a holy God. "We are therefore Christ's ambassadors," says the apostle, "as though God were making his appeal through us" (2 Cor. 5:18, 20). The charge to be "ambassadors" sounds so noble. We imagine ourselves being asked to don pith helmets and book passage on a sailing ship to take the gospel across blue water somewhere. But the reality of the apostle's words is much simpler, though no less noble. Yes, we are to represent Christ on distant shores if God calls us there, but mostly we are to represent our Savior to those he places in the context of our everyday lives. God makes his appeal through us as our lives show the face of Jesus to those with whom we share home, work, and worship.

Our worship is never primarily about pleasing ourselves—everyone knows that. Our worship is primarily about pleasing God—everyone knows that, too. But what we may forget is that our worship, no different than the rest of our lives, pleases God when we represent his Son through it. This is more than a matter of choosing music that is properly respectful or adequately relevant. Our worship should show the face of Jesus to those who have gathered and to those who need to gather to worship him. They see him when they understand his gospel—making our task to represent that gospel in all we do.

Discovering how we navigate the choices and tensions that inevitably arise when we attempt to represent Christ's lordship and love in our worship is the subject of the next chapters. The point of this chapter has simply been to highlight the natural conclusion drawn from previous chapters: the structure of a worship service is the story of Christ's ministry. Just as the content of the Sermon, the words of the hymns, and the administration of the sacraments should reflect gospel truth, so also should the pattern of the liturgy that includes them.

Our worship is not merely an arbitrary or traditional collection of ceremonial ordinances people are compelled to follow in order to make God happy. Worship defines the community context in which we re-present

Christ to his people and Christ is present with his people.[13] Worship should
not be so narrowly conceived as being only about reminding people of
their ethical obligations and doing proper things to honor God. Worship
is about renewing relationship with the present Christ. As we re-present
his redemptive ministry through the liturgy, God's people experience the
grace of the gospel and grow in their relationship with him. From these
blessings flow all the responses of honor and obedience that are true of
love for Christ (John 14:23).[14]

Older translations of the Bible offered the glorious insight that God
inhabits the praises of his people (Ps. 22:3 KJV). Our examination of
historical liturgies and biblical patterns of worship has enriched this understanding. God is not only enthroned on our praises, he indwells them
through the ministry of Christ's gospel that enables and forms our worship.
As our worship reflects his story, we become his face to his people, renew
his message among them, and present him to them.

13. Hughes Oliphant Old, *The Reading and Preaching of the Scriptures in the Worship of
the Christian Church*, vol. 1, *The Biblical Period* (Grand Rapids: Eerdmans, 1998), 341.
    14. William H. Willimon, *The Service of God: How Worship and Ethics Are Related* (Nash-
ville: Abingdon, 1983), 28, 80.

10

THE MISSION OF CHRIST-
CENTERED WORSHIP

Churches in our changing culture face many challenges regarding worship style. While theological controversies swirl about the nature of justification, explanation of the Trinity, gender responsibilities, and charismatic gifts, my experience in hundreds of North American churches says these discussions are few in comparison with worship controversies.[1] Without exception, every North American church I know has some level of tension regarding its worship style.

The reasons for these tensions are numerous: transience of church populations, the demise of denominations, family breakdown, fewer people worshiping in the churches of their youth, aging church populations, concern to stem the exodus of a younger generation, the influences of pop culture, four decades of contemporary worship music, the charismatic renewal, ecumenism, technological innovations, globalization, megachurch influences, a longing for authenticity, the erosion of traditional values, reactive fear in much of the church, neoconservatism, fresh challenges to contribute to cultural transformation, a longing for anchors amid rapid

---

1. Thomas G. Long, *Beyond the Worship Wars: Building Vital and Faithful Worship* (Herndon, VA: Alban Institute, 2001), 3; Matthew R. Moore, "Dear Church Family," distributed by Session to Briarwood Presbyterian Church, Birmingham, AL, January 27, 2002, 1.

cultural changes, rising interest in the global church, ancient-future church movements, and neo-Catholic movements.[2]

All of these factors, plus many more, have created a perfect storm to shipwreck any assumption that a church will be safe as long as it makes no decisions about its worship style. Even a choice not to change is a significant choice of direction in our present context of inescapable cultural crosscurrents. Our challenge and calling in such times is to worship God according to gospel priorities so that those Christ is rescuing from the storms of life can see his face and trust his heart.

Gospel Mission

Churches today inevitably make choices about whether their liturgy should be high church or low church, contemporary or traditional, simple or sophisticated—or an eclectic mix. Sadly, most only know how to make these choices based on the power and preferences of a dominant person or party in the church. As a consequence, worship style is determined by arbitrary rule ("I've decided . . ."), personal taste ("What I like is . . ."), church tradition ("What we have always done is . . ."), or cultural preference ("What the people will find acceptable, attractive, or enjoyable is . . ."). There is a better approach.

The church has a mission. God calls us to minister the gospel. Our worship should be an intentional expression of this biblical purpose.[3] Love for Christ compels us always to consider how we may re-present the gospel so as to bring the most glory to God and good to his people. This gospel is not only directed toward evangelism or foreign missions. The message of God's provision of grace is as vital for daily Christian living as it is for conversion. Without assurance of grace, we despair in our sin. Without reminder of grace, we depend on our own strength. Without rejoicing in grace, we presume the merit of our performance. Unless we make the communication of the gospel the frame and focus of our worship, our ceremonies possess only a form of godliness without the power of God (2 Tim. 3:5).

2. Duane Kelderman et al., *Authentic Worship in a Changing Culture* (Grand Rapids: CRC Publications, 1997), 16–34; Chris Armstrong, "The Future Lies in the Past: Why Evangelicals Are Connecting with the Early Church as They Move into the 21st Century," *Christianity Today*, February 2008, 24–26; Robert Lewis Shayon and Nash Cox, comps., *Religion, Television, and the Information Superhighway: A Search for a Middle Way* (Philadelphia: Waymark, 1994), 4.

3. James B. Torrance, *Worship, Community and the Triune God of Grace* (Downers Grove, IL: InterVarsity Academic, 1996), 41.

Necessities and Capacities

Concern to see the power of God among his people will require that we abandon no essential of worship that declares his glory. If we do not understand his glory, then we cannot give him proper praise nor rightly humble ourselves before him. Similarly, if we do not appreciate his grace, then our praise will be wrongly motivated, and guilt will either harden or crush us. Concern that God's people understand his glory and grace should direct us to design worship that ministers to the "necessities and capacities" of God's people (the terms are from the Westminster Larger Catechism, question 159).

For their spiritual health, God's people must honor his name, humble themselves, seek his grace, know his pardon, give him thanks, learn his ways, love his people, be his disciples, and walk in his peace. None of these "necessities" can be compromised without causing damage. Were any of these features of gospel health long absent from any believer's life, spiritual progress would be stunted and eventually fail. The truths of the progress of the gospel form the essential framework of our worship so that they shape the lives of the worshipers. This shaping cannot occur, however, if the worship is expressed in ways that are insensitive to the "capacities" of the worshipers.

The leaders of the Protestant Reformation showed sensitivity to the capacities of God's people by insisting that worship be in the common language of the people (rather than Latin). People who did not understand the words of the worship could not fully grasp the gospel the church proclaimed. The Reformers were not so concerned to change the essential structure of worship. In fact, their liturgies intentionally sought to reclaim the earliest Catholic liturgies that the Reformers believed were more reflective of New Testament worship.[4] There were various approaches to this reclamation, but none ignored the general gospel pattern of Christian worship. Liturgical choices continued to minister to the gospel necessities of the people even as their capacities for apprehending and appreciating the aspects of worship were carefully measured.

The Reformers' sensitivity to the capacities of the people extended far beyond language choices. Consideration of the cultural context and background of the people influenced many kinds of worship choices. As has already been discussed, Luther carefully weighed the placement of an Offertory because the practice of indulgences had so influenced the perceptions of his people. Calvin yielded to concerns about sacerdotalism in his

4. Howard L. Rice and James C. Huffstutler, *Reformed Worship* (Louisville: Geneva, 2001), 3.

choices about an Assurance of Pardon and the frequency of Communion, but he combated impressions of priestly privilege in choices regarding his own position in the service.

Both of these Reformers made music choices that they believed would allow people more readily to enter into the praise of God. Both eschewed the ornate preaching forms of their times in order to speak "plainly" for the people's understanding—an ethic echoed in the Westminster Confession of Faith and other precursors of modern evangelicalism. In fact, it is ironic that today some so highly regard the language of Puritan preaching that they want to press it upon contemporary congregations—ignoring the ethic of the Puritans, which was to preach in the language of their people.

Discerning the balance between the necessities and capacities of worshipers has never been easy, but it is always essential for those who minister with gospel priorities. Designing worship based on what people *need* to know and do, without considering what they *can* know and do is futile and unbiblical.[5] When Jesus and Paul ministered the gospel, they spoke with erudition to schooled scribes, and with simplicity to the common folk; with challenge to the self-righteous, and with sensitivity to the outcasts; with Jewish temple allusions to the Jews, and with pagan poetry allusions to the Gentiles. Always a gospel ethic involves "double listening," listening to both the world and the Word to ensure people can know what they must know and can worship as they must worship.[6]

Sensitivity versus Compromise

Sensitivity to worshipers' capacities goes awry when concern to communicate to those in our culture tempts us to be undiscerning about the realities of our culture. Jesus and Paul were willing to challenge religious traditions in order to communicate spiritual truth, but they were not naïve about their choices. They refused to be bound by conventions that would hinder the gospel, but they respected cultural norms that would enable them to keep the gospel credible and knowable. Jesus ministered to the woman at the well (which would have raised eyebrows about his message), but he did not accompany her alone to her home (which would have resulted in rejection of his message). Paul in Athens made allusion to an unknown God, but he did not make an offering at that altar. On Mars Hill the apostle quoted

5. Russell G. Shubin, "Worship That Moves the Soul: A Conversation with Robert King," *Mission Frontiers* 23, no. 2 (June 2001): 13.
6. Greg Perry, "Reforming Worship," *Reformed Theological Review* 61, no. 1 (April 2002): 46.

pagan poetry, but he carefully chose a passage that would underscore his message and not undermine his credibility. Concern for the witness of the gospel made Jesus and Paul willing to break with some traditions and willing to honor others.

Applications of these principles are always most difficult in the present tense. How do we minister to the necessities and capacities of people in our worship today? Their necessities require our faithfulness to the gospel. Our worship must reflect the truths of the ministry of Christ revealed in his Word. As previous chapters have demonstrated, the structure of our worship and the content of our words—said, read, demonstrated, prayed, and sung—communicate the message that God's people need. People's ability to understand and appropriate the message depends both on the work of the Spirit in their hearts and on worship leaders' willingness and ability to discern how to communicate in the cultural context.

Sensitivity to the cultural context does not mean automatic capitulation to cultural norms. For example, the expectation that a generation that has grown up with PowerPoint presentations and video marketing will want the same in worship can be quite naïve. Some in this generation feel so bombarded by all this cultural "noise" that they long for a place of quiet reflection.[7] Some persons who have experienced the dead spirituality of religious formalism will long for informality that communicates authenticity. Others who feel the aimlessness of a culture without heroes, institutions, or values to respect will seek churches that "feel like" church—where faith, at least, seems secure because continuities with the past are honored through traditional songs and symbols. Some will run from churches whose anachronistic music communicates lethargy and selfishness; others will run from churches too naïve to recognize their music is so "with it" that it carries secular baggage that many young people are desperate to escape.[8]

Gospel Priorities

Cultural signals are confusing and legitimate values can suggest conflicting choices, but navigating amid these waves is not hopeless. The gospel charts

7. Robert E. Webber, "How Will the Millennials Worship? A Snapshot of the Very Near Future," *Reformed Worship* 38, no. 2 (April–June 2001): 3.

8. See Timothy J. Keller's astute analysis in "Reformed Worship in the Global City" in *Worship by the Book*, ed. D. A. Carson (Grand Rapids: Zondervan, 2002), 195–98; also Long, *Beyond the Worship Wars*, 17; Kelderman et al., *Authentic Worship*, 65; Michael Horton, *A Better Way: Rediscovering the Drama of God-Centered Worship* (Grand Rapids: Baker Books, 2002), 164, 171.

our course. Not only can gospel priorities aid worship choices, but they can stop worship wars. In this era of church "shopping and hopping," biblical illiteracy, denominational indifference, population mobility, televised super preachers, and advertised worship styles, everyone has an opinion about worship. But those opinions are often uninformed individual preferences driven by a "sense" of what is right or pleasing, rather than by reasoned consideration of how the gospel can best be communicated to the specific people God is gathering for the ministry of this specific church.[9]

If gospel priorities do not determine worship choices, then people's preferences will tear the church apart. The variety of style possibilities combined with the usual mix of personalities, generations, newcomers, and old-timers will put church leaders under constant pressure to adjust worship. If personal preferences are allowed to call the shots, then worship tensions will be unavoidable. For example, my frequent church travels result in my often being asked (usually by unhappy persons) why so many churches have abandoned their "traditional" music. Yet when I press for clarification of what is meant by "traditional," I discover the term usually defines whatever church music the questioner grew accustomed to prior to age twenty-five. That music may be nineteenth-century English hymnody, early-twentieth-century revival and crusade songs, or "classics" from the 1970s Jesus Movement, but it is perceived as "traditional."

Well-meaning people can become convinced that this "traditional" music should dominate their church's worship because they can most genuinely enter into an attitude of worship through such music. There is nothing false or inauthentic in their worship. Nor is it necessarily wrong that their worship preferences reflect their cultural background. All worship styles reflect aspects of culture or else it would be impossible for believers in that culture to appreciate their worship. All believers will have worship preferences affected by their context and heritage. This is not wrong either. We only err when we fail to recognize that the cultural background affecting our preferences is not universal—and when we make our preferences rather than the gospel our worship guide.[10]

Gospel Ministry

Because of the differing worship perspectives vying for ascendancy in our churches, it has never been more important for church leaders to unite in a

9. Long, *Beyond the Worship Wars*, 78.
10. Lawrence Roff, *Let Us Sing* (Philadelphia: Great Commission Publications, 1991), 148–50.

worship approach that prioritizes gospel principles. Christ-centered worship can create harmony around a common mission even where personal preferences differ. Such worship requires leaders to identify the gospel calling of their specific church in its specific cultural setting. First, leaders should ask, "Who has God gathered to do ministry in this place?" As leaders identify the mix of personalities, backgrounds, talents, and gifts God has gathered, they will begin to understand their ministry resources.

Next, leaders should ask, "What is God calling us to do with these resources?" This question requires leaders to consider the spiritual and physical needs of those already gathered, as well as the needs of those this *specific* church has opportunity to reach and serve for Christ's sake.[11] A trip to the local chamber of commerce or to a Web site specializing in demographic studies may reveal the predominant kinds of people who are in (or who are coming to) the neighborhood a church wants to serve.[12] Similar studies may reveal neglected pockets of individuals no one has bothered to serve but who need the ministry of Christ. A Christ-centered church asks not only how to minister to those most like us but also how to minister to those who most need us.

All churches should periodically survey their congregations to determine the kinds of people its members see often at work, at play, or in family gatherings. Since most new people in a church are invited by a friend or family member, a church has no future whose people believe it cannot or will not minister to their friends and loved ones. A church also has no future if leaders only consider how to minister to the present generation. We are mistaken, of course, to let our children determine what our worship should be; we are also mistaken not to consider how their children may need to worship.[13]

Worship choices should never be segregated into meeting the needs of either those inside or those outside the present church community. Worship

11. David D. Bannerman, *The Worship of the Presbyterian Church* (Edinburgh: Andrew Elliot, 1984), 9–12.

12. Helpful Web sites on demographics: http://www.churchtoolbox.org/precept/html (general demographics); http://realestate.yahoo.com/re/neighborhood/main/html (presentation of demographic characteristics by ZIP code); http://www.bestplaces.net/html/cities.html (comparison of city demographics); http://factfinder.census.gov/servlet/AGSGeoAddressServlet?_program_year_50&-treeId=420&_lang=en&_sse=on (census data by street address); http://www.cluster1.claritas.com/MyBestSegments/Default.jsp?ID=20 (psychographic analysis for every ZIP code in America); http://www.arda.tm (churches by denomination and membership in every county in America); http://yp.yahoo.com/py/yploc.py?&clr=ypResults&stp=y&stx=85537085&desc=churches&qtx=&tab=B2C&country_in=us (church names and addresses by ZIP code); http://www.mislinks.org/church/chplant.htm (church planting resources); http://factfinder.census.gov/home/saff/main.html (census information).

13. Howard Vanderwall, ed., *The Church of All Ages* (Herndon, VA: Alban Institute, 2008), 4, 11.

priorities cannot ignore the needs of those already gathered in the body of Christ, because the primary purpose of any church is to enable the people of God rightly to honor God. At the same time, leaders must recognize that God's people cannot rightly honor him if they are unconcerned for the progress of his kingdom and the proclamation of his name. So worship choices also cannot ignore the needs of those God has yet to gather into the body of Christ. Leaders must be concerned always to deepen the church's "rootedness" and extend her "reach."[14] The apostle Paul reminds us of this internal/external balance when he tells the Corinthian church that in worship, "All . . . must be done for the strengthening of the church" (1 Cor. 14:26), but also encourages worship with intelligible words so that an unbeliever can understand the gospel (1 Cor. 14:23–25).

During his many years of fruitful ministry, noted churchman Edmund Clowney advised many to think of their corporate worship as "doxological evangelism."[15] His words were a reminder that true worship requires enthusiastic, respectful, and grateful praise of God, that is, doxology (from the Greek word for *praise*). If God's people gather to worship without evident gladness, awe, and security in God's redemptive provision and providential care, then their worship is defective. Thus, we must design worship to minister to the people God has already gathered in his name. At the same time, God's people must recognize that their evident joy and peace in a dark world are a light to the lost. Worship designed to enable God's people to rejoice in his goodness will also, of necessity, attract those who need to learn to rejoice and rest in him—and we cannot neglect them.[16] Healthy worship is one of the church's most effective evangelism tools; thus, we cannot forget the unbeliever even as we focus on enabling believers rightly to honor their God.[17]

When a local church's leaders have carefully discerned those (believers and unbelievers) to whom God is calling them to minister, then decisions regarding worship style can become a matter of gospel principles rather than personal preferences. The leaders can reason, "Our worship is supposed to be a re-presentation of the gospel to those in our spiritual care. So if we are presenting the gospel to them, what are the best ways to communicate the glory and goodness of God with the resources he has given us?"

14. Kelderman et al., *Authentic Worship*, 60; Bob Kauflin, *Worship Matters: Leading Others to Encounter the Greatness of God* (Wheaton, IL: Crossway, 2008), 189–91.
15. See Edmund Clowney, "The Singing Savior," *Moody Monthly*, July–August 1979, 42; also Timothy J. Keller's reflections on Clowney's work in Carson, *Worship by the Book*, 218–19.
16. Paul Waitman Hoon, *The Integrity of Worship: Ecumenical and Pastoral Studies in Liturgical Theology* (Nashville and New York: Abingdon, 1971), 59.
17. Kelderman et al., *Authentic Worship*, 69; Kauflin, *Worship Matters*, 203–4.

Gospel Unity

Answering these questions will require leaders to consider the necessities and capacities of those God has gathered and is gathering for that specific church's spiritual care. Yet, while such consideration may be a difficult task, it can also be a wonderfully uniting one. Leaders can lock arms in unity to support worship that promotes the gospel's purposes, even when it does not meet all of their or others' personal preferences. Personal preferences can still be taken into consideration because they are included in the discussion of people's necessities and capacities. But everyone should understand that these personal preferences do not trump gospel purposes. And when leaders unite under the rule of the gospel, the constant pressures from some parishioners to adjust worship for the sake of personal preferences can be resisted with explanations about the church's specific calling rather than with statements about counter-preferences.

The gospel priorities of Christ-centered worship make it plain why worship choices must be made and give a rationale for those choices. This rationale is based on biblical principles that can be explained to other leaders, to the congregation, and to those with contrary preferences. Leaders simply must keep reminding themselves and others that their style of worship is determined by what they have agreed effectively communicates the gospel in their specific context. Other churches with other people and other resources may well have other legitimate callings that determine other legitimate style choices. But those churches cannot and should not determine how the gospel can best be presented in a context they do not know or share.[18]

Even leaders who have contrary style preferences can unite in a higher gospel purpose without feeling they have compromised their values. Once they see that the main concerns of worship are about meeting biblical priorities rather than personal expectations, leaders can unite behind a worship style that does not entirely match their preferences because they are convinced it advances the gospel. Church leaders who have the mind of Jesus will consider others' interests above their own, and will consider Christ's purposes above all (Phil. 2:3–11). With such leaders to guide them, God's people can also unite in worship, not because they share the same preferences, but because they have a shared purpose: the presentation of the gospel for the glory of the Savior and the good of his people.

18. Marva Dawn, *Reaching Out without Dumbing Down: A Theology of Worship for the Turn-of-the-century Culture* (Grand Rapids: Eerdmans, 1995), 13.

Gospel Doxology

Just as the gospel cannot be limited by the preferences of a single generation or community, the worship that expresses God's good news must extend beyond all borders. The psalmist urges God's people, "Declare his glory among the nations, his marvelous deeds among all the peoples. For great is the Lord, and most worthy of praise" (Ps. 96:3–4a). With such perspective, the Old Testament writer anticipates the culmination of all ages when those from every nation, tribe, people, and language will stand before the throne of God and declare their salvation through Christ (Rev. 7:9–10). Christ-centered worship prepares us for such world-encompassing praise and stimulates the mission impulse that ushers it forward.

In the worship scenes of Revelation, the tribes and nations of the world do not give up their languages as they offer their praise. We continue to recognize the differences of their cultures even as they unite in praise of the Lamb that was slain. Their rich variety of backgrounds does not diminish his glory but underscores his rightful rule over all. God's glory is made more magnificent by the diverse ways people bring praise for the ministry of the Lamb.

Those who love the gospel and delight in its spread across nations, continents, and cultures rejoice in this "ethnodoxology"—the glorious praise of many peoples enriched by the different ways God has formed their languages and cultures.[19] As an orchestral work is made more glorious by many instrumental voices joined in a symphony of music, our worship grows in glory as we unite with very different voices to sing the wonders of the gospel. The manifold wisdom of God is apparent in the variety of his people's expressions, and the great grace of God is evident in the unity of their faith.[20]

Christ-centered worship enables this symphonic expression of the gospel as it expands across ages and locales, not by making rules about liturgical practices and preferences but by retelling the gospel story. As the gospel forms the content of our worship, it simultaneously forms its contours. We may tell the story in different languages and cultural expressions, but the fundamental story doesn't change.[21] The narrative consistency both protects the truth of the gospel and gives worship an unchanging structural core.

19. Shubin, "Worship That Moves the Soul," 11.
20. T. F. Torrance, "The Mind of Christ in Worship: The Problem of Apollinarianism in the Liturgy," in *Theology in Reconciliation* (Grand Rapids: Eerdmans, 1975), 213.
21. Bryan Chapell, John Frame, Joseph "Skip" Ryan, Roy Taylor, and Wade Williams, "MNA Guidelines for Church Planters on Principles and Practices of Worship," Presbyterian Church in America, October 2000, 3.

The gospel narrative does not simply form the structure of our worship; it simultaneously stimulates mission on behalf of the One we worship. The story of Christ-centered worship is the story of the God who has come to redeem his people. As we retell his story in our worship, our hearts are moved by his love and we want to tell the world of it.[22] We intuitively know that more glory will come to the One we worship if more people worship with us. As our worship resonates with the message of his love for us, our hearts resonate with love for him and his purposes.[23] More and more we come to understand that our worship is part of God's mission to make known his Son to our hearts and to the world.

22. Vernon M. Whaley, *Understanding Music and Worship in the Local Church* (Wheaton, IL: Evangelical Training Association, 1995), 24.
23. Kauflin, *Worship Matters*, 148–49.

11

THE ASPECTS OF CHRIST-CENTERED WORSHIP

With the understanding that the worship of the church universal is designed for re-presenting the gospel, we can begin to consider how to structure worship for each local church. Worship that follows the gospel pattern of Christ's grace in our lives will have his priorities. We will want to praise the glory and goodness of God, and we will want the effects of this praise to touch our hearts and be a witness to others. Gospel concerns will cause us not simply to evaluate the correctness of our liturgy, but also to consider how our worship ministers to the necessities and capacities of God's people. In short, we cannot be more concerned for propriety than for ministry. Our worship must express the redeeming grace its structure reflects and our hearts need.

The Values of Worship

This Christ-centered approach to worship should help us address issues that churches face as choices are made about the structure and style of their liturgy. Church leaders know they must make decisions about the liturgy based on their and their church's values. The task sounds straightforward enough. However, the job gets complicated because competing values so frequently seem to have equal validity. Leaders feel forced to reject one of the values stated in the following tandems that typically frame our worship controversies:

Typical Worship Issues

1. Structured vs. Free
2. Traditional vs. Relevant
3. Objective vs. Subjective
4. Doxological vs. Delightful
5. Solemn (dignified) vs. Celebrative (joyous)
6. Transcendent vs. Accessible
7. Common vs. Excellent
8. Emotional vs. Cognitive
9. Dialogical vs. Proclamatory
10. Historic vs. Contextualized
11. Saved- vs. Seeker-sensitive

These issues often are presented to worship leaders in the form of either/or scenarios: "Either our worship needs to be structured or free, emotional or cognitive, saved- or seeker-sensitive. . . . Which will it be? Choose!"

The problem with choosing between any of these values in Christ-centered worship is that there is biblical warrant for each.[1] If our goal is to present the gospel, then there has to be some structure to the truths we want to communicate. At the same time, the varieties of people and circumstances we address will necessitate judgment about how best to present those truths. The witness of the gospel requires some structure, but it requires some freedom too.

Balancing Our Values

Gospel balance needs to be applied to each of the tandem issues. We should not be forced to choose between being *traditional* or being *relevant*. Only the most arrogant congregation would say that God has taught nothing to its forefathers from which it can learn. And only the most self-absorbed congregation would say that it does not need to be concerned about making its worship relevant to the present generation.

Our worship must have *objective* elements. We do not teach the Trinity simply because it "feels" right. We claim the truth the Bible teaches because the holy Word of God is more dependable and authoritative than our *sub-*

---

1. Bob Kauflin, *Worship Matters: Leading Others to Encounter the Greatness of God* (Wheaton, IL: Crossway, 2008), 159–62.

jective feelings. At the same time, to worship without passionate love, joy, contrition, and thanksgiving denies the reality of the truths we claim.

Some claim that our worship should be entirely *doxological*, only concerned for the glory of God. But if God's people have no *delight* in his glory and their worship stimulates none, then we reasonably question whether his glory has been rightly presented or perceived. With great wisdom the Westminster divines not only urged preaching concerned for the glory of God; they also urged preaching with illustrations that delighted the people (see chapter 20, "Christ-Centered Sermons" in part 2). Mind and heart are both engaged in the best preaching, and in the worship that includes it.

Scripture contains texts that soar in *transcendent* thought, as well as passages made *accessible* by references to weeds and sheep. The Bible urges *solemnity* before God, and *joy* in his presence. Writers of Scripture may use *excellent* prose, or the language of *common* fishermen. Since the Scriptures that teach us how to worship and whom to worship use all of these means to share the gospel with us, our worship rightly employs all the same in order to present the gospel to God's people.

Orienting Our Values

Perhaps no set of competing values creates more worship controversy than the saved- versus seeker-sensitive tandem. The influences of the "seeker-oriented" worship services pioneered by Willow Creek Community Church in suburban Chicago are broad in North American church culture. The innovative ways in which Willow Creek and others have used music, drama, preaching, orders of service, service times, lighting, architecture, and even parking to serve the needs of the unchurched have taught many valuable lessons about gospel outreach.

In recent years, Willow Creek has also begun to examine whether it needs to focus more on the instructional depth of its ministry and worship.[2] This honest conclusion, drawn from equally bold self-assessment, underscores solid biblical principles. The first of these principles is that God primarily designs worship for his people to honor him. If our worship were ever truly and completely "seeker-oriented," then the purposes of worship would be turned upside down. If worship is more about people than about God, then it is not really worship of him. Second, if the worship of God's church is not primarily for God's people, then we deny them the worship they are obliged to give, and we rob God of the worship he is due from them.

2. Matt Branaugh, "Willow Creek's 'Huge Shift,'" *Christianity Today*, May 2008, 13.

Being entirely "seeker-*oriented*" is not really an option for Christ-centered worship.[3] But being "seeker-*sensitive*" is still an appropriate way to think about worship. Being "seeker-sensitive" is not the same as being "seeker-oriented."[4] We should remember that in the history of the church (see discussion in chapter 2) there have always been three groups to consider in the planning of worship: the communicants (adult believers), catechumens (children and adult converts learning the faith), and seekers (those examining whether they will claim the truths of the gospel).[5] The apostle Paul charges the church to be sensitive to the needs of seekers (see discussion in preceding chapter). They are not the focus of the church's worship, but the church is not to plan its worship without their needs in view (1 Cor. 14:23–25).

Witnessing Our Values

Worship is witness. By it, believers proclaim the goodness of the gospel to God, to one another, and to unbelievers. We do not focus on seekers. We do not forget them, either. In fact, the most effective churches prepare for unbelievers before they are present. Such churches consider the unchurched persons that God has placed in their ministry context and, then, adjust the language and style of the worship so that it can be apprehended by them. Some may complain that it makes no sense to plan worship for those who are not present, but such worship also prepares the hearts of those who are present to reach those who are not.

After the devastations of September 11, 2001, the churches of New York City swelled with unchurched people looking for something more trustworthy and enduring than glass and steel. Yet after only a few weeks, most of the churches had shrunk back to their original attendance. Redeemer Church in Manhattan, a church renowned for worship excellence and outreach, was an exception. Pastor Tim Keller explained, "If your church was not prepared for unbelievers before the tragedy, then once the tragedy happened, it was already too late to help them."

To some degree every church will need worship that is both traditional and relevant, doxological and delightful, emotional and cognitive, historical and contextualized, elementary and mature, saved- and seeker-sensitive. Healthy lives balance each of these considerations, and the Bible presents

3. Gary A. Parrett, "9.5 Theses on Worship: A Disputation on the Role of Music," *Christianity Today*, February 2005, 42.

4. Douglas Webster, "Seeker-Sensitive, Not Consumer-Oriented," *Discernment*, Spring–Summer 2005, 8–9.

5. Hughes Oliphant Old, *The Reading and Preaching of the Scriptures in the Worship of the Christian Church*, vol. 1, *The Biblical Period* (Grand Rapids: Eerdmans, 1998), 349.

the gospel in terms of each. The gospel is too good and too rich to be contained in one dimension of human expression. We deny the multidimensional wisdom of the gospel, the phases of our own lives, and the needs of persons unlike ourselves if we impose standards that limit worship to our preferences. Thus, worship wars erupt when anyone attempts to eliminate any one of the considerations in these tandems with regard to worship structure, preaching content, music style, Bible translation used, and so on.

The same God who inspired the Epistle to the Romans also penned Psalm 23. If some who relish the sophistication of Romans would dare to claim that God "dumbed down" the Scriptures when he inspired the simple Shepherd's Psalm, they would simply indicate they had confused excellence with complexity. Such persons also have yet to face issues in life that can make the simple truths of the gospel most precious—for themselves and others. There are times for our souls to soar to musical heights on the melodies of Mahler, and there are times to cling to the down-to-earth goodness of "Jesus Loves Me." Before we complain too stridently about a chorus being repeated two or three times, we may need to re-read Psalm 136 or give thanks that we do not have to repeat the *Kyrie* twelve times as Calvin required of his people in Strasbourg.[6]

Excellence in all dimensions of worship expression, including music, must not simply be defined by cultural standards of sophistication, but by the ability of the expression to strengthen, deepen, and develop faith. We should neither demean songs that a congregation knows and loves nor allow it never to move from them. Creating uncertain and muted praise by demanding highly sophisticated expression from an unprepared congregation denies God the passionate worship he deserves from his people. Yet to allow the congregation to settle for clichéd worship and unthinking routines does the same. The healthiest congregations with the most thoughtful worship engage in an eclectic mix of worship expression that keeps faith fresh, serves multiple generations, stays rooted in the past, blossoms toward the future, stimulates childlike love, strives for excellence in presentation, bridges cultural barriers, and encourages ever-greater understanding.[7]

The same apostle Paul who urged us to press on to the deeper truths of the gospel also taught us to express those truths plainly. He told us that God uses the simple things of the world to confound the wise, even as he chastised those who stayed with gospel milk when they should have

6. Michael S. Hamilton, "The Triumph of the Praise Songs," *Christianity Today*, July 1999, 35.

7. Thomas G. Long, *Beyond the Worship Wars: Building Vital and Faithful Worship* (Herndon, VA: Alban Institute, 2001), 63.

matured to meat (1 Cor. 3:2; cf. Heb. 5:12). He was willing to become all things to all men for the sake of the gospel, and the gospel commitments of our worship should compel us to do the same (1 Cor. 9:22). Gospel priorities require us to determine the degree to which our worship will emphasize values that must be held in tension, but these same commitments deny us the right to dispense with any of these values. Each has a role in communicating the truths of our Savior. The options that we have for incorporating the values become more apparent as we consider the aspects of Christ-centered worship (see below).

The Aspects of Worship

We have noted numerous times that the liturgies of the church have a generic gospel form. Though there are important exceptions, the aspects of historical worship structure consistently reflect its gospel core and content. It is also important, however, for us to remember that what is normative about our worship should not be determined by human tradition but by what makes the gospel accessible to the mind and heart. Our liturgy has a gospel form not because church history requires it (or could), but because the One we worship ministers to us in these redemptive terms.

We do not know Christ apart from the truths he has revealed about himself. These truths are always presented in the context of his redemptive ministry. Thus, we need the gospel pattern of our liturgy not only because our hearts need to feed on his grace, but also because we cannot truly worship Christ apart from the grace by which he has revealed himself to us. This realization makes now-familiar aspects of the gospel pattern of Christ-centered worship take on new significance. For now we must consider whether Christ can truly be known and worshiped if we neglect the grace-revealing aspects of the liturgy. This final representation of Christ-centered worship highlights the grace each aspect of the liturgy reflects:

Aspects of Christ-Centered Worship

1. Adoration (recognition of God's greatness and grace)
2. Confession (acknowledgment of our sin and need for grace)
3. Assurance (affirmation of God's provision of grace)
4. Thanksgiving (expression of praise and thanks for God's grace)
5. Petition and Intercession (expression of dependence on God's grace)
6. Instruction (acquiring the knowledge to grow in grace)
7. Communion/Fellowship (celebrating the grace of union with Christ and his people)
8. Charge and Blessing (living for and in the light of God's grace)

The Soul of Worship

With this perspective on the aspects of worship, I am suggesting that there is another way of approaching common debates about Christian liturgy. Those debates typically revolve around the issue of whether our worship should be more or less tied to a past tradition. Participants in these debates will amass personal, scriptural, or historic evidence to debate a specific order of worship elements (e.g., whether the Offering should precede or follow the Sermon, whether praise or prayer should start the service, whether the Lord's Prayer is said before or after the Lord's Supper), or to argue for the inclusion or removal of a specific practice (e.g., the Doxology after the Offering, an assurance of forgiveness, use of an ancient prayer or creed, music during Communion).

Too often these debates are narrowly focused, dealing with legitimate concerns about historical continuity and ministry effectiveness but forgetting the gospel perspective that should frame the entire discussion. Additionally, without the gospel as the organizing principle of Christian worship, well-meaning leaders attempt to organize worship around less-appropriate concepts (e.g., Trinity, sacrifice, covenant loyalty, community, kingdom, synagogue worship, ecclesial catholicity, early church continuity).

While these concepts are exceedingly important for the development of Christian orthodoxy and godly living, in themselves they are not the good news of the gospel.[8] For example, if the goal and pattern of our worship is merely to reflect the relationships of the Trinity, then our praise becomes satisfactory by the adequacy of our performance and we lose the joy of gratefully responding to the redemption Christ provides despite our inadequacy.[9] Concerns for both adequate performance and grateful praise will make us strive for excellence in worship expression, but only the latter truly honors God alone.

Worship primarily driven by concerns for propriety and acceptance feeds pride and burdens hearts. This is the inevitable consequence of making anything but the grace of the gospel the soul of our worship.[10] If our worship is not an expression of redemptive truths, it inevitably drifts from being a response to God's saving acts.[11] Instead, the worship itself begins to be perceived as saving acts generated by us—moving us to sacerdotal or

---

8. John H. Armstrong, "Thinking Out Loud (Again) on Worship," *Reformation and Revival Weekly Newsletter*, May 21, 2002, 1–3.

9. Kauflin, *Worship Matters*, 74–75.

10. James B. Torrance, *Worship, Community and the Triune God of Grace* (Downers Grove, IL: InterVarsity Academic, 1996), 22–23.

11. Robert E. Webber, *Worship Old and New: A Biblical, Historical, and Practical Introduction*, rev. ed. (Grand Rapids: Zondervan, 1994), 14.

cultic attitudes.[12] By re-presenting the gospel we remind ourselves that our worship is a response to God's grace, not an infusion or conjuring of it.[13] We are blessed by the reality of his presence but we do not create it.[14] The responses we offer in worship are only enabled by the power of the Spirit and are further evidence of God's grace, not the cause of it.[15]

Grace for the Heart

The centrality of grace in the aspects of worship, and the necessity of each aspect for a complete picture of Christ's ministry in our lives, should not simply signal priorities for the routines of corporate worship. The gracious character of each aspect of the liturgy should also remind us that worship is meant to refresh our hearts with God's goodness and strengthen our relationship with his Son. Worship is about renewing and deepening love for Christ. We do not experience this love without some guidance for its expression, but neither do we appreciate it with robotic adherence to a liturgy rule book.

Concern to honor Christ will keep us faithful to the pattern of Christ-centered worship, but concern to engage the heart through worship should keep us sensitive to the need for worship that is fresh, responsive to the needs of the congregation, and not simply governed by rote performance. One of the ways that we keep worship engaging is by letting each of the aspects of the liturgy do its work. Since the worship service is a re-presentation of the gospel, the thought, flow, timing, and order of each aspect of the service all need to reflect concern for how both thought and emotion are affected by prior and subsequent gospel aspects.[16]

For example, quick movement from high praise to abject confession may make theological and logical sense (the light of God's glory should make us recognize our sin), but the emotions may not have been given time to catch up. If the choir has begun the service with glorious praise that has lifted hearts from earthly ditches of worry to heavenly heights of hope, no one may be ready for a quick descent back into the mud of personal confession. This is not necessarily because hearts are cold to the truths of the gospel. Hearts may not be ready for a jarring transition precisely because they have been warmed and moved by gospel truths. The post-

---

12. Nicholas Wolterstorff, "The Reformed Liturgy," in *Major Themes in the Reformed Tradition*, ed. Donald K. McKim (Grand Rapids: Eerdmans, 1992), 290, 293.

13. Richard Foster, *Streams of Living Water: Celebrating the Great Traditions of the Christian Faith* (New York: Harper, 1998), 86.

14. Torrance, *Worship, Community and the Triune God*, 15, 21.

15. Peter Leithart, "For Whom Is Worship?" *New Horizons* 23, no. 4 (April 2002): 5.

16. D. A. Carson, ed., *Worship by the Book* (Grand Rapids: Zondervan, 2002), 48–52.

Westminster, Irish liturgy purposefully provided the option of inserting Scripture Sentences of adoration or an Affirmation of Faith between the opening Hymn of Praise and Corporate Confession. The insertion allowed the emotional Irish to keep from stripping heart gears as they moved from rapture to contrition.

Worship sensitivity rightly considers the emotional impact as well as the logical significance of each aspect of the liturgy. Leaders should be willing to plan and adjust the timing, flow, rhythm, style, and presentation of each aspect of worship so that hearts do not disengage from consideration of the Savior's grace. Sometimes people need time to reflect and "feel" the significance of the gospel in order to be able to relate deeply to the Savior who provides it. Other times they will need to be stirred to their feet and encouraged to lift their hands in worship because sitting still would encourage coldness or callousness. We cannot allow the impression that worship need only involve truth acquisition or ceremony performance and not the engagement of the heart.

12

The Components of Christ-Centered Worship

Worship stays fresh when we vary the ways that we present each of the aspects of Christ-centered worship. For example, the Reformers understood the importance of beginning worship with praise, but offered their adoration in a variety of ways (e.g., opening Scripture Sentences, Hymns of Praise, Choral Anthems). Their sensitivity helps us understand that while the gospel aspects of Christ-centered worship are always important, they do not always have to be offered in the same way.

The Components of Worship

A great variety of components of worship can be used to express aspects of our liturgy. The list below is not meant to be exhaustive, but it illustrates how varied the components of biblical worship can be.

Components of a Worship Service

1. Calls (scriptural, pastoral, choral, unison, responsive, songs and hymns, etc.)

2. Prayers (pastoral, unison, responsive, corporate, elder-led, congregant-offered, personal, silent, collect, scriptural, extemporaneous, ancient or contemporary form, hymn)
3. Scripture Readings (pastoral, unison, individual, choral, antiphonal, responsive)
4. Music (hymns, psalms, solos, choral anthems, choral-congregational responses)
5. Offerings and Collections
6. Creeds and Affirmations (Apostles', Nicene, Athanasian, catechisms, historical and contemporary writings)
7. Benedictions and Charges (scriptural, historical, extemporaneous)
8. Rubrics (i.e., explanations and transitions between worship aspects—see chapter 17 in part 2)
9. Sermon
10. Sacraments
11. Expressions of Fellowship
12. Testimonies and Ministry Reports
13. Oaths and Vows
14. Ordinations and Commissionings
15. Church Discipline
16. Fasting
17. Other (see discussion below)?

Often worship becomes staid when particular aspects of the liturgy are arbitrarily or traditionally limited to expression with specific components of worship.[1] For example, every week the pastor may read a portion of Scripture for the Call to Worship simply because that's what all previous pastors did and that's what the congregation expects. But the practice may have become so routine that no one really pays attention to the words anymore. Instead, the Call to Worship may simply have become a Pavlovian signal to find your seat, settle the kids, and look at the bulletin for the number of the first hymn (or look at the leader of the praise band for the downbeat of the first song).

In order for people's hearts and souls actually to enter into the adoration that is appropriate to begin their worship, they really have to consider why they are called to worship. This is far more likely if the Call to Worship is kept from being mere habit by occasionally being offered through a Choral Anthem, a Hymn of Praise, a special reading, or some other appropriate worship component. Jesus condemned "vain repetitions" in worship (Matt. 6:7 KJV). We should take care that our

---

1. Ronald E. Man, "Including Worship in the Seminary Curriculum" (unpublished manuscript), 17–20.

routines do not become ruts that inadvertently transgress his instructions. If the Doxology follows the Offering because of some law of the Medes and the Persians rather than because the ancient words sincerely reflect a congregation's praise for God's provision, something ought to change.

Fresh Worship

As long as its gospel purpose is fulfilled, each aspect of a Christ-centered liturgy may be expressed through a variety of worship components. If Confession of Sin has degenerated into the somber mumbling of corporate prayer whose oft-recited words no longer touch hearts, then that tradition should not be allowed to stifle real contrition. Consider some of the many options the different components of worship provide to help corporate confession be expressed legitimately and sincerely:

Options for Expressing Corporate Confession

Pastoral Prayer (form or extemporaneous)
Private Prayer
Unison Prayer (ancient or contemporary)
Responsive Reading
Scripture Reading
Corporate Hymn of Confession
Solo with Appropriate Message
Choral Anthem

I intend for this list of options for corporate confession to provide examples, not exhaust all alternatives. There are many more ways to express corporate confession with the components of worship. My goal is not to dictate how corporate confession must be offered, but to keep churches from abandoning gospel-needed confession because unnecessary routines have made it meaningless.

We do not have to abandon the gospel to keep worship alive; and we are more likely to keep multiple generations in worship when our liturgy is informed by our traditional routines rather than ruled by them. Always the church is required to honor past faithfulness, but we err in idolizing it with loyalty to its forms rather than to its faith. Just as corporate confession can be offered through a variety of worship components, so also can all the other aspects of Christ-centered worship (see examples below).

Aspects of Christ-Centered Worship	Worship Components Appropriate to Express Each Aspect
Adoration	Scriptural Call to Worship Extemporized Call to Worship Hymn/Song(s) of Praise *Gloria* Doxology *Sanctus* Antiphonal/Responsive Reading Choral Anthem Affirmation of Faith Creed
Confession	Pastoral Prayer (form or extemporaneous) Unison Confession (ancient or contemporary) Silent Personal Prayer Responsive Reading Scripture Reading Hymn/Song(s) of Confession *Kyrie* Collect Choral Anthem re: Confession Musical Solo re: Confession Combinations of Above
Assurance	Scripture Reading Responsive Reading Hymn/Song(s) of Assurance *Sursum Corda* Choral Anthem re: Assurance Musical Solo re: Assurance Fellowship Exchange (greeting one another with expression of Christ's love and peace) Combinations of Above
Thanksgiving	Regular Offering Special Collection(s) Prayer of Thanksgiving Hymn/Song(s) of Thanksgiving Doxology *Gloria Patri* Psalm of Thanksgiving Personal Testimony of Praise Scripture Reading Combinations of Above

Continued

Aspects of Christ-Centered Worship	Worship Components Appropriate to Express Each Aspect
Petition and Intercession	Pastoral Prayer Elder-led Prayers Silent Personal Prayer Intercessory Prayers for and from Congregants (e.g., prepared prayers, extemporaneous sentence prayers, prayer requests followed by pastoral prayer) Hymn/Song(s) of Petition *Kyrie* Combinations of Above
Instruction	Scripture Readings (pastoral, lay leader, unison, antiphonal, responsive, etc.) Mission, Ministry, or Personal Testimony Creeds and Affirmations Baptisms Ordaining or Commissioning Church Discipline Preparation Hymn/Song(s) Sermon
Communion/ Fellowship	Intercessions Testimonies Fellowship Expressions and Announcements Mercy/Alms Collections Diaconal Reports *Sanctus* *Gloria Patri* *Agnus Dei* Creed Recitations Communion Options: • Congregation Seated and Served • Congregation Processing (according to individual timing or in corporate patterns) • Congregation Partaking as a Meal
Charge and Blessing	Scripture Read or Recited Ordaining or Commissioning Historic or Contemporary Writing Extemporized Charge Benediction from Pastor *Benedictus* *Gloria Patri* *Nunc Dimittis* Choral Benediction Final Hymn/Song(s) with Appropriate Message Exchanges of Fellowship (dismissing one another with expressions of Christ's love and peace) Combinations of Above

If we do not allow such options to contribute to the freedom and fresh-ness of our worship, then our worship practices deny the grace the gospel pattern of our liturgy proclaims.[2] However, concern for others' ability to worship should caution us that such variety can seem scary and threaten-ing. If these options are applied with haste, apparent irreverence, and lack of respect for honored traditions, then we deny the grace of the gospel in other ways. Pastoral prudence, patience, and understanding of people should not be abandoned to impose worship variations that appear only to serve a new pastor's preference or a younger (or older) generation's likes. It may be helpful to instruct the congregation about its history, so that what appear to be innovations are ultimately understood to be expressions of values long embraced.

For example, those from Presbyterian and Baptist traditions influenced by the Westminster Assembly may be aided by knowing that most of the components of Christ-centered worship cited above appear in lists of wor-ship elements in the Westminster Confession of Faith (see Westminster Confession of Faith 21.5; 22.1, 5). If sharp persons in a congregation ques-tion whether we were right to place more elements on our list, then it may be helpful to acknowledge the appropriateness of their question. There has been some debate about whether these lists in the Confession were meant to be exhaustive, but this seems unlikely since other lists prepared by the Westminster divines differed (cf. Westminster Larger Catechism, question 108).

Confessing Our Filters

We will probably never be able to prepare an exhaustive list of worship components since our own cultural practices can unintentionally blind us to Scripture's instruction. The Westminster divines were incisive students of Scripture, but they failed to list testimony as an element of New Testament worship despite numerous biblical examples. The Reformers' own worship practices became a filter by which they interpreted testimonies as Sermons rather than as reports of God's grace in individuals' experience.

No doubt every generation has similar filters, and we are wise to remain humble before the testimony of Scripture as we determine the components that are appropriate for expressing our worship. *Fellowship* among believers was clearly an element of New Testament worship gatherings, but until we identify it as such we may demean components of our worship that may aid the congregation's expression of mutual care (e.g., exchange of

2. Lawrence Roff, *Let Us Sing* (Philadelphia: Great Commission Publications, 1991), 15–16.

greetings, announcements, sharing of needs).[3] Some day we may resurrect the "holy kiss" (Rom. 16:16; 1 Cor. 16:20; 2 Cor. 13:12; 1 Thess. 5:26) as a component of worship or see scriptural warrant for a new kind of "mission report" (see Acts 15:3) to which our present culture blinds us.

Drama is a controversial worship component of this moment in history. Skilled theologians debate whether there is scriptural warrant for such. This is clearly not the first time in church history this subject has been debated. It is equally clear that the gestures, expressions, and object lessons of traditional Sermons have elements of drama in them. Still, my suspicion is that the popularity of drama in worship will pass. History demonstrates that believers stay in worship not because of any one element that is particularly appealing but because of their trust of a church's leaders and the clarity of the gospel they proclaim with scriptural authority.

Over time, only what truly serves the ministry of the Word survives in worship. This does not mean that I am ready to condemn those who employ components of worship unfamiliar or unappealing to me. If their practice is based on an honest and faithful reflection of gospel principles and biblical precedent, then I also need to weigh Scripture's endorsement more than my sensibilities or others' acceptance. I know the health of the church will ultimately be determined by whether it bases its conclusions on scriptural evidence rather than any human opinion. Where Scripture holds sway, the church will always find its way. The same can be said about the various other worship controversies on the evangelical church horizon: use of icons, use of media clips, weekly Communion, liturgical dance, clerical garb, and so forth.

Options for the Order

Because the components of biblical worship can be as direct as a Scripture Sentence and as complex as a choral anthem, we do not always need to represent every aspect of worship with a separate component. The content of an opening hymn may include confession as well as praise. A choral anthem may include acknowledgment of God's power as well as assurance of his pardon. Charts in previous chapters also show how various Reformation liturgies include praise, confession, assurance, and petition in the pastoral prayer.

3. Robert G. Rayburn, *O Come, Let Us Worship: Corporate Worship in the Evangelical Church* (Grand Rapids: Baker Academic, 1980), 91; Roger Lovette, *Come to Worship: Effective Approaches for Worship Planning* (Nashville: Broadman, 1990), 178.

Contemporary services can wisely move a congregation through the aspects of adoration, confession, assurance, and thanksgiving in the song set that typically opens worship. An opportunity for gospel expression also occurs in the rubrics that knit together the components of a traditional worship service. A minister's brief explanation of why gospel understanding should move the congregation to the next component of worship (or a Scripture or hymn that prepares for the next component) may beautifully relate multiple redemptive truths. Combinations such as these indicate that the order of worship may be affected by the nature and content of the components without compromising the gospel pattern of the liturgy (see examples in part 2 of this book).

Grace for the Heart

Finally, as was mentioned earlier, the order of the liturgy may vary because of the overall character of a particular order of service.[4] Often the aspects of the worship service are related to a redemptive theme (e.g., God's providence, provision, mercy, shepherding, fatherhood, omniscience, presence, etc.). The way the heart processes these themes can appropriately vary. In the aftermath of a crisis, a congregation may need a Sermon on God's eternal care before people can adequately express praise for his providence. A congregation broken by the sin of its leaders may need to hear the assurance of God's mercy before adoration or confession is possible.

The typical gospel pattern of the liturgy is designed to preserve and promote the truths of God's grace, not to enforce the order of their presentation. A gospel pattern insensitive to gospel purposes serves no one. Insistence on any liturgical order without apparent concern for how human hearts process the gospel in different times and circumstances denies rather than affirms God's grace. While worship ordinarily reflects the natural progression of the gospel in the life of the believer, it is more important that no essential aspect of the gospel be excluded from Christ-centered worship than that each aspect always occur with the same emphasis or in the same order.

History and Scripture reflect much freedom regarding the use of worship components that express the aspects of our liturgy. We keep the components and the aspects of Christ-centered worship true to the gospel not by mandating a routine for their presentation but by careful examination of their

---

4. Hughes Oliphant Old, *Leading in Prayer: A Workbook for Worship* (Grand Rapids: Eerdmans, 1995), 362–63.

contents and effects. The components should have scriptural precedent, and the aspects should communicate grace. When our liturgy reflects these priorities then it will re-present the gospel through worship that serves the glory of God and the good of his people.

Between Idolatries

If I could peek into the office of most pastors or worship leaders preparing a worship service, I would expect to see a variety of worship tools at most desks: a Bible, a hymnal, a concordance (to help find Scripture texts), a worship sourcebook (with a variety of hymns, readings, prayers, calls, benedictions, etc.), and a computer screen (ready to toggle between a variety of Web sites or software tools loaded with worship resources). The wealth of resources is enough to overwhelm the inexperienced, and enough to allow the highly experienced quickly to pick a few hymns that echo the Sermon's theme, conduct a few computer searches for appropriate readings, and then thumb through a few pages of Scripture in order to plug this week's readings into last week's worship template and chug through another service. The "plug and chug" method will inevitably become the default process for worship leaders forced to prepare worship services according to an order strictly prescribed by traditions disconnected from present experience.

Worship leaders without such strictures and without knowledge of the importance of the faith history or principles their congregation needs for long-term health will find their wealth of resources no less a trap. Freedom from any standards will lead to endless innovation guided only by the leader's taste or the congregation's approval. This "taste and approve" method inevitably leads to an idolatry of personal experience as the appropriateness of worship is judged by how many people "like it a lot."

Between these idolatries of tradition and experience is Christ-centered worship whose aspects reflect an enduring gospel that shapes the contours of our services. As these aspects are expressed by various components that Scripture gives us the right to vary, our worship has the gospel anchors needed to keep it true and the scriptural freedoms needed to keep it fresh. When these are combined with the gospel goals of enabling God's people to honor him from their hearts and to represent him to their neighbors, then our worship becomes the voice of Christ in our midst. He again inhabits the praise of his people, and they become his witnesses through their worship. They honor him for his glory even as his glory radiates from them.

Glory Dancing

My hope in articulating the beauty and historicity of Christ-centered worship is to show how the church's worship has always been shaped by its understanding of the gospel. With this understanding, contemporary believers can exercise their right and responsibility to shape their own churches' worship based on Christ's ministry to and through them. Gospel purposes should shape our worship more than personal preferences or respected traditions. My intention has not been to take sides in the traditional/contemporary worship debate or to try to mandate a liturgy for all churches. Rather my goal has been to encourage church leaders to identify their churches' specific gospel calling as the basis for making decisions about worship approaches and resources that may be traditional, contemporary, or something even better.

Many such resources are discussed in part 2 of this book. The way to use these is not simply to choose from a smorgasbord of options for the sake of variety, but to consider how the wisdom of the church through time and across contexts can help us minister Christ to his people. By his Spirit our Lord has graced his church through the ages with great wisdom regarding how to maintain and present the gospel in worship. Our privilege and responsibility now is to mine this wisdom—refined through periods of both persecution and prosperity, amid challenges to both doctrine and piety, by both saints and sinners—to glorify Christ in our churches today. As we do so we will have opportunity not only to maintain continuity with Christ's witness among our forefathers, but also to extend his witness to generations to come.

My wife and I have often delighted to watch the sun's reflection dance on the waves of the sea, and we have been awed to think of the delight God took in creating such wonder. God's glory would have been adequately expressed had he just allowed the sun to penetrate the water, clarify its depths, illumine its colors, and provide the life of all within. All of this goodness would have been enough to bring him great glory, but still he was not done. He also made the waters to reflect his splendor so much that our eyes tear and our hearts thrill in beholding his glory. These are the privileges of our worship too.

God sent his Son to penetrate our darkness, cleanse our sin, share his righteousness, and give us new life where only death dwelt. If all we ever got to do in response was realize who God is and fall on our faces in humility and awe, then that would have been appropriate. And if, after he washed the dirt from our faces and the tears from our eyes, he had asked us to raise our hands in gratitude and our voices in songs of thanksgiving, then that would have been enough too. It would have been enough for him simply to ask us to praise him for such glory, but he did more.

He gave us worship that enables us to praise his glory *and* reflect it. Through our praise his glory dances in our hearts and shines before our neighbors. Awareness of this great privilege makes us want to shape our worship by the gospel. Our worship tools are not simply the shackles of a tradition or the idols of our innovation; they are the treasures we mine to offer him radiant love and highest honor. We use them to lift to him the hope of the gospel he provides as the greatest emblem of our praise and as the greatest expression of his glory. We design our worship to proclaim the gospel so that others can see his glory dancing in our hearts—and join the dance.

Part 2

GOSPEL WORSHIP RESOURCES

13

CALL TO WORSHIP

Shout for joy to the LORD, all the earth. Worship the LORD with gladness; come before him with joyful songs. Know that the LORD is God. It is he who made us, and we are his; we are his people, the sheep of his pasture. Enter his gates with thanksgiving and his courts with praise; give thanks to him and praise his name. For the LORD is good and his love endures forever; his faithfulness continues through all generations. (Ps. 100)

These joyful words of the psalmist that call God's covenant people to worship exemplify the qualities of a Call to Worship. In the historical practice of Christian churches across many traditions, a Call to Worship typically is a few lines of Scripture (or a combination of Scripture texts) expressed by a minister or worship leader at the beginning of a church service. In contemporary practice, a Call to Worship may be extemporized by the worship leader, presented by a choir, read responsively by the congregation, sung by a worship team, or included in an opening song, but the goal does not vary for those who understand the significance of these moments. The Call to Worship exhorts God's people to turn from worldly distractions and to focus hearts, minds, and actions on revering him. The beloved words of Psalm 100 well demonstrate the principles that

Adapted with permission from the author's foreword to *Calls to Worship: A Pocket Resource*, by Robert I. Vasholz (Ross-shire, Scotland: Christian Focus, 2008), 9–14.

for centuries have guided worship leaders in their expression and choice of words for the Call to Worship.

1. God calls us to worship. God's Word exhorts his people, "Shout for joy to the Lord," and, "Worship the Lord with gladness." In writing these words under the inspiration of the Holy Spirit, the psalmist is actually speaking for God as he calls the ancient people to worship. The example should remind us that a contemporary worship leader who uses the words of Scripture to call the congregation to worship still speaks on behalf of God. The host of the worship service is divine. We do not invite him to be present. He invites us to "come before him" (v. 2). God calls us from all other preoccupations to join the people he has redeemed in recognition, praise, and service of his omnipresent glory.

Because the Call to Worship is from God, we are reminded that he always initiates; we respond. This is a profound truth, not only for our salvation, but also for our worship of the One who saves us. The Call to Worship is not simply a perfunctory greeting of human cordiality but is at once a weighty responsibility and a joyful privilege. The worship leader issues God's invitation to join the heavenly throng that already and always praises him. The traditions of each church and occasion will help determine the appropriateness of gathering people from stray thoughts and conversations with informal words of welcome (e.g., "Good morning. How good to have you here in God's house!"), but the privileges and responsibilities of the Call to Worship that commences our focus on revering God are too good to displace with comments regarding the weather and yesterday's football game.

With a scriptural Call to Worship, God invites us by his Word to join the worship of the ages and angels. God does not simply invite us to a party of friends, or a lecture on religion, or a concert of sacred music—he invites us into the presence of the King of the Universe before whom all creation will bow and for whom all heaven now sings. With the Call to Worship, God's people are invited to participate in the wondrous praise that already and eternally enraptures the hosts of heaven. This awesome news and great privilege should be reflected with appropriate enthusiasm and joy by the worship leader in the Call to Worship. Such a call will typically lead directly into a corporate or choral Hymn of Praise as God's people respond to the blessings of worship into which they are called. A well-planned Call to Worship often reflects the theme of the service or the nature of the occasion so that the remaining elements of the service are a natural outflow of, and response to, the content of the call.

2. God calls us to respond to his revelation. By using the words of Scripture as a Call to Worship, the leader automatically urges God's people to respond to his disclosure of his own nature and purposes. This pattern established by the Call to Worship shapes the rest of the worship service. We do not approach God on our terms, but his. When he speaks, it is our obligation and privilege to respond appropriately in praise, prayer, repentance, testimony, encouragement of others, and service to what he declares about himself. This corporate dialogue in which we as God's people respond to God's revelation is the sacred rhythm of covenant worship that begins with the Call to Worship.

God reveals himself in Psalm 100: "Know that the LORD is God. It is he who made us" (v. 3). This revelation of God as Lord and Creator immediately leads the psalmist to exhortations for further exaltation: "Enter his gates with thanksgiving and his courts with praise; give thanks to him and praise his name" (v. 4). These words remind us that a Call to Worship has an imperative quality. We are not simply informing others of the attributes of God or creating a holy aura by the citation of a poignant Scripture passage. In the Call to Worship, the worship leader specifically calls God's people to respond to God's revelation.

Though it may seem obvious, it is often important to remind worship leaders that the text chosen for a Call to Worship is, in fact, a "call." In the Call to Worship the leader exhorts God's people to respond to the revelation of the divine nature and blessings. Thus, the text should call the people to shout, sing, praise, bow, bless, or in some other way express their worship of God. If the text itself does not have this imperative aspect (and virtually all texts chosen as calls to worship in historical liturgies do possess such an imperative), then the worship leader should provide a word or phrase that instructs God's people how to respond to the text cited. An added phrase as simple as, "In light of what God has told us about his love, let us worship him," can turn a Scripture that has no "call" quality into an appropriate Call to Worship.

3. *God calls us to respond to his redemption.* Because God invites our praise, we know our worship pleases him—somehow we have been made precious to him. The psalmist reminds us not merely that God made us, but also that "we are his; we are his people, the sheep of his pasture" (v. 3). As we face our weakness, frailty, and sin, it seems impossible that God would be pleased by us—or our praise. Yet, his invitation to worship is itself a revelation of his grace that makes us willing and able to respond to him. In fact, knowledge of God's redemptive qualities serves as the impetus for the climax of the psalmist's Call to Worship. The psalmist's adoration crescendos with these words: "Enter his gates with thanksgiving and his courts with praise" (v. 4); and the reasons follow: "For the LORD

is good and his love endures forever; his faithfulness continues through all generations" (v. 5).

The entire message of the gospel is not usually verbalized in the Call to Worship, but its features inevitably glisten. By a scriptural Call to Worship we understand that God welcomes us to his presence and invites us to participate in his purposes. Though we are weak, he is welcoming; though our iniquities are great, he remains inviting. The Call to Worship necessarily and simultaneously commends God's worthiness and consoles us in our unworthiness. We can come to him; he wants us, and he delights in our praise. All this reminds us that God has established our relationship with him by his grace and—far from releasing us from all holy obligations—that grace now compels our response of worship.

In the Call to Worship, God calls us to give him praise, but the command is not onerous. It is an invitation to respond to God's revelation of himself and his grace. In offering this invitation God is both host and honoree, and God's people are both invited and compelled by his mercy to give him glory. God gives us the privilege of welcome into his presence that we might reciprocate with the gift of worship. Right perception of this gift exchange encourages the worship leader to speak the Call to Worship with the warmth of heart and openness of gesture that such an occasion of mutual blessing deserves.

Call to Worship Examples

Leader-led Calls to Worship

1. Come, let us sing for joy to the LORD; let us shout aloud to the Rock of our salvation. Let us come before him with thanksgiving and extol him with music and song.

    (Ps. 95:1–2)

2. Shout for joy to the LORD, all the earth. Worship the LORD with gladness; come before him with joyful songs. Know that the LORD is God. It is he who made us, and not we ourselves; we are his people, the sheep of his pasture. Enter his gates with thanksgiving and his courts with praise; give thanks to him and praise his name.

    (Ps. 100:1–4)

3. Give thanks to the LORD, call on his name; make known among the nations what he has done. Sing to him, sing praise to him; tell of all

his wonderful acts. Glory in his holy name; let the hearts of those
who seek the LORD rejoice.

> *(Ps. 105:1–3)*

4. This is the day the LORD has made; let us rejoice and be glad in it.

> *(Ps. 118:24)*

5. "Our help is in the name of the LORD, the Maker of heaven and
   earth." Let us exalt his name together.

> *(Ps. 124:8; note the specific words of exhortation added by the
> worship leader at the end of the Scripture quotation. This addition
> allows the worship leader to use the original statement of truth as
> the basis for the Call to Worship.)*

6. The LORD is near to all who call on him, to all who call on him in
   truth. Seek the LORD while he may be found, call on him while he is
   near; let the wicked forsake his way and the evil man his thoughts.
   Let him turn to the LORD, and he will have mercy on him, and to
   our God, for he will freely pardon.

> *(Note this wedding of Ps. 145:18 and Isa. 55:6–7—passages of
> similar theme—into a unified Call to Worship. When performing
> such "wedding," we should take care not to ignore or twist the
> original meaning of the Word of God. At the same time, we should
> rejoice in the Bible's continuity and be willing to use passages that
> reinforce one another to exhort God's people to worship according
> to these great themes of Scripture.)*

7. Grace and peace to you who were dead in your sins,
   For God has made you alive with Christ and forgiven all your sins.
   Rejoice in the LORD and be glad, you righteous; sing, all you who
   are now upright in heart!

> *(from Col. 2:13–14; Ps. 32:11)*

8. "Praise be to the God and Father of our Lord Jesus Christ! In his
   great mercy he has given us new birth into a living hope through the
   resurrection of Jesus Christ from the dead, and into an inheritance
   that can never perish, spoil or fade—kept in heaven for you, who
   through faith are shielded by God's power until the coming of the
   salvation that is ready to be revealed in the last time." In this greatly
   rejoice.

> *(Note how 1 Pet. 1:3–5 is made a Call to Worship by the addition
> of final words of exhortation that closely echo the scriptural text.)*

9. "Worthy is the Lamb, who was slain, to receive power and wealth and wisdom and strength and honor and glory and praise! . . . To him who sits on the throne and to the Lamb [shall] be praise and honor and glory and power, for ever and ever!" Since he is so worthy, let us join with the hosts of heaven in offering the Savior our worship.

> (*Adapted from Rev. 5:12–13. Note again the exhortation added by the worship leader at the end of the Scripture quotation to make this glorious statement of truth a Call to Worship. Choral anthems or hymns that include such words may also make an appropriate Call to Worship.*)

Responsive or Antiphonal Calls to Worship

Typically the worship leader and the congregation alternate parts in responsive readings such as these below, with the worship leader beginning and the congregation responding (group responses are shown in bold). However, there are numerous ways to vary this pattern, such as the choir or one section of the congregation leading and the rest of the participants responding.

1. Sing to the LORD a new song; sing to the LORD, all the earth.
   Sing to the LORD, praise his name; proclaim his salvation day after day.
   [All]: Declare his glory among the nations, his marvelous deeds among all peoples.

   > (*Ps. 96:1–3*)

2. Give thanks to the LORD, for he is good;
   "His love endures forever."
   Let Israel say:
   "His love endures forever."
   Let the house of Aaron say:
   "His love endures forever."
   Let those who fear the LORD say:
   "His love endures forever."

   > (*from Ps. 118:1–4*)

3. "Holy, holy, holy is the Lord God Almighty, who was, and is, and is to come."

> "To him who sits on the throne and to the Lamb be praise and honor
> and glory and power, for ever and ever!"
>
> *(from Rev. 4:8; 5:13)*

4. "Praise our God, all you his servants, you who fear him, both small
   and great!"
   "Hallelujah! For our Lord God Almighty reigns. Let us rejoice and
   be glad and give him glory!"

   (from Rev. 19:5–7)

Alternative Suggestions

Calls to Worship can be developed from many additional texts, readings, hymns, and songs. A source that does not contain an obvious exhortation can usually be made into a very meaningful Call to Worship by adding one of the following (or similar) phrases:

1. In light of this glorious truth about our God, let us praise the Lord.
2. Now let us praise God from whom all these blessings flow.
3. Glorify the LORD with me; let us exalt his name together *(from Ps. 34:3)*.

Musical Examples

Such selections may be used as, before, or following a Call to Worship.

Traditional[1]

"All Creatures of Our God and King," by Francis of Assisi

"All People That on Earth Do Dwell," version of Psalm 100 by William Kethe

"Come, Christians, Join to Sing," by Christian H. Bateman

"Crown Him with Many Crowns," by Matthew Bridges

"Doxology," by Thomas Ken

---

1. "Traditional" and "contemporary" are confessedly "squishy" terms. A contemporary song could be forty years or days old; one that "sounds" traditional can be equally hard to place in time. I am tempted just to say, "You know what I mean." But, in general, "contemporary" here designates worship music written after 1960; often supporting simple and repetitive lyrics originally intended to stimulate emotional engagement in charismatic services (maturing trends have deepened lyrical content); and echoing popular music styles, rhythms, and instrumentation (think praise band vs. piano- or organ-led hymnody).

"Exalt the Lord, His Praise Proclaim," from Psalm 135 as in *The Psalter*, 1912

"Holy, Holy, Holy!" by Reginald Heber

"Mighty God, While Angels Bless Thee," by Robert Robinson

"O Come, My Soul," version of Psalm 103 as in *The Psalter*, 1912

"O for a Thousand Tongues to Sing," by Charles Wesley

"O Worship the King," by Robert Grant

"Praise Him! Praise Him!" by Fanny Crosby

"Praise, My Soul, the King of Heaven," by Henry F. Lyte

"Praise to the Lord, the Almighty," by Joachim Neander

"When Morning Gilds the Skies," original German translated by Edward Caswall

Contemporary

"All Hail King Jesus," by Dave Moody

"Blessed Be Your Name," by Beth and Matt Redman

"Come, Now Is the Time to Worship," by Brian Doerksen

"He Is Exalted," by Twila Paris

"Here I Am to Worship," by Tim Hughes

"How Great Is Our God," by Chris Tomlin, Jesse Reeves, and Ed Cash

"I Love You, Lord," by Laurie Klein

"I Will Rise Up," by Mike Ash

"Majesty," by Jack Hayford

"Meekness and Majesty," by Graham Kendrick

"O Lord, Our Lord, How Majestic Is Your Name," by Michael W. Smith

"Shout to the Lord," by Darlene Zschech

"We Are Marching in the Light of God," a South African folk song, administered by Walton Music

"We Bring the Sacrifice of Praise," by Kirk Dearman

"We Fall Down," by Chris Tomlin

"We Will Glorify," by Twila Paris

Choral

"Crown Him with Many Crowns," choral with congregation, arranged by Craig Courtney

"For the Beauty of the Earth," by John Rutter

"Holy, Holy, Holy!" arranged by Mark Hayes

"*Non Nobis Domine*," by Patrick Doyle, arranged by Graham Presket

"Now Sing We Joyfully Unto God," by Gordon Young

"Ode to Joy," by Ludwig van Beethoven

"O God, Beyond All Praising," by Gustav Holst, arranged by Jane Holstein

"Praise the Lord (Louez le Seigneur)," from Cameroon Processional Song, published by Earthsongs

"Rejoice, the Lord Is King," by John Darwall, arranged by Joel Raney

Text Resources for Additional Calls to Worship

Book of Common Prayer. San Francisco: HarperOne, 1983.

Book of Common Worship. Philadelphia: Board of Christian Education of the Presbyterian Church (USA), 1966, esp. 11–44.

Brink, Emily R., and John D. Witvliet, eds. *The Worship Sourcebook.* Grand Rapids: Calvin Institute of Christian Worship and Baker Books, 2004.

Rayburn, Robert G. *O Come, Let Us Worship: Corporate Worship in the Evangelical Church.* Grand Rapids: Baker Academic, 1980, esp. 303–13.

Vasholz, Robert I. *Calls to Worship: A Pocket Resource.* Ross-shire, Scotland: Christian Focus, 2008.

Music Resources for Additional Calls to Worship

Hymnals often include useful texts also.

African American Heritage Hymnal. Chicago: GIA Publications, 2001.

Baptist Hymnal. Nashville: LifeWay, 2008.

Hymnal 1982 According to the Use of the Episcopal Church. New York: Church Publishing, 1985.

The Hymnal for Worship and Celebration. Waco: Word Music, 1986.

Lutheran Service Book. St. Louis: Concordia, 2006.

Psalter Hymnal. Grand Rapids: CRC Publications, 2007.

Songs of Fellowship. Vols. 1–4. Eastbourne, UK: Kingsway Music, 1991–2008.

Trinity Hymnal. Rev. ed. Philadelphia: Great Commission Publications, 1990.

Trinity Psalter. Philadelphia: Great Commission Publications, 1994.

The Worshipping Church. Edited by Don Hustad. Carol Stream, IL: Hope Publishing, 1990.

14

Affirmation of Faith

An Affirmation of Faith provides for the expression of the church's most basic and deeply held beliefs. Through corporate reading, recitation, or singing of such an affirmation, the contemporary church expresses its continuity with the church of the ages and its solidarity with fellow believers across the world. By affirming what we believe, we renew our convictions, attest our continuing belief in the historical truths of Christianity, indicate our support of those who have been persecuted for their faith, humble ourselves before the truths of Scripture, provide testimony of our faith to our children and the watching world, declare our loyalty to our God, and renew in heart and mind the truths on which we will base our daily lives and on which we have staked the eternal destiny of our souls.

Affirmations of Faith are often made by reciting the ecumenical creeds—those historical statements of basic truths that believers in all times and places can profess (e.g., Apostles' Creed, Nicene Creed, Athanasian Creed). Church traditions that eschew the use of "man-made" creeds still may affirm core tenets of their faith in worship by using passages of Scripture or hymns that summarize core beliefs. If the Affirmation of Faith follows the Sermon—affirming what has been taught—the Sermon itself (or a source used in the Sermon) may provide fitting language for a corporate response. Care should be taken to make sure that such a contemporary or non-scriptural affirmation truly does contain concepts that can be affirmed in good conscience by all believers.

Affirmations of Faith are used in the context of the church's instruction (such as prior to or after a Scripture reading or Sermon) or with the church's testimony of its core beliefs (such as before or after a baptism or the Lord's Supper). The instruction and witness aspects of the Affirmation of Faith are often well served by using portions of catechisms and confessions that summarize a church's beliefs. Such affirmations can have many appropriate uses and places in a worship service. As mentioned earlier in this book, the Irish liturgy introduced an Affirmation of Faith after the opening hymn to provide emotional and conceptual transition from praise to confession.

Affirmation of Faith Examples

Affirmations of Faith

The following examples are typically read in unison.

1. Hear, O Israel: The LORD our God, the LORD is one. Love the LORD your God with all your heart and with all your soul and with all your strength.

   (*Deut. 6:4–5*)

2. God is our refuge and strength, an ever-present help in trouble. Therefore we will not fear, though the earth give way and the mountains fall into the heart of the sea, though its waters roar and foam and the mountains quake with their surging.

   There is a river whose streams make glad the city of God, the holy place where the Most High dwells. God is within her, she will not fall; God will help her at break of day. Nations are in uproar, kingdoms fall; he lifts his voice, the earth melts. The LORD Almighty is with us; the God of Jacob is our fortress.

   Come and see the works of the LORD, the desolations he has brought on the earth. He makes wars cease to the ends of the earth; he breaks the bow and shatters the spear; he burns the shields with fire.

   "Be still, and know that I am God; I will be exalted among the nations, I will be exalted in the earth."

   The LORD Almighty is with us; the God of Jacob is our fortress.

   (*Ps. 46*)

3. All of us who were baptized into Christ Jesus were baptized into his death. We were therefore buried with him through baptism into death in order that, just as Christ was raised from the dead through the glory of the Father, we too may live a new life. If we have been united with him like this in his death, we will certainly also be united with him in his resurrection. For we know that our old self was crucified with him so that the body of sin might be done away with that we should no longer be slaves to sin—because anyone who has died has been freed from sin. Now if we died with Christ, we believe that we will also live with him. For we know that since Christ was raised from the dead, he cannot die again; death no longer has mastery over him. The death he died, he died to sin once for all; but the life he lives, he lives to God.

(*Rom. 6:3–10, adapted*)

4. We believe: Christ died for our sins according to the Scriptures, that he was buried, that he was raised on the third day according to the Scriptures, and that he appeared to Peter, and then to the Twelve. After that, he appeared to more than five hundred of the brothers at the same time, most of whom are still living, though some have fallen asleep. Then he appeared to James, then to all the apostles, and last of all he appeared to Paul also. Christ has indeed been raised from the dead, the firstfruits of those who have fallen asleep.

For since death came through a man, the resurrection of the dead comes also through a man. For as in Adam all die, so in Christ all will be made alive. But each in his own turn: Christ, the firstfruits; then, when he comes, those who belong to him. Then the end will come, when he hands over the kingdom to God the Father after he has destroyed all dominion, authority, and power. For he must reign until he has put all his enemies under his feet. . . . When he has done this, then the Son himself will be made subject to him who put everything under him, so that God may be all in all.

(*1 Cor. 15:3–8; 20–28, adapted*)

5. Because of his great love for us, God, who is rich in mercy, made us alive with Christ even when we were dead in transgressions—it is by grace you have been saved. And God raised us up with Christ and seated us with him in the heavenly realms in Christ Jesus, in order that in the coming ages he might show the incomparable riches of his grace, expressed in his kindness to us in Christ Jesus. For it is by grace you have been saved, through faith—and this not from

yourselves, it is the gift of God—not by works, so that no one can boast. For we are God's workmanship, created in Christ Jesus to do good works, which God prepared in advance for us to do.

(*Eph. 2:4–10, adapted*)

6. I believe in God the Father Almighty, Maker of heaven and earth. I believe in Jesus Christ, his only Son, our Lord, who was conceived by the Holy Spirit, and born of the virgin Mary. He suffered under Pontius Pilate, was crucified, died, and was buried; he descended into hell. The third day he rose again from the dead. He ascended into heaven and is seated at the right hand of God the Father Almighty. From there he will come to judge the living and the dead. I believe in the Holy Spirit, the holy catholic church, the communion of saints, the forgiveness of sins, the resurrection of the body, and the life everlasting. Amen.

(*Apostles' Creed*)

7. We believe in one God, the Father Almighty, Maker of heaven and earth, of all things visible and invisible. And in one Lord Jesus Christ, the only-begotten Son of God, begotten of his Father before all worlds, God of God, Light of Light, very God of very God, begotten, not made, being of one substance with the Father; by whom all things were made; who for us and for our salvation came down from heaven, and was incarnate by the Holy Spirit of the virgin Mary, and was made man; and was crucified also for us under Pontius Pilate; he suffered and was buried; and the third day he rose again according to the Scriptures, and ascended into heaven, and is seated at the right hand of the Father; and he shall come again, with glory, to judge both the living and the dead; whose kingdom shall have no end. And we believe in the Holy Spirit, the Lord and giver of life, who proceeds from the Father and the Son; who with the Father and the Son together is worshiped and glorified; who spoke by the prophets; and we believe in one holy catholic and apostolic church; we acknowledge one baptism for the remission of sins; and we look for the resurrection of the dead, and the life of the world to come. Amen.

(*Nicene Creed*)

8. My only comfort in life and in death is that I am not my own, but belong—body and soul, in life and in death—to my faithful Savior Jesus Christ. He has fully paid for all my sins with his precious blood,

and has set me free from the tyranny of the devil. He also watches over me in such a way that not a hair can fall from my head without the will of my Father in heaven: in fact, all things must work together for my salvation. Because I belong to him, Christ, by his Holy Spirit, assures me of eternal life and makes me wholeheartedly willing and ready from now on to live for him.

(*Heidelberg Catechism, question 1*)

9. God is a Spirit, in and of himself infinite in being, glory, blessedness, and perfection; all-sufficient, eternal, unchangeable, incomprehensible, everywhere present, almighty, knowing all things, most wise, most holy, most just, most merciful and gracious, long-suffering, and abundant in goodness and truth.

(*Westminster Larger Catechism, question 7*)

10. Our God is All-Sufficient. He has made and upholds all things by the word of his power. One generation succeeds another, and we hasten back to the dust; the heavens we behold will vanish away like the clouds that cover them, the earth we tread on will dissolve as a morning dream. But our God is unchangeable and incorruptible; forever and ever, he is God over all, blessed eternally. Infinitely great and glorious is our God.

We are his offspring and under his care. His hands have made and fashioned us. He has watched over us with more than paternal protection and more than maternal tenderness. He holds our soul eternally, and will not allow us to be lost. His divine power has given us all things necessary for life and godliness. He has redeemed our lives from destruction, crowned us with lovingkindness and tender mercies, satisfied our mouths with good things, renewed our youth like the eagle's.

His Holy Scriptures govern every part of our lives, and regulate the discharge of all our duties, so that our lives may adorn the glory of his name in all things.

(*adapted from* Valley of Vision,
"*Second Day Morning: God Over All*")

11. Our God rules all things in wisdom, love, and power. He has made summer and winter, day and night, so that each of these revolutions serves our welfare and is full of his care and kindness. His bounty is seen in the relations that train us, the laws that defend us, the homes that shelter us, the food that builds us, the raiment that clothes us, the

continuance of our health, members, senses, understanding, memory, affections, and will. But as stars fade before the rising sun, he has eclipsed all these benefits with the wisdom and grace that purposed our eternal redemption. By his great mercy God laid our salvation on his mighty and willing Son, our Savior; One that is able to save to the uttermost. His name is Jesus. By his grace, his blood cleanses us from our sin. God imputes to us his righteousness, which justifies the guilty, and gives us title to eternal life and possession of his Holy Spirit. By this Spirit of life-giving wisdom and power we have faith to grasp God's promises, rejoice in our hope, turn from evil, and live for the glory of our Savior.

(adapted from Valley of Vision, *"Second Day Evening: Bounty")*

12. In life and in death we belong to God. Through the grace of our Lord Jesus Christ, the love of God, and the communion of the Holy Spirit, we trust in the one triune God, the Holy One of Israel, whom alone we worship and serve. We trust in Jesus Christ, fully human, fully God. Jesus proclaimed the reign of God: preaching good news to the poor and release to the captives, teaching by word and deed and blessing the children, healing the sick and binding up the brokenhearted, eating with outcasts, forgiving sinners, and calling all to repent and believe the gospel.

(from "A Brief Statement of Faith," The Book of Confessions, Part 1 of the Constitution of the Presbyterian Church [U.S.A.]. Published by the General Assembly of the Presbyterian Church [U.S.A.].)

Responsive or Antiphonal Affirmations of Faith

Typically the worship leader and the congregation alternate parts in responsive readings such as these below, with the worship leader beginning and the congregation responding (group responses are shown in bold). However, there are numerous ways to vary this pattern, such as the choir or one section of the congregation leading and the rest of the participants responding.

1. The Lord is my shepherd, I shall not be in want.
   He makes me lie down in green pastures,
   He leads me beside quiet waters,
   he restores my soul.
   He guides me in paths of righteousness
   for his name's sake.
   Even though I walk through the valley of the shadow of death,
   I will fear no evil, for you are with me;

Your rod and your staff, they comfort me.
You prepare a table before me in the presence of my enemies.
You anoint my head with oil;
my cup overflows.
Surely goodness and love will follow me all the days of my life,
And I will dwell in the house of the LORD forever.
> (Ps. 23)

2. Lord, you have been our dwelling place
throughout all generations.
Before the mountains were born,
or you brought forth the earth and the world,
from everlasting to everlasting you are God.
> (Ps. 90:1–2)

3. Blessed are the poor in spirit, for theirs is the kingdom of heaven.
Blessed are those who mourn, for they will be comforted.
Blessed are the meek, for they will inherit the earth.
Blessed are those who hunger and thirst for righteousness, for they will be filled.
Blessed are the merciful, for they will be shown mercy.
Blessed are the pure in heart, for they will see God.
Blessed are the peacemakers, for they will be called sons of God.
Blessed are those who are persecuted because of righteousness, for theirs is the kingdom of heaven.
Blessed are you when people insult you, persecute you and falsely say all kinds of evil against you because of me.
Rejoice and be glad, because great is your reward in heaven, for in the same way they persecuted the prophets who were before you.
You are the salt of the earth. But if the salt loses its saltiness, how can it be made salty again? It is no longer good for anything, except to be thrown out and trampled by men.
You are the light of the world. A city on a hill cannot be hidden.
Neither do people light a lamp and put it under a bowl. Instead they put it on its stand, and it gives light to everyone in the house.
In the same way, let your light shine before men, that they may see your good deeds and praise your Father in heaven.
> (Beatitudes, Matt. 5:3–16)

4. In the beginning was the Word, and the Word was with God, and the Word was God.

He was with God in the beginning.
Through him all things were made; without him nothing was made
  that has been made.
In him was life, and that life was the light of men.
The light shines in the darkness, but the darkness has not under-
  stood it.
**This was the true light that gives light to every man who comes into
  the world.**
He was in the world, and though the world was made through him,
  the world did not recognize him.
**For by him were all things created, that are in heaven, and that are
  in earth, visible and invisible.**
For by him all things were created: things in heaven and on earth,
  visible and invisible, whether thrones or powers or rulers or
  authorities; all things were created by him and for him.
He is before all things, and in him all things hold together.
  (from John 1:1–5, 9–10; Col. 1:16–17)

5. Do you believe in God the Father?
   **I believe in God, the Father almighty,
   creator of heaven and earth.**

   Do you believe in Jesus Christ, God's Son and our Lord?
   **I believe in Jesus Christ, God's only Son, our Lord,
   who was conceived by the Holy Spirit,
   born of the virgin Mary,
   suffered under Pontius Pilate,
   was crucified, died, and was buried.
   He descended to hell.
   On the third day he rose again;
   he ascended into heaven,
   he is seated at the right hand of the Father,
   from there he will come to judge the living and the dead.**

   Do you believe in the Holy Spirit?
   **I believe in the Holy Spirit,
   the holy catholic church,
   the communion of saints,
   the forgiveness of sins,
   the resurrection of the body,
   and the life everlasting.**
     (based on the Apostles' Creed)

6. What do you believe about the work of God?
We believe that God—
   who is perfectly merciful
   and also very just—
sent his Son to assume the nature
in which the disobedience had been committed,
   in order to bear in it the punishment of sin
   by his most bitter passion and death.

And what do you believe about the work of Jesus Christ?
We believe that Jesus Christ presented himself
in our name before his Father,
to appease his wrath
with full satisfaction
by offering himself
   on the tree of the cross
and pouring out his precious blood
   for the cleansing of our sins,
   as the prophets had predicted.

Why did he endure all this?
He endured all this
for the forgiveness of our sins.

What comfort does this give you?
We find all comforts in his wounds
and have no need to seek or invent any other means
to reconcile ourselves with God
than this one and only sacrifice,
once made,
which renders believers perfect forever.

> (*responsive from the Belgic Confession, articles 20–21,* Worship
> Sourcebook, *pp. 158–59*)

7. As followers of Jesus Christ,
   living in this world—
   which some seek to control,
   but which others view with despair—
   we declare with joy and trust:
   Our world belongs to God!
   From the beginning,

through all the crises of our times,
until his kingdom fully comes,
God keeps covenant forever.
Our world belongs to him!
God is King! Let the earth be glad!
Christ is Victor; his rule has begun. Hallelujah!
The Spirit is at work, renewing the creation. Praise the Lord!

(responsive from Our World Belongs
in the Worship Sourcebook #27, p. 163)

Alternative Suggestions

Affirmations of Faith can be developed from many additional texts, readings, hymns, and songs. Such sources can be adapted into meaningful affirmations by introducing them with one of the following (or similar) phrases:

1. Christian, what do you believe?
2. Now let us affirm our faith together by reading in unison (or responsively) these words from . . .
3. Let us profess our faith.
4. Let us join our hearts with the saints of the ages and Christians across the world by affirming what we believe by God's mercy and for Christ's sake in the power of his Spirit.
5. With one heart and voice let us profess the faith of the church at all times and in all places.

Musical Examples

The following selections may be used as, before, or after the Affirmation of Faith.

Traditional

"A Mighty Fortress," from Martin Luther, translated by Frederick Hedge
"Be Thou My Vision," from Irish traditional, translated by Mary Byrne
"Christ Is Made the Sure Foundation," from seventh-century Latin, translated by John Mason Neale
"*Gloria Patri*," from second-century Latin
"Great Is Thy Faithfulness," by Thomas O. Chisolm
"He Leadeth Me," by Joseph H. Gilmore

"His Eye Is on the Sparrow," by Civilla Martin

"I Cannot Tell," by William Young Fullerton

"I Greet Thee Who My Sure Redeemer Art," from *Strasbourg Psalter*, 1545, translated by Elizabeth Smith

"It Took a Miracle," by John W. Peterson

"My Hope Is Built on Nothing Less," by Edward Mote

"Our God, Our Help in Ages Past," from Psalm 90, by Isaac Watts

"There Is a Fountain Filled with Blood," by William Cowper

"There Is a Green Hill Far Away," by Cecil Frances Alexander

"This Is My Father's World," by Maltbie Babcock

"To God Be the Glory," by Fanny Crosby

"Whate'er My God Ordains Is Right," by Samuel Rodigast

Contemporary

"Arise, My Soul, Arise," by Charles Wesley, arranged by Indelible Grace

"Awesome God," by Rich Mullins

"Be Exalted, O God," by Brent Chambers

"Because He Lives," by William Gaither

"Before the Throne of God Above," by Charitie Lees Bancroft, modern tune by Vikki Cook

"Days of Elijah," by Robin Mark Click

"God Never Fails," by George Jordan

"He Knows My Name," by Tommy Walker

"My Tribute," by Andre Crouch

"I Will Follow You," by Bebo Norman

"In Christ Alone," by Keith Getty and Stuart Townend

"Jesus, Your Name," by Keith Getty and Ian Hannah

"The Love of Christ Is Rich and Free," by William Gadsby, modern tune by Sandra McCracken

"You Are My All in All," by Dennis Jernigan

"You Are My Hiding Place," by Michael Ledner

Choral

"And the Father Will Dance Over You," by Mark Hayes

"Creation Hymn," by Bryan Chapell, arranged by Craig Courtney

"God So Loved the World," by John Stainer

"He, Watching Over Israel," by Felix Mendelssohn

"How Can I Keep from Singing," by Robert Lowry, arranged by John Carter

"Jesu, Joy of Man's Desiring," by Johann Sebastian Bach

"My Song Is Love Unknown," by Samuel Crossman, arranged by Edwin Childs

"No More Night," by Walt Harrah, arranged by Russell Mauldin

"None Other Lamb," by Christina Rossetti, arranged by Craig Courtney

"On Jordan's Stormy Banks," from African American spiritual, arranged by Howard Helvey

"Sheep May Safely Graze," by Johann Sebastian Bach

"The Lord's Prayer," by Albert Malotte

"The Majesty and Glory of Your Name," by Linda Lee Johnson, arranged by Tom Fettke

Text Resources for Affirmations of Faith

Belgic Confession

Bennett, Arthur, ed. *The Valley of Vision: A Collection of Puritan Prayers and Devotions*. Carlisle, PA: Banner of Truth Trust, 1975.

Brink, Emily R., and John D. Witvliet, eds. *The Worship Sourcebook*. Grand Rapids: Calvin Institute of Christian Worship and Baker Books, 2004.

Heidelberg Catechism

London Confession

Westminster Confession of Faith and Larger and Shorter Catechisms

Music Resources for Affirmations of Faith

Hymnals often include useful texts also.

African American Heritage Hymnal. Chicago: GIA Publications, 2001.

Baptist Hymnal. Nashville: LifeWay, 2008.

The Hymnal for Worship and Celebration. Waco: Word Music, 1986.

Hymnal 1982 According to the Use of the Episcopal Church. New York: Church Publishing, 1985.

Lutheran Service Book. St. Louis: Concordia, 2006.

Psalter Hymnal. Grand Rapids: CRC Publications, 2007.

Songs of Fellowship. Vols. 1–4. Eastbourne, UK: Kingsway Music, 1991–2008.

Trinity Hymnal. Rev. ed. Philadelphia: Great Commission Publications, 1990.

Trinity Psalter. Philadelphia: Great Commission Publications, 1994.

The Worshipping Church. Edited by Don Hustad. Carol Stream, IL: Hope Publishing, 1990.

15

CONFESSION OF SIN

For modern sensibilities, confession of sin may seem an unappealing aspect of worship. It can be easy to succumb to the idea that dealing with sin is a turnoff that will steer people away from worship. But to such objections the church must turn a deaf ear for the good of God's people. While it is certainly possible (and sadly common) to force people to grovel without grace, it is impossible to know grace if we have no awareness of sin. Those in whom the Spirit of God dwells are longing to confess their sin in order to experience the mercy of God. In fact, we should question whether the gospel itself is present, if there has been no acknowledgment of sin. If, because of local traditions or tastes, a formal Confession of Sin raises too many red flags for inclusion in the worship service, the truths of the gospel still require there to be some form of confession in the songs, prayers, or preaching. The grace of God has no present glory if the sin it overcomes is not a present reality, and the ministry of Christ has no significance if the sin he came to defeat will not even be faced.

Of course, a Confession of Sin can be made unnecessarily onerous. Believers can be forced to mouth arcane forms that do not realistically state our struggles or represent our feelings. We can also get locked into conventional expressions that do not adequately represent our condition as a covenant people who are cherished by God despite our sin. To neglect the Scriptures telling us that the kindness of God leads to repentance (Rom.

2:4) will seem to make God's forgiveness conditional upon our repentance rather than making the certainty and completeness of his mercy the magnet of confession. We run to his arms with our sin-sick hearts because we know there is grace sufficient, boundless, and free already there. We repent because we are forgiven, not to gain forgiveness. In our confession we experience God's love because we confront our sin with the greatness of mercy that is already ours through faith in Christ, but we do not earn, gain, or force God's pity by the words or weight of our confession. We are forgiven because he was forsaken, not because our contrition is adequate. If God's forgiveness were gained by the adequacy of our repentance, then no one but his Son would know his care. But because our faith is in the finished work of that Child, we are cherished children of God despite our constant waywardness and the inevitable inadequacy of our confession.

John Newton's simple words, "Amazing grace, how sweet the sound, that saved a wretch like me," do not dodge the wretchedness of our sin. Still, the words touch us and draw us to confession because they so clearly strive to represent the awful consequences of our sin as honestly as they do the amazing grace of our God. Grace is all the more beautiful when we face the ugliness of our sin. But we do not confess our wretchedness to wallow in self-pity or merit divine mercy; we confess our destitution so that our hearts will be enraptured anew and motivated afresh by the riches of our Savior's love.

Confession passages of Scripture and the confession prayers of historical liturgies lead us into acknowledgment of the magnitude of our sin, but never without the aim of magnifying grace. In corporate worship, these confessions are often repeated in unison; but, they can also be prayed publicly by the worship leader on behalf of the people (as Ezra in Ezra 9, the Levites in Neh. 9, and Solomon in 1 Kings 8 confessed for the people). Prayers of confession may also be said or sung responsively by the congregation, used as individual meditations for silent prayer, or reflected in extemporaneous pulpit prayers that instruct God's people how to confess sin in their own hearts.

Consideration for congregations who reflexively oppose form prayers may confuse leaders about the nature of extemporaneous prayer. While it is true that a cursory reading of a form prayer may circumvent serious heart consideration, it is also true that an off-the-cuff, whatever-comes-to-mind-first prayer may fail to minister the Spirit's truths. Those whose extemporaneous prayers lead God's people into deep consideration of spiritual matters have meditated on God's Word day and night (Ps. 1:2). They have prepared themselves to pray by considering what God says to them personally, what he has said to his people over the centuries, and what his people face today. Prior reflection on these is the spiritual fuel that enables pulpit prayers to be spontaneous without being shallow, cliché-ridden, or even damaging.

Leaders of the Reformation believed that prayers of confession expressed essentials of the gospel renewal that was sweeping across the church. They rewrote ancient confessions to reflect a more biblical understanding of the nature of sin, grace, and repentance. The Reformers also adapted biblical prayers for corporate use in their churches. The prayer of confession in Daniel 9 became a model for Martin Bucer. The prayer of confession he developed for the church at Strasbourg became a model for Calvin's practice at Geneva. In turn, Calvin's pattern was reflected in the Book of Common Prayer by Thomas Cranmer in England, in the Book of Common Order by John Knox in Scotland, and in the Reformed liturgy contribution of Richard Baxter as he ministered among the English non-conformists.

In the historic liturgies, a Confession of Sin typically follows opening praise. Recognition of the greatness and goodness of God inevitably creates counter-recognition of our humanity and sin. The progress of the gospel in our hearts is, thus, naturally reflected in the contours of the worship service. We should not fail to recognize, however, that in worship as in life, there are many appropriate places to humble ourselves before God. We may also be ready to confess our sin after a reading of the law, or after a Sermon that has confronted us with the righteousness that God requires. Grace does not require a set place for our confession, but rather the recognition of its necessity.

Confession of Sin Examples

Confession of Sin

These are typically read as a unison prayer or individually in silent prayer.

1. Remember, O Lord, your great mercy and love, for they are from of
   old.
   Remember not the sins of my youth, and my rebellious ways:
   according to your love remember me, for you are good, O Lord. . . .
   For the sake of your name, O Lord, forgive my iniquity, though it is
   great.
   Turn to me and be gracious to me, for I am lonely and afflicted.
   The troubles of my heart have multiplied; free me from my anguish.

Look upon my affliction and my distress and take away all my sins.
(from Ps. 25:6–7, 11, 16–18)

2. Do not withhold your mercy from me, O Lord;
may your love and your truth always protect me.
For troubles without number surround me;
my sins have overtaken me, and I cannot see.
They are more than the hairs of my head, and my heart fails within
me.
Be pleased, O Lord, to save me;
O Lord, come quickly to help me.
(from Ps. 40:11–13)

3. Have mercy on me, O God, according to your unfailing love; according to your great compassion, blot out my transgressions.
Wash away all my iniquity, and cleanse me from my sin.
For I know my transgressions, and my sin is always before me.
Against you, you only, have I sinned and done what is evil in your
sight,
so that you are proved right when you speak, and justified when you
judge.
(from Ps. 51:1–4)

4. Almighty and merciful God, we have erred and strayed from your
ways like lost sheep.
We have followed too much the devices and desires of our own
hearts.
We have offended against your holy laws.
We have left undone those things which we ought to have done;
and we have done those things which we ought not to have done.
O Lord, have mercy upon us. Spare those who confess their faults.
Restore those who are penitent, according to your promises declared
to the world
in Christ Jesus, our Lord.
And grant, O merciful God, for his sake, that we may live a holy,
just, and humble life
to the glory of your holy name. *Amen.*
(traditional)

5. Merciful God, we confess that we have sinned against you in thought,
word, and deed,
by what we have done, and by what we have left undone.

We have not loved you with our whole heart and mind and strength.
We have not loved our neighbors as ourselves.
In your mercy forgive what we have been,
  help us amend what we are,
  and direct what we shall be,
so that we may delight in your will and walk in your ways,
  to the glory of your holy name.
Through Christ, our Lord. *Amen.*
  (*traditional*)

6. You asked for my hands, that you might use them for your purpose.
   I gave them for a moment, then withdrew them, for the work was
     hard.
   You asked for my mouth to speak out against injustice.
   I gave you a whisper that I might not be accused.
   You asked for my eyes to see the pain of poverty.
   I closed them, for I did not want to see.
   You asked for my life, that you might work through me.
   I gave a small part, that I might not get too involved.
   Lord, forgive my calculated efforts to serve you—
   only when it is convenient for me to do so,
   only in those places where it is safe to do so,
   and only with those who make it easy to do so.
   Father, forgive me, renew me, send me out as a usable instrument,
   that I might take seriously the meaning of your cross. *Amen.*
     (*a contemporary Confession of Sin
     from the* Worship Sourcebook #35, *p. 98*)

7. O God of Grace, Thou hast imputed my sin to my substitute, and
     hast imputed his righteousness to my soul, clothing me with a
     bridegroom's robe, decking me with jewels of holiness.
   But in my Christian walk I am still in rags; my best prayers are
     stained with sin; my penitential tears are so much impurity;
     my confessions of wrong are so many aggravations of sin; my
     receiving the Spirit is tinctured with selfishness.
   I need to repent of my repentance; I need my tears to be washed;
   I have no robe to bring to cover my sins, no loom to weave my own
     righteousness;
   I am always standing clothed in filthy garments, and by grace am
     always receiving change of raiment, for thou dost always justify
     the ungodly;

I am always going into the far country, and always returning home
   as a prodigal, always saying, Father, forgive me, and thou art
   always bringing forth the best robe.
Every morning let me wear it, every evening return in it, go out to
   the day's work in it, be married in it, be wound in death in
   it, stand before the great white throne in it, enter heaven in it
   shining as the sun.
Grant me never to lose sight of
   the exceeding sinfulness of sin,
   the exceeding righteousness of salvation,
   the exceeding glory of Christ,
   the exceeding beauty of holiness,
   the exceeding wonder of grace.

   (adapted from Valley of Vision, *"Continual Repentance")*

8. O most great, most just and gracious God; you are of purer eyes
   than to behold iniquity; but you hast promised mercy through
   Jesus Christ to all who repent and believe in him. Therefore,
   we confess that we are sinful by nature and that we have all
   sinned and come short of the glory of God. We have neglected
   and abused your holy worship and your holy name. We have
   dealt unjustly and uncharitably with our neighbors. We have
   not sought first your kingdom and righteousness. We have not
   been content with our daily bread.
You have revealed your wonderful love to us in Christ and offered us
   pardon and salvation in him; but we have turned away. We have
   run into temptation; and the sin that we should have hated, we
   have committed.
Have mercy upon us, most merciful Father! We confess you alone
   are our hope. Make us your children and give us the Spirit of
   your Son, our only Savior. Amen.

   (from a 1661 prayer of Richard Baxter, The Savoy Liturgy)

Responsive or Antiphonal Confessions of Sin

Typically the worship leader and the congregation alternate parts in
responsive readings such as these below, with the worship leader beginning
and the congregation responding (group responses are shown in bold).
However, there are numerous ways to vary this pattern, such as the choir
or one section of the congregation leading and the rest of the participants
responding.

1. Have mercy on us, O God, according to your unfailing love;
   according to your great compassion, blot out our transgressions.
   Wash away all our iniquity, and cleanse us from our sin.
   For we know our transgressions, and our sin is always before us.
   Against you, you only, have we sinned and done what is evil in your
       sight,
   so that you are proved right when you speak, and justified when you
       judge.
   Hide your face from our sins and blot out all our iniquity.
   Create in us a pure heart, O God, and renew a steadfast spirit within
   us.
   Do not cast us from your presence or take your Holy Spirit from us.
   Restore to us the joy of your salvation and grant us a willing spirit,
       to sustain us.
   You do not delight in sacrifice, or we would bring it;
   you do not take pleasure in burnt offerings.
   Our sacrifice, O God, is a broken spirit;
   a broken and contrite heart, O God, you will not despise.
   (from Ps. 51:1–4, 9–12, 16–17)

2. Father, we are sorry for the many times we have left you
       and chosen to satisfy our own selfish desires.
   For the times we have hurt the members of our families
       by refusing to do our share of the family tasks.
   Father, we have sinned. Forgive us.
   For the times we were unkind and impatient with those who needed
       our time and concern.
   Father, we have sinned. Forgive us.
   For the times we were too weak to stand up for what was right
   and allowed others to suffer because of our cowardice.
   Father, we have sinned. Forgive us.
   For the times we refused to forgive others.
   Father, we have sinned. Forgive us.
   (from More Children's Liturgies, *ed. Maria Bruck © 1981 by Mission-*
   ary Society of Saint Paul the Apostle in the State of New York.
   Reprinted by permission of Paulist Press, New York/Mahwah, NJ.)

3. God of everlasting love,
   we confess that we have been unfaithful
   to our covenant with you and with one another.
   We have worshiped other gods: money, power, greed, and convenience.

We have served our own self-interest
instead of serving only you and your people.
We have not loved our neighbor as you have commanded,
nor have we rightly loved ourselves.
Forgive us, gracious God,
and bring us back into the fullness
of our covenant with you and one another.
Through Christ, our Lord.

> *(responsive from the* Worship Sourcebook *#51, pp. 102–3)*

4. *Litany*
   O Lord,
   Have mercy upon us.
   O Christ,
   Have mercy upon us.
   O Spirit,
   Have mercy upon us.
   O God the Father in heaven,
   We beseech you, hear us.
   O God the Son, Redeemer of the world,
   We beseech you, hear us.
   O God the Holy Spirit, our Comforter,
   We beseech you, hear us.
   Be gracious unto us.
   Spare us, good Lord.
   Be gracious unto us.
   Help us, good Lord.
   Be gracious unto us.
   Save us, good Lord,
   from our sin;
   from our errors;
   from all evil.
   Good Lord, deliver us.
   [All]: Lord, have mercy upon us.

> *(variation of seven-fold litany of Gregory the Great, circa 600 AD)*

Alternative Suggestions

Confessions of Sin can be developed from many additional texts, read-ings, hymns, and songs. Such sources often can be adapted into a meaningful

Confession of Sin as the worship leader introduces or follows them with words that form a Call to Confession (see italicized below).

1. *The psalmist testifies:*
    Blessed is he
        whose transgressions are forgiven,
        whose sins are covered.
    Blessed is the man
        whose sin the LORD does not count against him
        and in whose spirit is no deceit.
    When I kept silent, my bones wasted away through my groaning all
        day long.
    For day and night your hand was heavy upon me;
        my strength was sapped
        as in the heat of summer.
    Then I acknowledged my sin to you and did not cover up my iniquity.
    I said, "I will confess my transgressions to the LORD"—
        and you forgave
        the guilt of my sin.
    *Therefore let all of you who would know God's forgiveness not keep
    silent but acknowledge your sin and confess your transgression to
    the Lord in this time of prayer.*
                        (adapted from Ps. 32:1–6)

2. *We sing:*
    Not what my hands have done can save my guilty soul;
        not what my toiling flesh has borne can make my spirit whole.
    Not what I feel or do can give me peace with God;
        not all my prayers and sighs and tears can bear my awful load.
    *But Christ can bear it all, can forgive it all, and he is willing. Therefore
    let us bow before his throne of grace, confess our sin, and acknowl-
    edge our inadequacy to correct it or compensate for it apart from
    him. And let us by such repentance claim the wonderful pardon and
    peace he alone can give.*
                        (adapted from "Not What My Hands Have Done,"
                        by Horatius Bonar)

3. "Come now, let us reason together,"
        says the Lord.
    "Though your sins are like scarlet,
        they shall be as white as snow;

though they are red as crimson,
    they shall be like wool."
*So that we would know this wonderful cleansing, let us respond to
the God who gives us such good reason to come to him and confess
our sin to him.*

(Isa. 1:18)

4. *The proof of God's amazing grace is this:*
While we were still sinners, Christ died for us.
Let us then approach the throne of grace with confidence,
so that we may receive mercy and find grace to help us in our time
    of need.

(adapted from Rom. 5:8 and Heb. 4:16)

5. *God's Word declares to us:*
    If we claim to be without sin,
    we deceive ourselves and the truth is not in us.

God's Word also assures us:
    If we confess our sins,
    he is faithful and just and will forgive us our sins
    and purify us from all unrighteousness.

Therefore let us now confess our sin to God.

(adapted from 1 John 1:8–9)

6. O Lord, open my lips,
    and my mouth will declare your praise.
You do not delight in sacrifice, or I would bring it;
    you do not take pleasure in burnt offerings.
The sacrifices of God are a broken spirit;
    a broken and contrite heart,
    O God, you will not despise.
*Our God tells us that the sacrifice he most desires is a broken and
contrite heart. Let us bring him such sacrifice now in our prayers of
confession.*

(Ps. 51:15–17)

7. O Lord, you have searched me
    and you know me.
You know when I sit and when I rise;
    you perceive my thoughts from afar.

You discern my going out and my lying down;
    you are familiar with all my ways.
Before a word is on my tongue
    you know it completely, O Lord.
In the light of God's complete knowledge of our thoughts and ac-
tions, let us confess our sins to him and claim the grace of the One
who loves us and gave himself for us despite knowing the worst
about us.
             (Ps. 139:1–4)

8. Let the wicked forsake his way
    and the evil man his thoughts.
Let him turn to the Lord, and he will have mercy on him,
    and to our God, for he will freely pardon.
God promises his pardon to those who will forsake their pride and
plead for his mercy. I urge you in these next moments to make such
a plea your own as you confess your sin in private prayer to the God
who delights to show mercy.
             (adapted from Isa. 55:7 and Mic. 7:18)

Musical Examples

The following selections may be used as, before, or following a Confession of Sin.

Traditional

"Ah, Holy Jesus, How Hast Thou Offended," by Johann Heermann
"Beneath the Cross of Jesus," by Elizabeth Clephane
"Come Thou Fount of Every Blessing," by Robert Robinson
"I Was a Wandering Sheep," by Horatius Bonar
"Man of Sorrows," by Philip Bliss
"My Faith Looks Up to Thee," by Ray Palmer
"None Other Lamb," by Christina Rossetti
"Not What My Hands Have Done," by Horatius Bonar
"O Sacred Head Now Wounded," by Bernard of Clairvaux, translated by
    Paul Gerhardt
"When I Survey the Wondrous Cross," by Isaac Watts

Contemporary

"Change My Heart, O God," by Eddie Espinosa

"From Depths of Woe I Raise to Thee," from Psalm 130, by Martin Luther, arranged by Indelible Grace

"God Be Merciful to Me," from Psalm 51 as in *The Psalter*, 1912, arranged by Indelible Grace

"How Deep the Father's Love," by Stuart Townend

Choral

"Behold the Lamb of God," from Messiah, by George Frideric Handel

"Behold the Lamb of God," by Craig Courtney

"Jesus, Lover of My Soul," arranged by Mark Hayes

"Lamb of God, What Wondrous Love," by Russell Kane and Allan Petker, music by Gabriel Fauré

"Lamb of God," by Twila Paris

"*Pie Jesu*," by Andrew Lloyd Webber

"*Pie Jesu*," from Requiem in D Minor, by Wolfgang Amadeus Mozart

"Wash Me Thoroughly," from Chandos Anthem no. 3, by George Frideric Handel

"Where Can I Run?" by Kurt Kaiser

Text Resources for Confessions of Sin

Bennett, Arthur, ed. *The Valley of Vision: A Collection of Puritan Prayers and Devotions*. Carlisle, PA: Banner of Truth Trust, 1975, esp. 121–77.

Book of Common Worship. Philadelphia: Board of Christian Education of the Presbyterian Church (USA), 1966, esp. 11–80.

Brink, Emily R., and John D. Witvliet, eds. *The Worship Sourcebook*. Grand Rapids: Calvin Institute of Christian Worship and Baker Books, 2004.

Old, Hughes Oliphant. *Leading in Prayer: A Workbook for Worship*. Grand Rapids: Eerdmans, 1995.

Rayburn, Robert G. *O Come, Let Us Worship: Corporate Worship in the Evangelical Church*. Grand Rapids: Baker Academic, 1980, esp. 303–13.

Music Resources for Confessions of Sin

Hymnals often include useful texts also.

African American Heritage Hymnal. Chicago: GIA Publications, 2001.

Baptist Hymnal. Nashville: LifeWay, 2008.

Hymnal 1982 According to the Use of the Episcopal Church. New York: Church Publishing, 1985.

The Hymnal for Worship and Celebration. Waco: Word Music, 1986.

Lutheran Service Book. St. Louis: Concordia, 2006.

Psalter Hymnal. Grand Rapids: CRC Publications, 2007.

Songs of Fellowship. Vols. 1–4. Eastbourne, UK: Kingsway Music, 1991–2008.

Trinity Hymnal. Rev. ed. Philadelphia: Great Commission Publications, 1990.

Trinity Psalter. Philadelphia: Great Commission Publications, 1994.

The Worshipping Church. Edited by Don Hustad. Carol Stream, IL: Hope Publishing, 1990.

16

ASSURANCE OF PARDON

No element of the gospel is more essential than the good news that in Christ Jesus we have received pardon from sin. The Assurance of Pardon in a worship service announces God's forgiveness. Shame is past, guilt is gone, and divine mercy is ours. We have peace with God because Jesus paid the penalty for our sin on the cross. It pleased God to apply our punishment to him who was without sin, and to grant his holiness to us who are unrighteous. By faith we are united to Christ and may rest in the knowledge that we are as precious to God as his own Child.

Concerned to distinguish themselves from Roman Catholics, Protestant churches have sometimes been hesitant to include a formal Assurance of Pardon in their worship services. We do not want the minister to assume (or be presumed to have) the role of a priest granting absolution. Dear to our convictions is the priesthood of *all* believers. We believe all God's people have immediate access to his grace without the need of a human intermediary. We do not want any to think that they require a priest's (or preacher's) intercession to gain access to God's mercy. As valid as this concern is, it should not stop worship leaders from reminding God's people of heaven's mercy in a service designed to reflect gospel truths. As noted earlier in this book, John Calvin argued at Geneva that Roman Catholics should not be the only ones to hear the glory of God's pardon in their worship.

Concerns about "priestly" presumption can be allayed by taking care to remove the "I" from any Assurance of Pardon. Instead of saying, "I grant you God's pardon," the minister should always communicate God as the grantor: "Now hear the pardon God grants you because of the ministry of Christ Jesus," or, "Hear now this good news provided by the God of mercy." Such phrases followed by a brief Scripture passage attesting to the grace of God make it clear that the pardon is from God, not from the minister. If the congregation is encouraged to respond to the scriptural assurance with, "Thanks be to God," then there is further reinforcement of the idea that our pardon is from God alone. A church striving to make its services accessible to unchurched persons may not find this kind of "liturgical" response desirable, but it can still provide an assurance of God's pardon in Scriptures quoted, responsive readings chosen, prayers offered, or songs sung.

While the minister should not assume the role of a priest in giving an Assurance of Pardon, there is no more critical time to reflect the nature of Christ in manner or expression. Such precious words of pardon from the assaults of sin and shame should not be said in funeral tones or routine flatness. Joy should resonate in the words of the minister. The goodness of the gospel should pour from the heart with a voice warmed by grace, with a face softened by love, and with eyes that meet hurting eyes with the assurance of the Father's mercy. God's people should know his peace by the way the minister expresses the Assurance of Pardon.

Assurance of Pardon Examples

Assurances of Pardon

1. When I kept silent, my bones wasted away through my groaning all day long. For day and night your hand was heavy upon me; my strength was sapped as in the heat of summer. Then I acknowledged my sin to you and did not cover up my iniquity. I said, "I will confess my transgressions to the LORD"—and you forgave the guilt of my sin.

   (Ps. 32:3–5)

2. The LORD is compassionate and gracious, slow to anger, abounding in love. . . . He does not treat us as our sins deserve or repay us according to our iniquities. For as high as the heavens are above the earth, so great is his love for those who fear him; as far as the east is from the west, so far has he removed our transgressions from us. As

a father has compassion on his children, so the LORD has compassion on those who fear him; for he knows how we are formed, he remembers that we are dust.

(Ps. 103:8, 10–14)

3. He was pierced for our transgressions, he was crushed for our iniquities; the punishment that brought us peace was upon him, and by his wounds we are healed. We all, like sheep, have gone astray, each of us has turned to his own way; and the LORD has laid on him the iniquity of us all.

(Isa. 53:5–6, adapted)

4. Who is a God like you, who pardons sin and forgives the transgression of the remnant of his inheritance? You do not stay angry forever but delight to show mercy. You will again have compassion on us; you will tread our sins underfoot and hurl all our iniquities into the depths of the sea.

(Mic. 7:18–19)

5. For God so loved the world that he gave his one and only Son, that whoever believes in him shall not perish but have eternal life.

(John 3:16)

6. But God demonstrates his own love for us in this: While we were still sinners, Christ died for us. Since we have now been justified by his blood, how much more shall we be saved from God's wrath through him!

(Rom. 5:8–9)

7. Therefore, there is now no condemnation for those who are in Christ Jesus.

(Rom. 8:1)

8. He himself bore our sins in his body on the tree, so that we might die to sins and live for righteousness; by his wounds you have been healed.

(1 Pet. 2:24)

9. By true faith in Jesus Christ,
I am right with God
and heir to life everlasting.

Even though my conscience accuses me
> of having grievously sinned against all God's commandments
> and of never having kept any of them,
and even though I am still inclined toward all evil,
nevertheless, without my deserving it at all,
out of sheer grace, God grants and credits to me
the perfect satisfaction, righteousness, and holiness of Christ,
> as if I have never sinned nor been a sinner,
> as if I had been as perfectly obedient
> as Christ was obedient for me.
All I need to do
is accept this gift of God with a believing heart.

(from Heidelberg Catechism, questions 59–60)

Responsive or Antiphonal Assurances of Pardon

Typically the worship leader and the congregation alternate parts in responsive readings such as these below, with the worship leader beginning and the congregation responding (group responses are shown in bold). However, there are numerous ways to vary this pattern, such as the choir or one section of the congregation leading and the rest of the participants responding.

1. What then, shall we say in response to this?
   If God is for us, who can be against us?
   He who did not spare his own Son,
   but gave him up for us all—
   how will he not also, along with him, graciously give us all things?
   Who will bring any charge against those whom God has chosen?
   It is God who justifies.
   Who is he that condemns? Christ Jesus, who died—more than that,
   who was raised to life—is at the right hand of God
   and is also interceding for us.
   Who shall separate us from the love of Christ?
   Shall trouble or hardship or persecution or famine
   or nakedness or danger or sword?
   No, in all these things we are more than conquerors
   through him who loved us.
   For I am convinced that neither death nor life,
   neither angels nor demons,
   neither the present nor the future,
   nor any powers, neither height nor depth,
   nor anything else in all creation,

will be able to separate us
from the love of God that is in Christ Jesus our Lord.
(from Rom. 8:31–35, 37–39)

2. While it is true that we have sinned,
it is a greater truth that we are forgiven
through God's love in Jesus Christ.
To all who humbly seek the mercy of God I say,
in Jesus Christ your sin is forgiven.
Thanks be to God.
*(from The Book of Common Worship © 1991. Reprinted by
permission of The Presbyterian Church in Canada.)*

3. May God, who said, "Let light shine out of darkness," make his light
shine in our hearts to give us the light of the knowledge of the glory of
God in the face of Christ Jesus who has saved us from all our sin.
Amen.
(from 2 Cor. 4:6)

Alternative Suggestions

Assurances of Pardon can be developed from many additional texts,
readings, hymns, and songs. Such sources can be adapted into meaningful
assurances by introducing or following them with a phrase such as:

1. Since God has promised us this grace, you have his assurance of
   pardon and peace.
2. Receive this good news of the grace of our Lord Jesus Christ.
3. Because of the love of God, the sacrifice of his Son, and faith granted
   by the Holy Spirit, you are forgiven.
4. By the grace of God, you are forgiven. Now live in the power of his
   peace.

Musical Examples

The following selections may be used as, before, or following an Assurance of Pardon.

Traditional

"*Agnus Dei*," from Latin traditional

"Amazing Grace!" by John Newton

"And Can It Be That I Should Gain," by Charles Wesley

"By Grace I'm Saved," by Christian L. Scheidt

"I Heard the Voice of Jesus Say," by Horatius Bonar

"I Know Whom I Have Believed," by Daniel Whittle

"Jesus, Thy Blood and Righteousness," by Nikolaus Ludwig von Zinzendorf

"Let Us Love and Sing and Wonder," by John Newton

"My Faith Has Found a Resting Place," by Lidie Edmunds

"O Sacred Head, Now Wounded," by Bernard of Clairvaux, translated by Paul Gerhardt

"Redeemed, How I Love to Proclaim It!" by Fanny Crosby

"Rock of Ages," by Augustus Toplady, modern arrangement by James Ward

"There Is Power in the Blood," by Lewis Jones

Contemporary

"A Father to the Fatherless," by Paul Oakley

"Before the Throne of God Above," by Vicki Cook

"Behold What Manner of Love," by Patricia Van Tine

"He Looked beyond My Fault," by Dottie Rambo

"Here is Love," by Robert Lowry

"I Could Sing of Your Love Forever," by Martin Smith

"In Christ Alone," by Keith Getty and Stuart Townend

"Oh, to See the Dawn," by Keith Getty and Stuart Townend

"Poor Sinner, Dejected with Fear," by William Gadsby, arranged by K. Bowser and P. Jones

"The Love of Christ Is Rich and Free," arranged by Indelible Grace

"There Is a Redeemer," by Melody Green and Keith Green

"Who Am I," by Mark Hall

"You Are My All in All," by Dennis Jernigan

"You Are My King," by Billy James Foote

Choral

"Amazing Grace," arranged by John Rutter

"Behold the Lamb of God," by Craig Courtney

"Cast Your Burden upon the Lord," by Felix Mendelssohn

"God So Loved the World," from *The Crucifixion*, by John Stainer

"He Shall Feed His Flock/Come Unto Him," from *Messiah*, by George Frideric Handel

"My Shepherd Will Supply," words by Isaac Watts, arranged by Virgil Thomson

"O, the Deep, Deep Love of Jesus," arranged by Gilbert Martin

"Salvation Is Created," by Ivan Tschesnokoff

"Steal Away," (solo) from African American spiritual, arranged by H. T. Burleigh

"There Is a Balm in Gilead," from African American spiritual, arranged by William Dawson

"Worthy Is the Lamb," from *Messiah*, by George Frideric Handel

Text Resources for Assurances of Pardon

Book of Common Worship. Philadelphia: Board of Christian Education of the Presbyterian Church (USA), 1966, esp. 351–52.

Brink, Emily R., and John D. Witvliet, eds. *The Worship Sourcebook*. Grand Rapids: Calvin Institute of Christian Worship and Baker Books, 2004.

Old, Hughes Oliphant. *Leading in Prayer: A Workbook for Worship*. Grand Rapids: Eerdmans, 1995.

Rayburn, Robert G. *O Come, Let Us Worship: Corporate Worship in the Evangelical Church*. Grand Rapids: Baker Academic, 1980.

Music Resources for Assurances of Pardon

Hymnals often include useful texts also.

African American Heritage Hymnal. Chicago: GIA Publications, 2001.

Baptist Hymnal. Nashville: LifeWay, 2008.

Hymnal 1982 According to the Use of the Episcopal Church. New York: Church Publishing, 1985.

The Hymnal for Worship and Celebration. Waco: Word Music, 1986.

Lutheran Service Book. St. Louis: Concordia, 2006.

Psalter Hymnal. Grand Rapids: CRC Publications, 2007.

Songs of Fellowship. Vols. 1–4. Eastbourne, UK: Kingsway Music, 1991–2008.

Trinity Hymnal. Rev. ed. Philadelphia: Great Commission Publications, 1990.

Trinity Psalter. Philadelphia: Great Commission Publications, 1994.

The Worshipping Church. Edited by Don Hustad. Carol Stream, IL: Hope Publishing, 1990.

17

RUBRICS

TRANSITIONS

A rubric was once the decorative text or instruction that appeared in red ink (rubric means "red") in medieval documents. In worship services, rubrics are the little directions that appear in the bulletin or are voiced by the worship leader to lead the congregation through the conduct of worship. The rubrics are not the major elements of the worship service, but rather are the instructive transitions that tell the congregation what to do *and* why. Rubrics verbally tie together key aspects of the worship service, explaining their purpose and sequence in relation to the theme(s) of the entire service.

Skilled use of rubrics helps the worship service to make sense and move along with clarity, purpose, and attitudes appropriate for each element. A rubric can be as simple as, "Turn with me to page 359 in the hymnal," or as instructive as, "Now that we have confessed our sin to God, we long for the assurance of his pardon. The apostle John gives us this assurance with these words . . ." By use of such rubrics a worship leader theologically ties the content of a previous worship component to the one that follows in order to weave a "gospel logic" into the liturgy. Skilled worship leaders may also encourage congregants to use a component of the service (a hymn, prayer, or reading) to prepare in a specific way (confession, reflection, praise) for the next component. In this way the components of the worship service themselves help lead people through the gospel progression.

At the same time that the rubrics highlight the gospel message woven through the worship service, the wording of the rubrics themselves may also reflect an overall theme of the worship service. If the theme (often determined by the main subject of the Sermon) is something like "Our Good Shepherd," then we tend to expect the Scriptures and hymns to reflect that theme. But the service will be even more cohesive and theologically rich if the words transitioning into and out of readings, offerings, hymns, and so on also echo the theme. As with other components of the worship service, worship leaders may wisely choose to put the words of ancient prayers or passages in contemporary language to make rubrics meaningful to present-day worshipers. While many rubric forms are suggested below, the most common practice of worship leaders is to create rubrics extemporaneously by echoing key words of an accompanying hymn, reading, prayer, psalm, or other Scripture to highlight the theme(s) of a service or the purpose of particular worship components. Rubrics are most typically read aloud by the worship leader alone.

Without rubrics, a worship service is just a spill of spiritual vegetables (we know the individual pieces are good for us, but they have no apparent order or purpose). With rubrics, a worship service becomes a gospel feast carefully prepared and sequenced to communicate the grace of God. But this caution is needed: too many rubrics or rubrics that are too long distract from the meal. They should enrich the courses designed for our spiritual dining, not compete with them.

Examples of Rubrics Accompanying Scripture Reading

Texts Read Prior to the Scripture Reading

1. Blessed is the man who does not walk in the counsel of the wicked
   or stand in the way of sinners or sit in the seat of mockers.
   But his delight is in the law of the LORD,
   and on his law he meditates day and night.
   (Ps. 1:1–2)

2. The law of the LORD is perfect, reviving the soul. The statutes of the LORD are trustworthy, making wise the simple. The precepts of the LORD are right, giving joy to the heart. The commands of the LORD are radiant, giving light to the eyes.
   (Ps. 19:7–8)

3. The ordinances of the LORD are sure and altogether righteous. They
   are more precious than gold, than much pure gold; they are sweeter
   than honey, than honey from the comb. By them is your servant
   warned; in keeping them there is great reward.

   (*Ps. 19:9b–11*)

4. Teach me your way, O LORD, and I will walk in your truth;
   Give me an undivided heart, that I may fear your name.

   (*Ps. 86:11*)

5. Give me understanding, and I will keep your law and obey it with
   all my heart.
   Direct me in the path of your commands, for there I find delight.
   Turn my heart toward your statutes and not toward selfish gain.
   Turn my eyes away from worthless things; preserve my life according
   to your word.

   (*Ps. 119:34–37*)

6. I will praise you with an upright heart as I learn your righteous
   laws.

   (*Ps. 119:7*)

7. As the rain and the snow come down from heaven, and do not return
   to it without watering the earth and making it bud and flourish,
   so that it yields seed for the sower and bread for the eater, so is my
   word that goes out from my mouth: It will not return to me empty,
   but will accomplish what I desire and achieve the purpose for which
   I sent it.

   (*Isa. 55:10–11*)

8. All Scripture is God-breathed and is useful for teaching, rebuking,
   correcting and training in righteousness, so that the man of God
   may be thoroughly equipped for every good work.

   (*2 Tim. 3:16–17*)

9. Hear now the Word of the Lord.

10. This is God's holy, inspired, and inerrant Word.

Prayers for Illumination Prior to Scripture Reading

A particular contribution of the Reformers was the re-introduction of the Prayer for Illumination. This prayer is used primarily (but not exclusively) for the Scripture text read prior to the Sermon. The Prayer for Illumination reflected the Reformers' understanding that the same Spirit who inspired the Word needed to be operative in the hearts of ministers and their hearers for them to have true (authentic) insight into the meaning of Scripture (see 1 Cor. 2:14). Without the work of the Holy Spirit, the Word of God was only print on a page or propositions for reflection. But through the Spirit working "by and with the Word in our hearts" (Westminster Confession of Faith 1.5), we would truly know conviction of our sin, release from our guilt, and the joy of our salvation. In more colloquial terms ministers say, "Unless the Spirit lifts his hand from the page, we cannot see it."[1] The statement helps us understand that a Prayer for Illumination is really a petition for the active work of the Spirit in the hearts of God's people so that his Word will be heard, understood, and lived. Whether a Prayer for Illumination is read from Scripture, recited from a traditional form, or extemporized (as is most common), it is a reminder to all that the preacher's message is only the second Sermon; the first has been offered by the Spirit in his Word. Apart from the Spirit's work, the words that follow will mean nothing.

1. May the God of our Lord Jesus Christ, the glorious Father, give you the Spirit of wisdom and revelation, so that you may know him better. I pray also that the eyes of your heart may be enlightened in order that you may know the hope to which he has called you, the riches of his glorious inheritance in the saints, and his incomparably great power for us who believe.

    (from Eph. 1:17–19)

2. Almighty, gracious Father, forasmuch as our whole salvation depends upon our true understanding of your Holy Word, grant to all of us that our hearts, being freed from worldly affairs, may hear and apprehend your Holy Word with all diligence and faith, that we may rightly understand your gracious will, cherish it, and live by it with all earnestness, to you praise and honor; through our Lord Jesus Christ.

    (from Martin Bucer, Strasbourg Psalter *of 1537)*

1. Colloquial as stated by Elder D. J. Ward, pastor of Main Street Baptist Church, Lexington, KY.

3. Most gracious God, our heavenly Father! in whom alone dwells all fullness of light and wisdom: Illumine our minds, we beseech you, by your Holy Spirit, in the true understanding of your Word. Give us grace that we may receive it with reverence and humility unfeigned. May it lead us to put our whole trust in you alone and so to serve and honor you, that we may glorify your holy name and edify our neighbors by good example. And since it has pleased you to number us among your people, help us to give you love and homage that we owe, as children to our Father, as servants to our Lord. We ask this for the sake of our Master and Savior, Jesus Christ.

(from John Calvin, as in Baird's Presbyterian Liturgies, *p. 37)*

4. Heavenly Father, we ask now that you would send the same Holy Spirit who inspired this Word to open our hearts to its truth. Please remove from us apathy, cynicism, callousness, or rebellion, so that we may really be hungry for this bread of life that feeds our souls, nourishes our hearts for your work, and fills us with the joy that is our strength. This we ask for the honor and glory of your dear Son and our dear Savior, Jesus Christ, in whose name we pray. Amen.

Responses After the Scripture Reading

Typically the worship leader and the congregation alternate parts in responsive readings such as these below, with the worship leader beginning and the congregation responding (group responses are shown in bold). However, there are numerous ways to vary this pattern, such as the choir or one section of the congregation leading and the rest of the participants responding.

1. This is the Word of the Lord.
Thanks be to God.

2. The gospel of the Lord
Praise to you, O Christ.

3. "All men are like grass, and all their glory is like the flowers of the field; the grass withers and the flowers fall, but the word of the Lord stands forever."
Amen.

(from 1 Pet. 1:24b–25)

Examples of Music Accompanying Scripture Reading or Prior to the Sermon

Traditional

"Blessed Jesus, at Your Word," by Tobias Clausnitzer
"Break, Thou, the Bread of Life," by Mary Lathbury
"Come, Holy Ghost, Our Hearts Inspire," by Charles Wesley
"How Firm a Foundation," originally from Rippon's *Selection of Hymns*, 1787
"Shine Thou upon Us, Lord," by John Ellerton
"The Spirit Breathes upon the Word," by Willam Cowper

Contemporary

"As the Deer," by Martin Nystrom
"Breathe," by Marie Barnett
"Open Our Eyes, Lord," by Bob Cull
"Open the Eyes of My Heart," by Paul Baloche
"Spirit of the Living God," by Daniel Iverson

Examples of Rubrics Accompanying Prayer

1. The eyes of the LORD are on the righteous and his ears are attentive to their cry.

    (Ps. 34:15)

2. The righteous cry out, and the LORD hears them; he delivers them from all their troubles. The LORD is close to the brokenhearted and saves those who are crushed in spirit.

    (Ps. 34:17–18)

3. Trust in him at all times, O people; pour out your hearts to him, for God is our refuge.

    (Ps. 62:8)

4. God says to his people: ". . . call upon me and come and pray to me, and I will listen to you. You will seek me and find me when you seek me with all your heart." Let us therefore seek the Lord now in prayer.

    (from Jer. 29:12–13)

5. Jesus taught us: "Ask and it will be given to you; seek and you will find; knock and the door will be opened to you. For everyone who asks receives; he who seeks finds; and to him who knocks, the door will be opened." We now need his care, so let us ask and seek and knock in prayer.

   (from Matt. 7:7–8)

6. Do not be anxious about anything, but in everything, by prayer and petition, with thanksgiving, present your requests to God. And the peace of God, which transcends all understanding, will guard your hearts and your minds in Christ Jesus.

   (Phil. 4:6–7)

7. We do not have a high priest who is unable to sympathize with our weaknesses, but we have one who has been tempted in every way, just as we are—yet was without sin. Let us then approach the throne of grace with confidence, so that we may receive mercy and find grace to help us in our time of need.

   (Heb. 4:15–16)

8. This is the confidence we have in approaching God: that if we ask anything according to his will, he hears us. And if we know that he hears us—whatever we ask—we know that we have what we asked of him.

   (1 John 5:14–15)

Examples of Rubrics Accompanying Hymns and Songs

Prior to a Hymn or Song of Praise

1. I will give thanks to the LORD because of his righteousness and will sing praise to the name of the LORD Most High.

   (Ps. 7:17)

2. I will praise you, O LORD, with all my heart; I will tell of all your wonders. I will be glad and rejoice in you; I will sing praise to your name, O Most High.

   (Ps. 9:1–2)

3. Sing to the LORD, you saints of his; praise his holy name.

   (Ps. 30:4)

4. Because your love is better than life, my lips will glorify you. I will praise you as long as I live, and in your name I will lift up my hands. My soul will be satisfied as with the richest of foods; with singing lips my mouth will praise you.

(Ps. 63:3–5)

5. I will sing of the LORD's great love forever; with my mouth I will make your faithfulness known through all generations. I will declare that your love stands firm forever, that you established your faithfulness in heaven itself.

(Ps. 89:1–2)

6. Come, let us sing for joy to the LORD; let us shout aloud to the Rock of our salvation. Let us come before him with thanksgiving and extol him with music and song.

(Ps. 95:1–2)

7. Sing to the LORD a new song; sing to the LORD, all the earth. Sing to the LORD, praise his name; proclaim his salvation day after day. Declare his glory among the nations, his marvelous deeds among all peoples.

(Ps. 96:1–3)

8. Say among the nations, "The LORD reigns." The world is firmly established, it cannot be moved; he will judge the peoples with equity. Let the heavens rejoice, let the earth be glad; let the sea resound, and all that is in it; let the fields be jubilant, and everything in them. Then all the trees of the forest will sing for joy; they will sing before the LORD, for he comes, he comes to judge the earth. He will judge the world in righteousness and the peoples in his truth.

(Ps. 96:10–13)

9. Shout for joy to the LORD, all the earth. Worship the LORD with gladness; come before him with joyful songs.

(Ps. 100:1–2)

10. Praise the LORD. Praise God in his sanctuary; praise him in his mighty heavens. Praise him for his acts of power; praise him for his surpassing greatness. Praise him with the sounding of the trumpet, praise him with the harp and lyre, praise him with tambourine and dancing, praise him with the strings and flute, praise him with the clash of

cymbals, praise him with resounding cymbals. Let everything that has breath praise the LORD. Praise the LORD.

> (*Ps. 150*)

Prior to a Hymn or Song Reflecting on a Worship Theme

1. Exalt the LORD our God and worship at his holy mountain, for the LORD our God is holy.

> (*from Ps. 99:9, for a theme relating to God's holiness*)

2. I will sing of your love and justice; to you, O LORD, I will sing praise.

> (*from Ps. 101:1, for a theme relating to God's love and justice*)

3. Let us now use this song as . . .
   a. a prayer of confession to our God.
   b. a reminder of the assurance we have of God's grace.
   c. a petition for God to open our hearts to his Word.
   d. an affirmation of our faith in the good providence of our God.
   e. an expression of our joy in our God's grace and mercy.
   f. an affirmation of our commitment to do as God's Word says.

Examples of Rubrics Accompanying the Offering

1. Tell the Israelites to bring me an offering. You are to receive the offering for me from each man whose heart prompts him to give.

> (*Exod. 25:2*)

2. Each of you must bring a gift in proportion to the way the LORD your God has blessed you.

> (*Deut. 16:17*)

3. Honor the LORD with your wealth, with the firstfruits of all your crops.

> (*Prov. 3:9*)

4. Freely you have received, freely give.

> (*Matt. 10:8*)

5. The apostle Paul reminds us that God does not grant us the privileges of work and provision merely to sustain ourselves: "In everything I

did, I showed you that by this kind of hard work we must help the weak, remembering the words the Lord Jesus himself said: 'It is more blessed to give than to receive.'"

(*Acts 20:35b*)

6. For you know the grace of our Lord Jesus Christ, that though he was rich, yet for your sakes he became poor, so that you through his poverty might become rich.

(*2 Cor. 8:9*)

7. Remember this: Whoever sows sparingly will also reap sparingly, and whoever sows generously will also reap generously. Each man should give what he has decided in his heart to give, not reluctantly or under compulsion, for God loves a cheerful giver.

(*2 Cor. 9:6–7*)

8. And do not forget to do good and to share with others, for with such sacrifices God is pleased.

(*Heb. 13:16*)

Examples of Music Accompanying the Offering

Traditional

"All Things Are Thine," by John Whittier
"Christ Shall Have Dominion," version of Psalm 72 in *The Psalter*, 1912
"Praise, My Soul, the King of Heaven," by Henry Lyte
"We Give Thee But Thine Own," by William Walsham How

Contemporary

"Give Thanks with a Joyful Heart," by Henry Smith
"You Are My All in All," by Dennis Jernigan
"Lord, You Are More Precious Than Silver," by Lynn Deshazo

Text Resources for Rubrics

Bennett, Arthur, ed. *The Valley of Vision: A Collection of Puritan Prayers and Devotions.* Carlisle, PA: Banner of Truth Trust, 1975, esp. 121–77.

Brink, Emily R., and John D. Witvliet, eds. *The Worship Sourcebook*. Grand Rapids: Calvin Institute of Christian Worship and Baker Books, 2004.

Old, Hughes Oliphant. *Leading in Prayer: A Workbook for Worship*. Grand Rapids: Eerdmans, 1995.

Rayburn, Robert G. *O Come, Let Us Worship: Corporate Worship in the Evangelical Church*. Grand Rapids: Baker Academic, 1980, esp. 303–13.

Music Resources for Rubrics

Hymnals often include useful texts also.

African American Heritage Hymnal. Chicago: GIA Publications, 2001.

Baptist Hymnal. Nashville: LifeWay, 2008.

Hymnal 1982 According to the Use of the Episcopal Church. New York: Church Publishing, 1985.

The Hymnal for Worship and Celebration. Waco: Word Music, 1986.

Lutheran Service Book. St. Louis: Concordia, 2006.

Psalter Hymnal. Grand Rapids: CRC Publications, 2007.

Songs of Fellowship. Vols. 1–4. Eastbourne, UK: Kingsway Music, 1991–2008.

Trinity Hymnal. Rev. ed. Philadelphia: Great Commission Publications, 1990.

Trinity Psalter. Philadelphia: Great Commission Publications, 1994.

The Worshipping Church. Edited by Don Hustad. Carol Stream, IL: Hope Publishing, 1990.

18

HISTORIC COMPONENTS

The historical uses of most of the liturgical components below are discussed in chapters 2 and 3 of this book. My intention in listing these components here is not to insist on, or even endorse, their use in all contemporary worship. My goal is simply to shine the wisdom of the historical church on our present practice.

The worship components below are densely scriptural and have instructed and encouraged believers across many centuries. By studying the content and use of such texts, we can discover how they or similar words may be used in various aspects of our worship services to communicate gospel truths. For example, in the three centuries since Thomas Ken penned the words of our "Doxology," the hymn has assumed an almost petrified place after the Offering in many churches. But the content of the hymn (especially if all original verses are included) indicates that it could also be used as an Affirmation of Faith before or after intercessory prayer. The Doxology is also a fitting response to the reading of Scripture. Some churches begin their worship with this Doxology; others use it as an ascription of praise prior to or after a Benediction. All these uses are appropriate given the content of the words Ken originally wrote to provide a unified ending for three separate hymns: "Morning Hymn," "Evening Hymn," and "Midnight Hymn."

To expand their usefulness, a number of the following components have also been set to music (both traditional and contemporary). As is true of much that we learn from church history, naïveté would lead us simply to mimic or idolize past worship practices. We would also be naïve (or arrogant) to presume the Lord could teach us nothing from the wisdom of centuries of saints who have preceded us. The church of Jesus Christ requires both continuity with the past and creativity in the present to give testimony to the power of his Spirit for all ages.

Gloria
("Glory")

Glory to God in the highest,
and peace to his people on earth.
Lord God, heavenly King, almighty God and Father,
we worship you, we give you thanks, we praise you for your glory.
Lord Jesus Christ, only Son of the Father,
Lord God, Lamb of God,
you take away the sin of the world: have mercy on us;
you are seated at the right hand of the Father; receive our prayer.
For you alone are the Holy One, you alone are the Lord,
You alone are the Most High, Jesus Christ,
with the Holy Spirit, in the glory of God the Father. Amen.

Example of a Collect prayer: Almighty God, to whom all hearts are open, by whom all desires are known, and from whom no secrets are hid; cleanse the thoughts of our hearts by the inspiration of your Holy Spirit, that we may perfectly love you and worthily magnify your holy name, through Jesus Christ our Lord. Amen.

Doxology
("Praise")

Praise God from whom all blessings flow;
Praise him all creatures here below;
Praise him above ye heavenly host;
Praise Father, Son and Holy Ghost.

Gloria Patri
("Glory to the Father")

Glory be to the Father and to the Son and to the Holy Ghost,
As it was in the beginning, is now and ever shall be, world without
    end. Amen.

Te Deum Laudamus
("We Praise thee, O God," historically sung to reflect the outline
of the Apostles' Creed)

We praise thee, O God
we acknowledge thee to be the Lord
All the earth doth worship thee
the Father everlasting.
To thee all the angels cry aloud
the heavens and all the powers therein.
To thee cherubim and seraphim do continually cry
Holy, Holy, Holy,
Lord God of Sabaoth; heaven and earth
are full of the majesty of thy glory.
The glorious company of apostles praise thee.
The goodly fellowship of the prophets praise thee.
The noble army of martyrs praise thee.
The Holy Church
throughout all the world doth acknowledge thee;
the Father of an infinite majesty;
thine honourable true and only Son;
also the Holy Ghost the Comforter.
Thou art the King of Glory, O Christ.
Thou art the everlasting Son of the Father.
When thou tookest upon thee to deliver man,
thou didst not abhor the Virgin's womb.
When thou hadst overcome the sharpness of death,
thou didst open the kingdom of heaven to all believers.
Thou sittest at the hand of God in glory of the Father.
We believe that Thou shalt come to be our Judge.
We therefore pray thee, help thy servants,
whom thou hast redeemed with thy precious blood.
Make them numbered with thy saints in glory everlasting
O Lord save thy people
and bless thine heritage.
Govern them and lift them up for ever.
Day by day we magnify thee;
and worship thy name, ever world without end.
Vouchsafe, O Lord to keep us this day without sin.
O Lord, have mercy upon us, have mercy upon us.
O Lord, let thy mercy lighten upon us, as our trust is in thee.
O Lord in thee have I trusted let me not be confounded.

Sursum Corda
("Lift your hearts")

Presider: The Lord be with you.
People: And with thy spirit.
Presider: Lift up your hearts.
People: We lift them up unto the Lord.
Presider: Let us give thanks to the Lord our God.
People: It is meet and right so to do.

Sanctus
("Holy")

Holy, holy, holy, Lord God of Hosts:
Heaven and earth are full of thy glory.
Hosanna in the highest.
Blessed is he that cometh in the name of the Lord.
Hosanna in the highest.

Benedictus
("Blessed")

Blessed is he who comes in the name of the Lord.
Hosanna in the highest.

Agnus Dei
("Lamb of God")

Lamb of God, who takes away the sins of the world, have mercy
    upon us.
Lamb of God, who takes away the sins of the world, have mercy
    upon us.
Lamb of God, who takes away the sins of the world, grant us peace.

Nunc Dimittis
("Now dismiss")

Now dismiss Thy servant, O Lord, in peace, according to Thy word: For
mine own eyes hath seen Thy salvation, which Thou hast prepared in the
sight of all the peoples, a light to reveal Thee to the nations and the glory
of Thy people Israel.

Aaronic Benediction

May the Lord bless you and keep you; may He make His face to shine on
you and be gracious to you; may He lift up His countenance on you and
give you peace.

Trisagion
("Three times holy")

Holy God,
Holy and mighty,
Holy immortal One,
Have mercy upon us.

Litany

O Lord,
Have mercy upon us.
O Christ,
Have mercy upon us.
O Spirit,
Have mercy upon us.
O God the Father in heaven,
We beseech you, hear us.
O God the Son, Redeemer of the world,
We beseech you, hear us.
O God the Holy Spirit, our Comforter,
We beseech you, hear us.
Be gracious unto us.
Spare us, good Lord.
Be gracious unto us.
Help us, good Lord.
Be gracious unto us.
Save us, good Lord,
from our sin;
from our errors;
from all evil.
Good Lord, deliver us.
[All]: Lord, have mercy upon us.

Text Resources for Historic Components

Book of Common Prayer. San Francisco: HarperOne, 1983.

Book of Common Worship. Philadelphia: Board of Christian Education of the Presbyterian Church (USA), 1966, esp. 351–52.

Brink, Emily R., and John D. Witvliet, eds. *The Worship Sourcebook*. Grand Rapids: Calvin Institute of Christian Worship and Baker Books, 2004.

Old, Hughes Oliphant. *Leading in Prayer: A Workbook for Worship*. Grand Rapids: Eerdmans, 1995.

Rayburn, Robert G. *O Come, Let Us Worship: Corporate Worship in the Evangelical Church*. Grand Rapids: Baker Academic, 1980, esp. 303–13.

Music Resources for Historic Components

Hymnals often include useful texts also.

African American Heritage Hymnal. Chicago: GIA Publications, 2001.

Baptist Hymnal. Nashville: LifeWay, 2008.

Hymnal 1982 According to the Use of the Episcopal Church. New York: Church Publishing, 1985.

The Hymnal for Worship and Celebration. Waco: Word Music, 1986.

Lutheran Service Book. St. Louis: Concordia, 2006.

Psalter Hymnal. Grand Rapids: CRC Publications, 2007.

Songs of Fellowship. Vols. 1–4. Eastbourne, UK: Kingsway Music, 1991–2008.

Trinity Hymnal. Rev. ed. Philadelphia: Great Commission Publications, 1990.

Trinity Psalter. Philadelphia: Great Commission Publications, 1994.

The Worshipping Church. Edited by Don Hustad. Carol Stream, IL: Hope Publishing, 1990.

19

SCRIPTURE-READING HISTORY
AND PRACTICE

So Moses wrote down this law and gave it to the priests, the sons of Levi, who carried the ark of the covenant of the Lord, and to all the elders of Israel. Then Moses commanded them: "At the end of every seven years . . . during the Feast of Tabernacles when all Israel comes to appear before the Lord your God at the place he will choose, you shall read this law before them in their hearing. Assemble the people—men, women and children, and the aliens living in your towns—so they can listen and learn to fear the Lord your God. . . ." (Deut. 31:9–12)

These verses formally introduce the institution of Scripture reading in the history of Christian worship. No longer binding his communication to the ephemeral thunderings on Sinai, the spatially confined burning bush, or the fleeting prophetic pronouncement, God now commands the repetition of a text as his immanent and permanent voice among his people. Thus, reading the Word of God becomes the very core of worship, affording each hearer an opportunity for ongoing, personal encounter with the divine.[1] In essence, Scripture is God's voice incarnate for the church in all ages.

1. J. Edward Lantz, *Reading the Bible Aloud* (New York: Macmillan, 1959), 43.

Scriptural Roots

The homage reserved for presenting God's recorded Word is evident in the honored position the reading of Scripture has held in the liturgy, doctrine, and history of the Christian church. The verses above from Deuteronomy schedule the public review of the arrangements of the covenant between God and his people.[2] Thus, as early as the Pentateuch, oral reading of Scripture becomes a normative worship practice. Because these books of Moses laid the foundation for the Jewish concept of all covenantal worship, this practice of public reading assumes seminal significance for later developments in Christian worship.[3]

As the Jewish worship tradition developed, standards emerged for the habitual reading of various Scriptures in the synagogue. The liturgy essentially consisted of two readings, the first of which came from the Law (i.e., the books of Moses), and the second came from the Prophets (see Luke 16:16; Acts 13:15).[4]

It is important to note that while Scripture reading was required in synagogue worship, preaching was optional.[5] Preaching naturally developed in ordinary worship services as an exposition or application of what was read, but Sermons were derivative of the readings.[6] Further, as was demonstrated annually in the Passover observances of individual families, worship of the highest order could always be oriented around the Word and prayer without sermonic exposition.[7] The Christian church did not revoke this aspect of its Jewish worship heritage nor subordinate the importance of Scripture readings. Instead, the readings were expanded.

New Testament worship services echoed the Jewish synagogue patterns for prayers, readings, and exposition, but apostolic writings were added to the canonical materials (cf. 1 Thess. 2:13).[8] As the Old Testament prophets

2. R. K. Harrison, "Deuteronomy," in *New Bible Commentary Revised*, ed. D. Guthrie and J. A. Motyer (Grand Rapids: Eerdmans, 1970), 202; Meredith Kline, "Dynastic Covenant," *The Westminster Theological Journal* 23 (1960): 13, 15.

3. Richard G. Moulton, *The Literary Study of the Bible* (Boston: D. C. Heath, 1906), 268.

4. Pius Parsch, *The Liturgy of the Mass*, trans. H. E. Winstone, 3rd ed. (St. Louis: B. Herder, 1957), 72.

5. Arthur T. Pierson, *How to Read the Word of God Effectively* (Chicago: Moody Bible Institute, 1925), 3–4; Lantz, *Reading the Bible Aloud*, 3.

6. Edwin C. Dargan, *A History of Preaching*, vol. 1 (New York: Hodder and Stoughton, 1905), 39.

7. Joseph A. Jungman, *The Mass of the Roman Rite*, rev. ed., trans. Francis Brunner (New York: Benzinger Bros., 1950), 8; *The Union Hagadah*, rev. ed. (Central Conference of American Rabbis, 1923).

8. J. H. Srawley, *The Early History of the Liturgy*, The Cambridge Handbooks of Liturgical Study, 2nd ed. (Cambridge: Cambridge University Press, 1957), 188; Dargan, *History of Preaching*, 39; Karl Young, *The Drama of the Medieval Church* (Oxford: Clarendon, 1933), 16.

arranged for the perpetuation of their message in the readings of the temple, the New Testament messengers created literature for repeated use in the church (Acts 15:23–31; Col. 4:16; 1 Thess. 5:27). In his Colossian letter Paul commands, "After this letter has been read to you, see that it is also read in the church of the Laodiceans and that you in turn read the letter from Laodicea" (Col. 4:16). The Scripture poem of Philippians 2:6–11 is apparently intended for liturgical use, and Paul specifically commands his protégé Timothy, "Devote yourself to the public reading of Scripture, to preaching and to teaching" (1 Tim. 4:13).

Readings of the newer writings did not replace the Old Testament readings, but augmented them. That the apostolic writings were being read in the churches along with the ancient Scriptures is apparent from Peter's commentary on Paul (2 Pet. 3:16) and Paul's own commands for the continued use of the Psalms (Eph. 5:19; Col. 3:16). Further, the reading of the New Testament Gospels and Epistles, with their many Old Testament quotations and analogies, would necessarily keep both testaments echoing in the church.

Early Church Practice

Sensing the continued respect of the apostolic writers for the older Scriptures, the church continued publicly reading from both testaments in the early centuries of the Christian era. By the end of the fourth century, the dominant liturgical pattern included three readings: one from the Old Testament and two from the New—an Epistle and a Gospel. The last reading was always from one of the Gospels, and the people stood during this reading.[9]

In addition to having a minister, other officiant, or lay person reading Scripture, the church has made God's Word integral to worship through a variety of approaches. Responsive readings may involve the congregation by having the people read passages or verses in a public dialogue with the reader, as was apparently the expectation for some psalms (e.g., Pss. 113–16). A litany involves the congregation by having it repeat a key phrase or set of phrases in response to a reader. Again, this follows a pattern evident in the psalms (e.g., Pss. 118 and 136). An antiphonal reading has one segment of the congregation respond to (or echo) a reading from another segment of the congregation, as was practiced by Israel on Mounts Ebal and Gerizim (see Deut. 27 and Josh. 8). Variations of these practices

9. James D. Robertson, *Minister's Worship Handbook* (Grand Rapids: Baker Academic, 1974), 52.

may occur as portions of Scripture are assigned to the choir, readers in the congregation, or persons of different ages or genders in the congregation, or as the congregation simply responds to the Scripture reading with a unison "Amen," "Praise the Lord," or "Thanks be to God" (e.g., Deut. 27; 1 Chron. 16:36; Neh. 8:6).

The importance of Scripture reading in worship, however, should not be judged entirely on its liturgical heritage, even if that heritage is ancient and honorable. The importance of Scripture reading should rather be weighed on the biblical principle that liturgical history and practice only serve to underscore: the inherent efficacy of God's Word (Phil. 1:18).[10]

Theological Foundations

According to Scripture, the Word of God possesses inherent power. The Word of God creates: "God said, 'Let there be light,' and there was light" (Gen. 1:3); "For he spoke, and it came to be; he commanded, and it stood firm" (Ps. 33:9). The Word of God controls: "He sends his command to the earth; his word runs swiftly. He spreads the snow like wool and scatters the frost like ashes. He hurls down his hail like pebbles. . . . He sends his word and melts them . . ." (Ps. 147:15–18). The Word of God persuades: "'Let the one who has my word speak it faithfully, . . .' declares the Lord. 'Is not my word like fire . . . and like a hammer that breaks a rock in pieces?'" (Jer. 23:28–29). The Word of God performs God's purposes: "As the rain and snow come down from heaven, and do not return to it without watering the earth . . . so is my word that goes out from my mouth: It will not return to me empty, but will accomplish what I desire and achieve the purpose for which I sent it" (Isa. 55:10–11).

The dynamic power of the Word of God is fully manifested in the New Testament through the divine Logos, Christ. As the work of creation came through the Word of God, the work of new creation (i.e., redemption) is through the Word of God, Jesus, through whom "all things were made" (John 1:3), and who continues "sustaining all things by his powerful word" (Heb. 1:3). Christ's redemptive power and the power of his Word henceforth become inseparable in the New Testament images with Logos (the Incarnate Word) and logos (the inscripturated Word) becoming so reflexive as to become practically an identity. The apostle James says, "He chose to give us birth through the word of truth . . ." (James 1:18). The same play on words is used by Peter: "For you have been born again, not of perish-

---

10. See the discussion of the following paragraphs also in the author's *Christ-Centered Preaching: Redeeming the Expository Sermon*, 2nd ed. (Grand Rapids: Baker Academic, 2005).

able seed, but of imperishable, through the living and enduring word of God" (1 Pet. 1:23). Thus, it is not merely prosaic to insist that the reader of Scripture should serve the text, for if the Word is the mediate presence of Christ, service is due. Paul rightly instructs Timothy, and today's pastor, to be "a workman . . . who correctly handles the word of truth" (2 Tim. 2:15), for "the word of God is *living and active*. Sharper than any double-edged sword, it penetrates even to dividing soul and spirit, joints and marrow; it judges the thoughts and attitudes of the heart" (Heb. 4:12; emphasis mine).

Historical Controversy

As with most key features of the Christian worship service, the reading of Scripture has also occasionally been the focus of abuse and controversy. Early French Huguenots often eschewed preaching on the assumption that human interpretation necessarily polluted the purity of God's Word. Later debates in England boiled between Puritans and the established church over John Whitgift's rhetorical question, "Is not the Word of God as effectual when it is read as when it is preached? Or is not reading preaching?"[11] The divergent viewpoints were argued expertly and expansively by Whitgift when he was Bishop of Worcester, and also by the Puritan scholar, Thomas Cartwright.[12]

Whitgift's insistence on the sufficiency of readings, though argued on theological grounds, was a political necessity. In order to suppress Puritan teachings and provide services in parishes whose ministers had been removed (i.e., defrocked, imprisoned, or executed), a series of approved readings and homilies were prepared so they could be read in the churches.[13] Approved clergymen made the rounds through the rebel churches, presenting nothing but these readings.[14]

Cartwright argued for the Puritans,

It may be that God doth work faith by reading only, especially where preaching cannot be, and so he doth sometimes without reading by a wonderful

11. Donald J. McGinn, *The Admonition Controversy* (New Brunswick, NJ: Rutgers University Press, 1949), 176. The great debate between Whitgift and Cartwright is conveniently abridged in this most helpful work, which topically arranges the original arguments of Cartwright's *Admonition* (1572), Whitgift's *Answere* (1572), Cartwright's *Replye* (1573), Whitgift's *Defense* (1574), and Cartwright's *Second replie* (1575) and *The rest of the second replie* (1577).
12. Edwin Hall, *The Puritans and their Principles*, 2nd ed. (New York: Baker and Scribner, 1846), 108; McGinn, *Admonition Controversy*, 145–47.
13. Hall, *Puritans*, 110–12.
14. Ibid., 109.

work of his Spirit; but the ordinary ways whereby God regenereth his children is the Word of God which is preached.[15]

Whitgift adroitly replied,

> Did not St. Paul preach to the Romans when he writ to them? . . . Was not the reading of Deuteronomy to the people a preaching?[16]

The fact thrown into historical relief by the Elizabethan controversy is that Scripture reading is an inherent and indispensable feature of Christian worship. Even when events were so exceptional as to cause the merits of reading Scripture to be weighed against preaching, no one argued for excising Scripture from worship. The Puritan preachers insisted that preaching be an exposition of Scripture.[17] While they vigorously opposed "bare readings,"[18] they never argued for bare preaching (i.e., preaching apart from Scripture reading).

Modern Concerns

Since the Reformation, divergent commitments to fixed forms of worship—exemplified in conflicts between English Puritans and established church leaders—have influenced Scripture reading practices in Protestantism. Traditions valuing non-prescribed forms of worship tend to de-emphasize Scripture readings—viewing interpretation of the Word in preaching as the focus of worship. Traditions maintaining a high regard for ritual often organize worship around Scripture readings in liturgical forms while giving less attention to formal exposition of those texts.

Recent movements in a number of denominations have sought to unite the strengths of both worship traditions by re-emphasizing the inherent efficacy of the Word of God, promoted by both its reading and preaching. Musical and dramaturgical influences have also added new creativity and power to the way Scripture is "read" in both regular and special services. The force of these movements stems from the ancient ethic—confirmed throughout the church's liturgy, theology, and history—that the public reading of Scripture is a touchstone of authentic worship.

15. McGinn, *Admonition Controversy*, 180.
16. Ibid., 186–87.
17. Irvonwy Morgan, *The Godly Preachers of the Elizabethan Church* (London: Epworth, 1965), 25.
18. McGinn, *Admonition Controversy*, 180.

Individual Responsibilities

When Scripture reading is assigned to individuals, textual care begins with a commitment to understand what is to be read. The classic work of John Broadus, *On the Preparation and Delivery of Sermons*, observes,

> To read well is a rare accomplishment. It is much more common to excel in singing or in public speaking. Good preachers are numerous compared with good readers. The requisites to good reading are several. First, one must have great quickness of apprehension. . . .[19]

The primary need for understanding the text is derived from the doctrine that the Scriptures have truths of inherent power to communicate. While readers are not the sources of this power, they can be the conduits for it, unless through their oral interpretations they corrupt the truths. Readers can fail to group words or phrases properly, begin or end a selection in inappropriate contexts, speak in tones wholly foreign to the sentiment of the text, or, in short, by a myriad of variables fail to communicate what the text says. It is not enough merely to read words, even if the words sound excellent. "The reader needs to understand that it is not he that is speaking, but the selection."[20] The ancient Levites "read from the Book of the Law of God, making it clear and giving the meaning so that the people could understand what was being read" (Neh. 8:8). This remains the duty of modern readers.

To give the meaning requires searching it out. Reading, no less than preaching, is an exegetical task. It requires an exploration of language, history, and context. Though weak in other areas, Woolbert and Nelson's *The Art of Interpretive Speech* offers significant insight for another task of the oral reader who would serve the text. They write, "The ideal of the interpreter should be to do what the writer would do if he were a competent speaker and could meet face to face in conversation those who are to read what he writes."[21] Readers should be concerned to make climactic what the writer intended to be the climax, to connote feelings appropriate for the sense of the passage. In the words of Paul, we are to "rejoice with those who rejoice; mourn with those who mourn" (Rom. 12:15). "It is not the reader's task to alter or embellish the selection but rather to restrict

19. John A. Broadus, *On the Preparation and Delivery of Sermons*, ed. Jesse B. Weatherspoon, rev. ed. (London: Hodder and Stoughton, 1944), 360.

20. Harold A. Brack, *Effective Oral Interpretation for Religious Leaders* (Englewood Cliffs, NJ: Prentice-Hall, 1964), 16.

21. C. H. Woolbert and S. E. Nelson, *The Art of Interpretive Speech* (New York: F. S. Crofts, 1929), 19.

himself to the content of the selection as it is actually expressed."[22] In this way oral reading becomes a type of exposition of Scripture, and its presentation becomes a tool for both communicating and discovering the truths within the text.

Spiritual Responsibilities

Such intimate knowledge of the text is not immediately accessible to readers. In order to reflect authentically the latent light in the Scriptures, readers must first be illuminated inwardly. Readers should search out the propositional truths of the text, so that they can reflect what the writer wishes to communicate. In order to feel these truths readers must not abandon their thinking but personalize it. Scripture inherently intends a spiritual dynamic, and readers must internalize the truths if they are to be able to express their full intent. This approach is not mysticism or mechanical elocution but more closely reflects the nineteenth-century expressionism of American educator S. S. Curry. Curry crusaded for "the necessity of working 'within outward,' of being a unified person in which the mind stimulated the body to natural expression."[23]

On a spiritual plane, Curry's concepts are especially pertinent. For until the readers have experienced the inward work of the Word, they have not truly understood what there is to communicate. The apostle Paul explains,

> No one knows the thoughts of God except the Spirit of God. We have not received the spirit of the world but the Spirit who is from God, that we may understand what God has freely given us. This is what we speak, not in words taught us by human wisdom but in words taught by the Spirit, expressing spiritual truths in spiritual words. (1 Cor. 2:11–13)

The text cannot fully be served until it has been understood. It cannot be understood until it has been spiritually digested. Once this internalization has taken place, then a competent reading will truly be a "spontaneous overflow of powerful feelings."[24] These feelings will naturally flow when the interpreter of the Word of God outwardly is a listener to the Word of God inwardly.

22. Brack, *Effective Oral Interpretation*, 16.
23. Paul Edwards, "The Rise of Expression," in *Performance of Literature in Historical Perspectives*, ed. David W. Thompson (Lanham, MD: University Press of America, 1983), 488.
24. Jack Stillinger, ed., *William Wordsworth: Selected Poems and Prefaces* (Boston: Houghton Mifflin, 1965), 460.

Having spiritually attuned internal ears further enables readers to serve the text by communicating its power over their own hearts. J. Edward Lantz in *Reading the Bible Aloud* says, "The reader has a threefold responsibility regarding mood, as he has regarding other elements of reading... namely adequately to express the moods inherent in the material; to express his own true response to them and not be deceptive; and, finally, to create and establish the proper moods in his listeners. . . ."[25] Audience responsibilities will be dealt with shortly. Lantz's second comment is the one immediately germane. In essence, Lantz observes that readers should yield themselves to Scripture's inherent power and seek to communicate their responses to that power in their reading. In doing so, readers add their own testimonies to the truths the Scriptures espouse, and so further illumine them.

In no way is this reflection of personal experience meant to imply that the inherent efficacy of Scripture resides in the virtue of the people relating it. Nor is this to connote that the scriptural truths are buried until they are excavated by the existential experience of a particular reader. Rather, the beauty of seeing that personal experience has a role in Scripture reading is the realization that God is perpetually turning another facet of the jewel of Scripture toward our spiritual eyes so that increasingly we may appreciate its value. There are not divergent truths in any one propositional statement of Scripture, but there are many angles from which to see the truth in the statement. That four different ministers read a text in four different ways does not necessarily indicate any wrong reading (provided the readings authentically reflect the meaning of the text and the reader's experience with it). God variously gifts the people of his church (1 Cor. 12:4), saying this is historically done in order for "you [to] have been enriched in every way—in all your speaking and in all your knowledge . . ." (1 Cor. 1:5).

Understanding Responsibilities

A century and a half ago, Archbishop Whately expertly balanced the need to express the intention of the author with the experience of the reader, saying,

> It is not, indeed, desirable that in reading the Bible, for example, or anything which is not intended to appear as his [i.e., the reader's] own composition, he should deliver what are, avowedly, another's sentiments in the same style, as if they were such as arose in his own mind; but it is desirable that he should

25. Lantz, *Reading the Bible Aloud*, 53.

deliver them as if he were reporting another's sentiments, which were both fully understood, and felt in all their force by the reporter. . . .[26]

In a modern reworking of Whately, Lantz concludes,

> Do not strive to impersonate the author. . . . As a reader you are an interpreter speaking the thoughts of the author and recreating his moods; but you speak as yourself, with your own identity, just as you sing music that some other person has composed.
>
> Your interpretation of the passage may be different from that of someone else. . . . You even have the privilege of interpreting the same material differently at different times . . . *provided you do not distort the intended meaning of the author.*[27]

Summarizing the reader's duty to the text, the greatest responsibility is understanding the text. Analysis of the thought, mood, wording, historical context, and impact on the readers themselves are all vital to a competent interpretation of the text. Little has been said thus far regarding the actual tools of expression (voice, volume, pitch, tone, gesture, pause, etc.). Some of this will follow in the discussion of the reader's responsibility to the audience. But too concentrated a discussion on tools can create a mechanical or artificial reading.

In general, readers can be confident of their interpretation if they have taken time to develop a natural facility with the speaking tools, and then apply their skills to interpretation based on "a thorough understanding of the matter, and a re-creation in the reader of the writer's mood and feeling."[28] Lantz also advises, "An effective method of making the reader come alive is to think of what you are reading while you are reading it."[29] All these hints share the larger concern of the honored Broadus:

> To read the Bible really well is a difficult task. . . . The lack of full intellectual and spiritual sympathy with Scripture . . . so often prevents our entering fully in to the sense. There is a common tendency to be subdued by mistaken reverence into a uniform tone, devoid of real expression. . . . It is all sacred, and in reading even its less striking devotional parts there should be a prevailing solemnity; but this solemnity does not forbid a rich variety of expression, as many readers appear to imagine.[30]

26. Brack, *Effective Oral Interpretation*, 16.
27. Lantz, *Reading the Bible Aloud*, 92 (emphasis added).
28. Ibid., 42.
29. Ibid., 73.
30. Broadus, *Preparation and Delivery*, 362.

Sacramental Responsibilities

Broadus's concern for honoring the text has received much emphasis thus far. His further concern for a "rich variety of expression" brings another subject into focus. Competent oral interpreters care about how they are being heard as well as what is being heard.[31] David Thompson writes,

> The reader faces in both directions at once, toward the literature as the source of his inner gestures and toward the audience whose imagination these gestures reach out to and capture. . . . He apparently communicates the story or poem out to us, but actually he leads us to a communion in it.[32]

The sacramental perspective is beautiful and especially appropriate for the ministration of an inspired text which can perform an inward grace. As the servant of the body in this communion, readers must make every effort to assist the listener in approaching the altar of the Word. In a note complementary to his advice on competently serving the text (cf. note 27 above), Lantz says, "think of them [i.e., the listeners] as you read and be eager to have each one of them comprehend your meaning."[33]

Preparation Responsibilities

In order to have the listener comprehend and commune with the text, readers need to render two basic services to the audience: (1) they must conscientiously remove obstacles from the listener's path to the Word; and (2) they must not so flurry around or fumble through the obstacles that they becomes a hindrance themselves.

"As sharers of a piece of literature we do not dispense it, but rather we lead our listeners into a more perceptive beholding of it," says Harold Brack.[34] Leading the listener rudimentarily involves the utilization of good speaking skills. Of primary importance is a dynamic voice able to reflect nuances in the text (through pitch, pause, tempo, tone, force, emotion, etc.), while being amply projected and enabling distinct articulation. Ebenezer Porter in his 1831 *Rhetorical Reader* underscores the attention that articulation deserves if the listener is not to be led astray:

31. Brack, *Effective Oral Interpretation*, 17.
32. David W. Thompson, "Interpretive Reading as Symbolic Action," *Quarterly Journal of Speech* 42, no. 4 (1956): 394.
33. Lantz, *Reading the Bible Aloud*, 90.
34. Brack, *Effective Oral Interpretation*, 17.

Good articulation is to the ear, what a fair handwriting . . . is to the eye. Who has not felt the perplexity of supplying a word, torn away by the seal of a letter. . . . The same inconvenience is felt from a similar omission in spoken language; with this additional disadvantage, that we are not at liberty to stop, and spell out the meaning by construction.[35]

Proper articulation necessitates becoming familiar with a text before presenting it so that pronunciations, word groupings, and punctuations may be correctly expressed. Nothing so immediately destroys the thought of the text and the credibility of the reader as words mispronounced or phrases mistreated. It is easy to read a question as though it were a statement or an exclamation as a question, if we have not read *and* spoken the material privately prior to a public reading. The best readers know that verbs and modifiers nuance the meaning of most sentences. Reading the text out loud in private will help prepare us to emphasize these key terms so that we give an accurate interpretation of the text as we read before others.

Expression Tools

Gesture should also be added to the list of tools at the reader's disposal to lead the listeners to communion with the text. Quintillian observed, "The face is what is most expressive. . . . It is often equivalent in expressiveness to what can be said in many words."[36] Other physical gestures are also powerful communication tools. Some of the Elizabethans, with John Bulwer, went so far as to suggest that between voice and bodily action, voice was the less effective communication tool.[37] Whether or not this evaluation is correct, it is nonetheless clear that readers' body actions can greatly enhance their presentation.[38] As with other aspects of interpretation, gestures need not be standardized for any particular selection in order to relate the text appropriately. Paul Campbell writes, "On a huge stage in a 5,000 seat auditorium, a performer may need to raise both hands skyward to get the same effect that a simple upward glance would achieve in a ten by twenty foot room."[39]

35. Ibid., 23.
36. Ibid., 66.
37. Bertram Joseph, "The Dramatic and Rhetorical Speaker's 'Person' and 'Action' in the English Renaissance," revised by Wallace Bacon, in *Performance of Literature in Historical Perspective*, ed. David W. Thompson (Lanham, MD: University Press of America, 1983), 462.
38. Gerald Kennedy, *His Word through Preaching* (New York: Harper and Row, 1947), 73.
39. Paul N. Campbell, *Oral Interpretation* (New York: Macmillan, 1966), 120.

Campbell's comments are a reminder that readers serve an audience that is not only a spectator of the presentation but a co-creator. The nature, size, emotions, needs, and character of the audience are all directly involved in how the selection will, and should, be related.[40] Readers must not change the meaning of the text because of the features of their audience, but they are obligated to assess the composition of their audience in order to relate the meaning of the text. Gestures that would powerfully express the meaning of a text on stage could obscure the meaning of the text in histrionics in a Sunday school classroom.[41] Readers who will not permit their audience a voice in their own expression of the text will deny themselves one of their most powerful creative tools, while cutting the audience off from effective communion with the Word.

Reading as Interpretation

To the extent that interpreters make their readings vulnerable to the needs of their listeners, they reveal some of themselves in the presentation of every selection. By their emphases, gestures, and even choice of selection readers inherently reveal their own communion with both the text and the audience. Therefore it is especially vital that readers of Scripture make sure there is quality in both species of this personal eucharist that they will be offering to others in the form of their own character. Brack rightly advises, "For the religious leader, oral interpretation should be another way in which he expresses Christian love for his hearers."[42]

If love is going to be expressed, it cannot be strained, affected, or artificial without eventually becoming either transparently false or obliquely ineffectual. Aristotle taught that the speaker's *ethos*, or character, was the most powerful agent of persuasive oratory.[43] Thomas Wright, the evangelical scholar of Victorian England, said that the action of the speaker's voice and body is the spring flowing from a fountain composed of *vox* (voice), *vultus* (countenance), and *vita* (life).[44] Life, and the quality of that life, will inevitably be reflected and unveiled in the self-revelation of oral performance. Therefore, it is vital that the living testimony of readers be consistent with the Scriptures they present. In today's parlance: "Don't talk

40. Ruth Finnegan, *Oral Poetry* (Cambridge: Cambridge University Press, 1977), 214; Harold Scheub, "Performance of Oral Narrative," in *Frontiers of Folklore*, ed. William R. Bascom, AAAS Selected Symposium 5 (Boulder, CO: Westview, 1977), 54.
41. Geoffrey Crump, *Speaking Poetry*, rev. ed. (London: Dennis Dobson, 1964), 4.
42. Brack, *Effective Oral Interpretation*, 22.
43. Aristotle, *Rhetoric* 1.2.
44. Joseph, "Dramatic and Rhetorical Speaker's 'Person' and 'Action,'" 462.

the talk if you don't walk the walk." This is true of all Christian witness, including that inherent in the reading of Scripture, for "can a blind man lead a blind man? Will they not both fall into a pit?" (Luke 6:39).

Reading as Divine Service

In the conformity of their own lives to Scripture, oral readers simultaneously become competent servants of both the text and the audience. They are faithful servants of the Word not only because they obey its principles but also because in their obedience they experience the graces that enable them to read with the power of sympathy, sincerity, and integrity. But even as they master their service to the text, oral readers serve their audience. Their integrity makes their reading palatable to the hearers who need to feed on the Word but will not take their bread from a tainted hand. Further, their inner experiences with the Word enable them to serve the hearers better by seasoning their nourishment with the fruit of their own spiritual encounter. Thus, while oral readers set the stage for the communion between God's Word and his people with the tools of understanding and the techniques of delivery, ultimately the stage requires the commitment of the readers' own hands and hearts if the drama is to achieve its full potential. S. S. Curry concludes,

> The reading of the Scriptures must never be perfunctory or merely formal. It should not be a mere authoritative presentation of facts or proclamation of words. . . . The reader must live his ideas at the time of utterance. . . . He can manifest to others the impressions made on his own being. . . . [For] when one soul is made to feel that another soul is hearing a message from the King of kings, he too bows his head and hears the voice of the Infinite speaking in his own breast.[45]

45. S. S. Curry, *Vocal and Literary Interpretation of the Bible* (New York: Macmillan, 1903), 132.

20

CHRIST-CENTERED SERMONS

E xpository preaching has a simple goal: to say what God says. Expository preachers presume that true spiritual health can only be effected by the Spirit of God. That Spirit inspired the Word of God as his only infallible witness to the minds and hearts of his people (2 Tim. 3:16–17). As the Spirit works by and with the Word in our hearts, God teaches us all that is needed for our spiritual lives. Thus, the chief goal of preachers should be to say what the Holy Spirit has said in the Bible. The most dependable way to do this is to explain the meaning of biblical texts and show how they apply to the lives of believers. Such explanation drives the preacher to serious study of God's Word for careful articulation both of its original meaning and present significance. Making sure God's people know what God has said and why he has said it is the tandem goal of expository preaching.

Preaching with God's Goals

But we need to be clear that the preacher's concern should not only be instructive. God is active in his Word, convicting the heart, renewing the

---

This chapter is used with permission and adapted from the author's "The Necessity of Preaching Grace for Progress in Sanctification," in *All for Jesus: A Celebration of the 50th Anniversary of Covenant Theological Seminary*, ed. Robert A. Peterson and Sean Michael Lewis (Ross-shire, Scotland: Christian Focus, 2006).

mind, and strengthening the will. This means that preaching is not simply an instructive lecture; it is a redemptive event. If we only think of the Sermon as a means of transferring information, then we will prioritize making the message dense with historical facts, moral instruction, and memory retention devices that prepare people for later tests of formal doctrine or factual knowledge. Such tests are rare. And most persons' ability to remember a Sermon's content in following days can devastate the ego of a preacher whose primary goal is the congregation's doctrinal or biblical literacy.

The needed reordering of priorities will not come by emptying the Sermon of biblical content, but by preparing it for spiritual warfare and welfare. Our primary goal is not preparing people for later tests of mind or behavior, but rather humbling and strengthening the wills of God's people within the context of the Sermon. Because God is active in his Word, we should preach with the conviction that the Spirit of God will use the truths of his Word *as we preach* to change hearts now! As hearts change, lives change—even when Sermon specifics are forgotten (Prov. 4:23).

Preachers must do careful study of God's Word (2 Tim. 2:15), but should marshal facts, doctrine, and application along with the dynamics of pastoral ethos and pathos to address the will of listeners (1 Thess. 2:8). The efficacy of our preaching should not primarily be judged by what persons remember, but by how they live in the wake of our messages. Of course, they will live biblically only if we have informed them accurately of the Bible's content. If our Sermons are not credible, accurate, or organized, then we undermine the truths that transform hearts. Still, the primary goal of the Sermon is not to inform the mind, but rather to confront the mind and heart with biblical truths in order to conform the will to Christ's purposes.

The preacher's obligation to transform as well as inform should compel us to ensure that our Sermons are an instrument of God's grace as well as a conduit for his truth. My concern for excavating grace principles from all Scripture has an intensely personal origin. The inadequacies of my preaching were torturing me, and I wondered whether I should leave the ministry. I could not figure out what was wrong. Church members complimented my preaching, but their own lives were consistently plagued by depression, addictions, and anger with each other. I had to question, "If I am such a good preacher, then why are the people I serve doing so badly?" Ultimately, I determined that a central reason for their despair, their escapist compulsions and their judgmental impatience with one another, was a pattern of thought that I was unintentionally encouraging.

Preaching God's Whole Counsel

The pattern of thought that I reinforced was not immediately apparent to me because I believed that my preaching was faithful to the commands of God's inerrant Word. The same Bible that attests to my Savior's virgin birth, sinless life, substitutionary atonement, physical resurrection, Great Commission, and sovereign rule also calls God's people to holiness. I knew that I could not embrace all that is dear to me in God's Word without also embracing its commands. So, I preached the whole counsel of God as I understood it.

Week after week, I told the imperfect people in my church to "do better." But this drumbeat for improvement, devoid of the encouragements and empowerments of grace, actually undermined the holiness that I was seeking to exhort. When God's people hear only the imperatives of the Word, they are forced to conclude that their righteousness is a product of their efforts. There are only two possible reactions to such preaching: Some will reason, "I will never meet God's requirements," leading them to despair. Others will assert, "I have measured up to what God requires—at least, compared with other people," leading to spiritual pride that manifests itself in the body of Christ as arrogance and sometimes intolerance.

Preaching the Redemptive Context

I recognized that these reactions were symptoms of spiritual maladies. What I needed to learn was that the cure was not preaching less of Scripture, but more. In particular, I needed to learn to preach each text in its redemptive context. Paul writes in Romans, "For everything that was written in the past was written to teach us, so that through endurance and the encouragement of the Scriptures we might have hope" (Rom. 15:4). Scanning the scope of the law and the prophets, the apostle is able to say that all was intended to give us hope. All Scripture has a redemptive purpose. No Scripture is so limited in purpose as to give us only moral instruction or lifestyle correction. Paul says that even the law itself functions as our "schoolmaster to lead us to Christ" (Gal. 3:24 KJV). Jesus also said that all "the law and the prophets" testified of him (cf. Luke 24:27; John 5:39).

Yet, we will call into question the accuracy of Paul and Jesus on this point if we think of messianic revelation only in terms of explicit mention of the person of Christ. Vast portions of both the Old and New Testaments make no explicit mention of Christ. Even the prophetic books that predict the coming Messiah contain much material that does not have Jesus as the direct subject. Christ surely knew this when, in Luke's account of the Savior's post-resurrection teaching, we read that "beginning with Moses and all the Prophets, he explained to them what was said in all the Scriptures concerning himself" (Luke 24:27). How can Jesus offer such exposition, and by corollary require such exposition from us, if the text does not make direct reference to him?[1]

In his discussions of the law, Paul helps us understand the varying dimensions of the Bible's redemptive hope. Though Paul never denies the efficacy of obedience, he explains that, through the law, he died to the law. The righteous requirements of the holiness of God that were always beyond his grasp signaled the death of hope in human achievement for spiritual life. The moral instruction of a holy God revealed that no one was capable of holiness by his own efforts. Our best works are judged but filthy rags in the Old Testament (Isa. 64:6), and the Savior echoes, "So you also, when you have done everything you were told to do, should say, 'We are unworthy servants; we have only done our duty'" (Luke 17:10).

The same law that reveals the requirements of God's holiness also reveals the inescapable reality of our unholiness. Because of the great disproportion between our best works and God's righteousness, we are always and forever incapable of the righteousness that would reconcile us to a holy God. This hardly seems a redemptive message. It would not be, were it not for the alternative it demands.

By revealing the holy nature of the God who provides redemption and the finite nature of humanity that requires redemption, the law points to the necessity of a Redeemer and prepares the human heart to seek him. The law, however, is only one aspect of Scripture that may help flesh out the person and work of Christ without making explicit mention of him.

Christ-centered exposition of Scripture does not require us to unveil depictions of Jesus by mysterious alchemies of allegory or typology; rather, it identifies how every text functions in furthering our understanding of who Christ is, what the Father sent him to do, and why. The goal is not to make a specific reference to Jesus magically appear from every camel track of Hebrew narrative or every metaphor of Hebrew poetry (leading to allegorical errors), but rather to show where every text stands in relation to the person and work of Christ, whose grace alone achieves our salvation.

Such an interpretive approach will always take the preacher to the heart of covenantal and Reformed theology by requiring discernment of the progressive and ever-present revelation of God's sovereign grace through Scripture. Discerning the gracious character of God in his revelation also rescues Reformed theology from its tendencies to narrow faith to abstract

---

1. See the author's *Christ-Centered Preaching: Redeeming the Expository Sermon*, 2nd ed. (Grand Rapids: Baker Academic, 2005), 275–76.

principles and points of debate. By consistently preaching of the God who traverses the universe he created in order to redeem his creatures by his blood, we become relationally bound to the reality of a living and loving Lord.[2] Our listeners become so bound as well—truly linked to God in heart rather than being proud of thoughts or practices that they feel distinguish them from others who are less informed or less good.

Discerning the Redemptive Context

A primary approach to discerning the redemptive nature of a biblical text is identifying how the passage predicts, prepares for, reflects, or results from the person and work of Christ.[3] This approach includes what is known as the redemptive/historical method, which seeks to identify how the passage furthers the progress or understanding of what Christ has done or will do in redemptive history. Prophecies obviously *predict* Christ and explain much of what he will do. The temple sacrifices predict what Christ will do, but also typologically *prepare* the people of God to understand the nature of the atoning work of the Savior. The relationship of Hosea and Gomer not only prepares the covenant people to understand how God will love Israel despite her sin, but also *reflects* the need for and nature of God's pardoning mercy in all ages. Our ability to seek that pardoning mercy at the throne of grace is a *result* of our great High Priest going before us to prepare the way and to make petitions on our behalf.

Dead Ends and Bridges

The preceding four categories of redemptive/historical explanation (predicting, preparing, reflecting, and resulting) are not, and should not be, rigidly segregated. Instead, preachers bear the greatest expository fruit when they understand that what they are seeking to expose to the view of God's people are the gospel truths that presage and apply God's work of redemption in Christ. Entire epochs and genres of Scripture serve special purposes in revealing the dimensions of grace that will ultimately be accomplished and applied in Christ.[4] For example, the period of the judges not only reveals the power of divine aid; it also demonstrates the folly of

2. Sidney Greidanus, *Preaching Christ from the Old Testament* (Grand Rapids: Eerdmans, 1999), 54.

3. Chapell, *Christ-Centered Preaching*, 282–88.

4. Sidney Greidanus, *The Modern Preacher and the Ancient Text: Interpreting and Preaching Biblical Literature* (Grand Rapids: Eerdmans, 1988), 166.

seeking to do what each person finds acceptable in his own eyes to maintain a covenant people. The kingship of Israel similarly demonstrates the folly of depending on human leaders to establish a righteous rule for the covenant people. The Old Testament takes us down many such redemptive *dead ends* for the purpose of turning us from human to divine dependence.[5]

By way of contrast, some aspects of Scripture function as redemptive *bridges* that allow the covenant people to progress in their understanding of redeeming grace. The Lord's calling and preservation of the diminutive nation of Israel serves as a perpetual statement that God's mercy is not extended only to the strong, capable, and deserving (Deut. 7:7). The provision of the manna in the wilderness, as well as of the prophets of the Word, helps all subsequent generations remain confident in God's provision of living bread—his Word (John 6:35; 1 Cor. 10:3, 16). Again, these categories should not be rigidly maintained. The temple sacrifices are at one level a dead end, in that they demonstrate that the blood of bulls and goats could never fully atone for sin. Yet at another level the sacrificial system is also a bridge to the understanding of what God would do for the nations through the Lamb of God.

Other classifications also function well in relating the many varieties of Scripture passages to the person and work of Christ.[6] The goal is not to determine a master metaphor that will provide a proper niche for all passages. Such pigeonholing of texts typically limits the implications of the Bible's own rich variety of metaphors that are used to relate redemptive truth (e.g., kingdom, family, Sabbath, tree). What we should not lose sight of among the infinite possibilities for redemptive interpretation is the necessity of exposing the truths of grace that all Scripture is designed to help us see.[7]

Macro- and Micro-Interpretations

We should always observe the text through spectacles whose lenses are these questions: (1) How is the Holy Spirit here revealing the nature of God that provides redemption? and (2) How is the Holy Spirit here revealing

---

5. Chapell, *Christ-Centered Preaching*, 305–6.

6. Edmund Clowney, *The Unfolding Mystery: Discovering Christ in the Old Testament* (Phillipsburg, NJ: Presbyterian and Reformed, 1988), 9–16.

7. Jonathan Edwards proposes such an approach in his "Letter to the Trustees of the College of New Jersey," saying, "The whole of it [Christian theology], in each part, stands in reference to the great work of redemption by Jesus Christ" as the "*summum* and *ultimum* of all divine operations and decrees." See Clarence H. Faust and Thomas H. Johnson, eds., *Jonathan Edwards* (New York: American Book, 1935), 411–12.

the nature of humanity that requires redemption? As long as we use these lenses to observe the text, we will interpret as Christ did when he showed his disciples how all Scripture spoke of him.

Asking these two questions (i.e., using these two lenses) maintains faithful exposition and demonstrates that redemptive interpretation does not require the preacher to run from Genesis to Revelation in every Sermon in order to expound a text's redemptive truths. While there is nothing wrong with such macro-interpretations, it is also possible—and often more fruitful—to identify the doctrinal statements or relational interactions in the immediate text that reveal some dimension of God's grace. The relational interactions in such micro-interpretations can include how God acts toward his people (e.g., providing strength for weakness, pardon for sin, provision in want, faithfulness in response to unfaithfulness) or how an individual representing God provides for others (e.g., David's care for Mephibosheth, Solomon's wisdom recorded for others less wise).[8]

Focusing on Our Fallen Condition and the Divine Solution

In essence, redemptive exposition requires that we identify an aspect of our fallen condition that is addressed by the Holy Spirit in each passage that he inspired for our edification, and then show God's way out of the human dilemma.[9] Such a pattern not only exposes the human predicament that requires God's relief but also forces the preacher to focus on a divine solution. Our salvation rests in his provision. God's glory is always the apex purpose of the Sermon. The vaunting of human ability and puffing of human pride vanish in such preaching, not because imperatives of the law of God are minimized, but because God is always the hero of the text.[10] He enables our righteousness, pardons our unrighteousness, and provides for our weakness.

Preaching the Grace of Holiness

This consistent preaching of the dimensions of God's grace does not render superfluous the commands of the law, but rather honors their authority by providing the biblical motivation and enablement necessary for our obedience. The fear that the regular preaching of grace will lead to antinomianism is sometimes justified. The human heart is more than capable

8. Chapell, *Christ-Centered Preaching*, 306–8.
9. Ibid., 48–52 and 299–305.
10. Ibid., 289–95.

of abusing grace to excuse sin. Those who are reacting to legalistic backgrounds often overcompensate for their gospel-weak past by launching into law-deaf pastimes. Still, despite this danger, there is no legitimate alternative to preaching the grace that underlies all biblical testimony. Such preaching does not define grace as the world does—a license to do as I please—but rather as the Bible teaches: a mercy so overwhelming that it compels me to do what pleases God.[11]

Grace-based preaching does not eliminate the moral obligations of the law. The Bible's standards reflect the character of God and are provided for our good and his glory. The preaching of grace should not negate the law but provide an antidote for pride in its performance and an incentive for conscientiousness in its observance.[12]

Motivating Holiness by Grace

The motivating power of grace is evident in Christ's words, "If you love me, you will obey what I command" (John 14:15). Because the redemptive interpretation of Scripture leads to Sermons marked by consistent adulation of the mercy of God in Christ, hearts in which the Spirit dwells are being continually stoked with more cause to love God.[13] This love becomes the primary motivation for Christian obedience as hearts in which the Spirit dwells respond with love for their Savior.[14] For the believer, there is no greater spiritual motivation than grace-stimulated love—not fear, or guilt, or gain (though each of these can have secondary roles in God's motivation hierarchy if they are not separated from love).[15] And as our love results in discipleship that demonstrates the beauty and blessing of walking with God, greater love for him grows and stimulates even more desire for obedience. Because we love him, we love what and whom he loves. Thus, we delight to walk in his ways and serve his people, giving ourselves to the testimony of his grace and the purposes of his kingdom.

11. J. I. Packer, *Rediscovering Holiness* (Ann Arbor: Servant Press, 1992), 75.

12. Westminster Shorter Catechism, question 1; Westminster Larger Catechism, questions 32, 97, 168, 174, and 178; Heidelberg Catechism, questions 1, 2, 32, and 86; Westminster Confession of Faith 16.2; 19.6, 7; 20.1; 22.6.

13. See Chapell, *Holiness by Grace* (Wheaton, IL: Crossway, 2001), 154; and *Christ-Centered Preaching*, 321.

14. Thomas Chalmers, "The Expulsive Power of a New Affection" in *History and Repository of Pulpit Eloquence*, ed. Henry C. Fish, vol. 2 (New York: Dodd, Mead and Co., 1856), 326. See also Walter Marshall, *The Gospel Mystery of Sanctification* (1692; repr., Grand Rapids: Reformation Heritage, 1999).

15. Chapell, *Holiness by Grace*, 29–31; and *Christ-Centered Preaching*, 320–23.

The Bible recognizes no definition of grace that excuses sin or encourages moral license. The burning love for God fueled by the consistent preaching of grace makes those in whom the Spirit dwells want to follow the commands that please him. This is why the apostle Paul could say that the grace of God teaches us to say no to ungodliness and worldly passions (see Titus 2:12). When grace is properly perceived, the law is not trashed; it is treasured. Because we love God, we want to honor the standards that honor him and pursue kingdom priorities that further his purposes in the world.

In grace-based preaching, the rules do not change; the reasons do.[16] We serve God *because* we love him, not *in order* to make him love us. After all, how could production of more filthy rags make God love us? He releases us from the performance treadmill that (falsely) promises to provide holiness through human effort, but the effect on the heart is love that is more constrained to please him. God's overwhelming and unconditional mercy ensures that there is now no condemnation for those who are in Christ Jesus (Rom. 8:1). But, rather than promoting license, this kindness leads to repentance (Rom. 2:4). We *want* to turn from the sin that grieves the One we love (Eph. 4:30).

Motivating Holiness by the Cross

The primary message that stimulates such love is the cross. Contemporary theologians sometimes wince at such statements because they seem to slight the resurrection, second coming, and other key redemptive events. It is certainly true that, without the resurrection, the cross would have signaled nothing but a gory death on a distant hill. Both the victory over sin accomplished by the resurrection and the vindication of righteousness promised in the consummation are vital truths for perseverance in Christian faithfulness. Still, when Paul wrote to the Corinthians that he resolved to preach nothing among them but Christ crucified, he reflected a profound understanding of humanity (1 Cor. 2:2). The Father's gift of his Son stirs the heart at its deepest level to make it tender toward God, receptive of his Word, and zealous for his will.

The old preaching imperative, "make much of the blood," reflects great wisdom about human motivation. The cross stimulates love for God, the resurrection zeal for his purposes, and the second coming perseverance in his cause. All are necessary, but God's mercy toward the undeserving—as it unfolds through Scripture and culminates in the cross—is still the mes-

16. Chapell, *Christ-Centered Preaching*, 312.

sage that programs the heart to receive and employ all the other truths of the gospel.

The primary reason we must preach the grace of God from all the Scriptures is not so that we will master an interpretive skill, or even produce correct exegesis. Biblical theology practiced merely as a science of interpretation encourages theological debate and spiritual pride as we strive to find and promote the master metaphor that will unite all Scripture (e.g., kingdom, covenant, creation-fall-redemption-consumation, family). These are helpful lenses through which to see the structure of Scripture, but the true goal of redemptive preaching is to expound the ways in which God progressively and consistently shows dimensions of his mercy in all ages so that we will understand Christ's sacrifice more fully and, consequently, love him more.[17] Any practice of biblical theology that does not include this relational aim[18] is misdirected.

We should study the Scriptures so that we may glorify God and enjoy him (Westminster Shorter Catechism, question 1). Without a profound love for him, we can do neither. Love for him leads us to seek him, serve him, repent to him, and live for him. All the requirements of love for God find their impulse at the cross. From there radiate many implications and imperatives, but still the cross is the center for the heart seeking God.

Enabling Holiness by Union with Christ

Christ's victory on the cross provides freedom from both the guilt and power of sin. The apostle Paul reminds us that, because Jesus resides in us, we possess the resurrection power that raised Jesus from the dead (Gal. 2:20; Eph. 1:18–23). John adds, "Greater is he that is in you than he that is in the world" (1 John 4:4 KJV). This is more than a promise that Jesus will add to our strength or aid our resolve. Because we are in union with Christ, his righteous status becomes ours, and his Spirit's power now enables us to resist the sin that he reveals to us.[19] In the terms of classic theology, once we were not able not to sin (*non posse non peccare*), but now we are able not to sin (*posse non peccare*).[20] Enough of the influence of our sin nature

---

17. Geerhardus Vos, "The Idea of Biblical Theology," a pamphlet form of Vos's inaugural address upon assuming the new chair of biblical theology at Princeton Seminary (Covenant Theological Seminary Library, n.d.; 1895 probable), 16. This address in elaborated form became the introduction of Vos's *Biblical Theology* (1948; repr., Grand Rapids: Eerdmans, 1975).

18. Graeme Goldsworthy, *Preaching the Whole Bible as Christian Scripture* (Grand Rapids /Cambridge, UK: Eerdmans, 2000), 92–96.

19. Chapell, *Holiness by Grace*, 52–63 and 140–43.

20. John Murray, *Principles of Conduct* (Grand Rapids: Eerdmans, 1957), 216–21.

persists that we will not perfectly perform his will until we are with Jesus in eternal glory (*non posse peccare*), but even now we are freed from Satan's lie that we cannot change. Sin has no more dominion over us (Rom. 6:14–18). We can make progress against the besetting sins of our lives because we are alive in Christ—whose resurrection power indwells us.

The release of sin's guilt *and* the reception of Christ's benefits are the more complete gospel of grace. Sometimes preachers preach only a partial gospel, indicating that the debt of our sin has been paid by the suffering of Christ (i.e., his passive righteousness). This is a glorious and precious truth for all Christians who know their need of forgiveness. Yet, even if our debt has been paid, it is still possible to live with a sense of inadequacy and humiliation because of our sin. It is as though we recognize that our debt has been paid, but, though we are grateful, our spiritual math still indicates that we have only a zero-sum balance: Christ's death on our behalf makes us feel guilty and small rather than free of debt.

To counter such feelings, we need the full benefits of the gospel. We have not only been freed of our debt; we have also been supplied with Christ's righteousness (resulting from his active and passive righteousness). Before God, we are already accounted as heirs of heaven, co-heirs with Christ, and children of God (Rom. 8:16–17). This adoption signals our worth and preciousness to God prior to our entry into heaven. So sure is our status and so rich is our righteousness that our Heavenly Father already considers us holy and pleasing to him (Rom. 12:1) and has already seated us in heavenly places (Eph. 2:6). Because we are in union with Christ, his status is ours (Gal. 2:20; 1 Cor. 1:30; 2 Cor. 5:21). Though we are striving with the power of Christ's Spirit to overcome sinful thoughts and actions in our lives, God has already reckoned us holy by his grace, which is embraced through our faith. Our positional sanctification gives us the foundation for our progressive sanctification.[21] In an intentional turn of words, it is because our feet are firmly planted in heaven that we have the foundation to resist the assaults of Satan on earth.

Preaching the Indicatives of the Gospel

Future grace awaits us in glory, but we already possess its status through the certainty of the promises of God and the guarantee of the Spirit in us (2 Cor. 5:5). The mark of that Spirit is not the absence of sin in our lives,

---

21. See the author's *In the Grip of Grace* (Grand Rapids: Baker Books, 1992), 54–58; and Jerry Bridges, *The Discipline of Grace: God's Role and Our Role in the Pursuit of Holiness* (Colorado Springs: NavPress, 1994), 108.

but the presence of new desires and new power to overcome temptation (Rom. 8:5–15). When we weep over our sin, we may question whether the power of the Spirit is real in us. But, in a wonderful confirmation of our status as new creatures in Christ, the grief we feel for sin is the assurance of our salvation.[22] Before the Spirit filled us, our hearts were—and only could be—hostile to God. But now when we sin, we hate it. The hatred of sin and godly sorrow for its expression are the evidence of the Spirit in us and heaven before us. Were not the Spirit in us there could be no sorrow for sin (other than the sorrow of consequences). But when we truly grieve that our sin has grieved the Spirit, trampled on the blood of our Savior, and offended our Heavenly Father, then we evidence a heart renewed by the Spirit and secured for eternity.

Hatred of sin, freedom from past guilt, possession of Christ's righteousness and power, and assurance of future grace combine to equip Christians for the holy race God calls us to run. However, it is important to remember that all of these truths rest on the person and work of Jesus Christ. There will be no progress in the Christian life without the past, present, and future grace of our Lord. Jesus said, "Apart from me you can do nothing" (John 15:5). No sentence in Scripture more underscores the need for Christ-centered preaching. The grace of God that is ultimately revealed in Christ frees us from our guilt and enables us to obey. Preaching that seeks to issue imperatives (what to do) from a biblical text without identifying the indicatives of the gospel (who we are by grace alone) to which the text points robs listeners of their only source of power to do what God requires.[23]

Most preachers approach the text with only one question in mind: What does this text instruct me to tell my people to do? But if we only tell people what to do without leading them to understand their dependence on the Savior to obey, then they will either be led to despair (I cannot do this) or false pride (If I work hard enough, I can do this). No one can serve God apart from Christ. A message full of imperatives (e.g., Be like . . . a commendable Bible character; Be good . . . by adopting these moral behaviors; Be disciplined . . . by diligence in these practices) but devoid of grace is antithetical to the gospel. These "be messages" are not wrong *in* themselves, but *by* themselves they are spiritually deadly because they imply that our path to God is made by our works.[24]

22. Chapell, *In the Grip of Grace*, 32–37.
23. H. Ridderbos, *Paul: An Outline of His Theology* (Grand Rapids: Eerdmans, 1975), 253.
24. Chapell, *Christ-Centered Preaching*, 289–95.

When we preach a biblical imperative in isolation from grace, we take what should be a blessing and make it as deadly for the soul as an untreated cashew nut is for the body. Africans love the sweetness and nourishment of the cashew nut, but they know that the nut in its natural form can be deadly. Unless heat is added, cyanide contained in the nut will poison those who ingest it. Similarly, the imperatives of the law are good and nourishing for the Christian life—unless the warmth of the gospel is lacking. When no explanations of grace accompany the preaching of the law, it also becomes spiritually deadly, creating despair for those who honestly realize that they cannot fully meet the law's requirements or stimulating pride in those who wrongly imagine that they can.[25]

Without a foundation of grace, striving for holiness only sinks the soul in a quagmire of human inadequacy. We must remember that even our best works deserve God's reproof unless they are sanctified by Christ (Westminster Confession of Faith 16.5). God delights in our good works only when they are presented in Christ (Westminster Confession of Faith 16.6). This means that, even if we do not mention Jesus by name in the explanation of a text, we must show where the text stands in relation to his grace in order to provide hope that the obligations of the text will be fulfilled.[26] Just as the necessity of a Christ-focus in all preaching is indicated by Jesus' words, "Apart from me, you can do nothing," so also the power of such a focus is indicated in Paul's words, "I can do all things through Christ who strengthens me" (Phil. 4:13 NKJV).

Preaching the Walk of Faith

How does this strengthening actually occur? All pastors recognize that people are constantly asking how they can access the power that God promises through Christ. This is a difficult question for preachers—and perhaps the difficulty explains why the question is so often ignored or simply relegated to the category of those things that are the fruit of more human endeavor. Though most sermons focus on telling people what to do, the imperatives are rarely new or unknown. What remains hidden for most people is knowing how to do what they know they should do but fail repeatedly to do. Until the preacher answers the "how" question, people remain in a spiritual quandary, regardless of the correctness of the

25. John Calvin, *Institutes of the Christian Religion*, ed. John T. McNeill, trans. Ford Lewis Battles. Library of Christian Classics (Philadelphia: Westminster, 1960), 2.7.1–3, 9.

26. Chapell, *Christ-Centered Preaching*, 303.

imperatives preached.[27] For example, preachers may assure people that if they pray harder, longer, and with greater faith, then they will gain the power of God. This instruction is indeed true, but it ignores the paradox that the power we seek *in* our prayer is required *for* our prayer. We cannot pray (or obey any other command of God) adequately apart from the enabling power of God.

Believing the Shepherd of Grace

The power that enables true obedience is from God, and we access it through a walk of faith. We walk with God by leaning on his strength, resting in the goodness of his providence, and believing his Word. This trust relationship is ultimately the source of our strength.[28] We act with the strength that comes from the simple faith that the Good Shepherd will be true to his Word and will accomplish what is right for us as we obey him.

The power of this faith does not reside in the strength or degree of our spiritual expression, but rather resides in the power and goodness of the One in whom we trust.[29] As an elevator is effective not on the basis of the strength of the person who walks in, but on the basis of the strength of the cable and motors that power it, so also our blessing depends not so much on any strength in us as on relying on the power of God. Obedience is a result of faith in the grace of God and is not a means to produce his grace. Blessings flow from obedience—but even these are the product of the grace in which we trust.

The power that results from this grace comes initially from the belief that what God's Word says is true. The Bible says that those who place their faith in Christ are new creatures who have the power to resist sin (2 Cor. 5:17). If we do not believe this, then we have no power to combat the sin. We cannot obey if we do not believe we can. Yet if we believe that God has already provided the assurance and resources for victory—no matter how great the opposition—then we will act and we will overcome. If we do not believe that God has forgiven our past, then there will be no reason to risk failure or deny our lusts now or in the future. Yet if we believe that our past is forgiven, our present is blessed, and our future is secure, we will repent of sin and return to our walk with him.[30]

27. Ibid., 323–27.
28. Chapell, *Holiness by Grace*, 52–62, 85–88, and 107.
29. Ibid., 193–203.
30. Ibid., 141–43.

Engaging the Disciplines of Grace

The reason that we engage in the Christian disciplines of prayer, Bible reading, worship, and fellowship is not to bribe God to act in accord with his nature, but to feed our faith in his unchanging nature so that we will consistently act in accord with his Word. Too many Christians practice the disciplines of the Christian life with the intention of turning God's face toward them and inclining his heart to favor them. They forget that God has loved them with an eternal and infinite love. He turned his face from our sin when he placed that sin on his dying Son, but now he never looks away from us and his heart never ebbs in affection for us. Every act of providence is for our eternal good and flows from his infinite love. Communing with God in prayer, understanding his ways through his Word, and embracing his glory and goodness through Christian fellowship and worship are means by which enabling grace fills our lives. These disciplines of grace are nourishments of the faith that we need in order to act in accord with God's purposes. They do not force or leverage God's hand but enable us to see it, grasp it, and receive the blessings it provides. The Christian disciplines do not earn blessings but guide us into the paths where God's grace has planted his blessings.

If God's blessings depended on the adequacy of our performance of his requirements, then we would know no blessings and would eventually turn from him. We practice the disciplines of the Christian life not with the expectation that they would ever be sufficient in quality or duration to merit God's favor, but with the expectation that they will help us better to know, love, and trust him.[31] The disciplines defeat this purpose if they are preached as payment to a god with an insatiable appetite for human sweat and tears.

The Christian disciplines can be compared to the nourishment that parents encourage their children to eat. If parents promise their love only on the condition that children will eat, then the children may very well clean their plates, but they will grow up hating the food that nourishes them—and, ultimately, hating the parents who made their love subject to a child's abilities. By contrast, the parents who promise unconditional love may still struggle with the eating habits of their children, but as the children mature they will naturally love that which nourishes them and the hands that provide it. In a similar way, preaching of the Christian dis-

31. John Murray, *The Collected Writings of John Murray*, vol. 4, ed. Iain H. Murray (Carlisle, PA: Banner of Truth Trust, 1982), 233; Thomas Manton, *A Treatise of the Life of Faith* (Ross-shire, Scotland: Christian Focus, 1997), 65; C. S. Lewis, *Mere Christianity*, rev. ed. (New York: Macmillan, 1952), 59–61; and Bridges, *Discipline of Grace*, 13–19 and 78–79.

ciplines helps God's people mature and cherish these aids to faith when they perceive that such practices nourish their growth in grace rather than purchase it.[32]

Confidence in the mercy of the Father purchased solely by the blood of his Son, belief in our new nature and secure future provided entirely by our union with Christ, and trust in God's paths and providence consistently nurtured by the disciplines of grace—all these combine to constitute the walk of faith that the Spirit uses to stimulate repentance and empower faithfulness. The first lesson of this walk of faith for preachers is that, while we must convict of sin, we are not finished preaching until we have also convinced of grace. Full application of the Word requires us to expound grace that not only teaches God's people *what* and *whom* to follow, but *why* to follow (out of love for him) and *how* (in dependence on him). The second lesson is equally vital: without love there is no faith to empower obedience. Faith is the confidence that God is present, sovereign, and good (Heb. 11:1, 6). We will put no faith in one we do not love. The faith that empowers the Christian life requires love for God.

The Key to Enabling Power

Christian preaching must consistently proclaim the grace of God, because in helping God's people to love him we enable them to serve him. The *why* is the *how*; motive and enablement unite in holiness.[33] Great love for God is great power for obedience. This is not only because love is necessary for true faith, but also because love is power. We will only do, and can only do, what we love most to do. We cannot long and well do a job that we hate doing. Though we may persist for a while, ultimately our loss of enthusiasm will lead to a loss of quality in our work. Even if our work remains good, it will not be as good as it could have been had we served with our whole hearts. Even if we do well a task that we find distasteful, it is only because we have a compelling love for the fruit of our labors or an ideal that is fulfilled by our work.[34]

We ultimately do only that which produces or honors what we most love. Persons who sin but claim that they still love God may not think that they are lying, but in the moment that they sinned, the individuals loved the sin more than they loved God. Such persons are no different than an adulterer who says to his wife, "The other woman meant nothing to me;

32. Chapell, *Holiness by Grace*, 56–57.
33. Chapell, *Christ-Centered Preaching*, 326.
34. Murray, *Principles of Conduct*, 226.

I still love you." The man may still love his wife, but in the moment of the sin, he loved the other person—or, at least, the passion—more than he loved his wife.

Preaching the Christ-focus of all Scripture is not simply an interpretive scheme or an exegetical device; it is regular exposure of the heart of God in order to ignite love for him in the hearts of believers. We preach grace to fan into flame zeal for the Savior. Our goal is not merely academic but also relational and spiritual. We consistently expound the gospel truths that pervade Scripture in order to fill the hearts of believers with love for God that drives out love for the world. The reason is simple: people are not tempted by what they have no desire to do. The only reason sin has any power in our lives is because we love it. If the sin had no attraction for us, it would have no power over us.

When love for Christ dominates our affections, sin loses its allure and, consequently, loses its power. Love for Christ is the power of obedience.[35] Preaching that floods the heart with affection for the Savior simultaneously loosens the hold of false idols on our hearts, chokes the appeal of sin, nourishes the desire for holiness, and stimulates zeal for kingdom purposes. When love for Christ is preeminent, doing his will is our greatest compulsion and joy. Thus, the joy of the Lord is our strength (Neh. 8:10), and helping to produce this joy is the great privilege of Christ-centered preaching.

Preaching remains a joy when pastors discern that their task is not to harangue or lay guilt on parishioners to bring them into servile duty, but rather to fill them up with love for God by extolling the wonders of his grace. Too many preachers leave ministry or become ineffective in it because they perceive their lot in life to be whipping recalcitrant parishioners into more diligent service. Of course, preaching must condemn sin and challenge the slothful, but without the context of love such ministry becomes a burden to all—including the minister. There is a better way to preach.

The better way always connects Scripture's commands with the motives and enablement of grace. Imperatives do not disappear from such preaching, because the commands of God are an expression of his nature and of his care for us. Still, the imperatives are always founded on the redemptive indicatives that give people confidence in God's faithfulness even in the face of their failures. We discourage people from basing their justification on their sanctification (i.e., determining whether they are right with God based on the quality or quantity of their religious performance), and

---

35. Chapell, *Holiness by Grace*, 107–9; and *Christ-Centered Preaching*, 326.

instead encourage them to live in the assurance of the completed work of Christ on their behalf.[36]

When our people perceive the present value of the blood of Christ, then they serve God with growing confidence of his blessing rather than with increasing dread of, or callousness to, his frown. Those who know that their forgiven status and family position are not jeopardized by the weaknesses of their present humanity live in loving service to Christ, rather than in self-justifying competition and judgment of each other.[37]

Preaching the Power of Joy

Consistent preaching of the gospel's assurances drives despair and pride from the Christian life. As a consequence, congregations find that spiritual fatigue, competitiveness, and insensitivity wane; in their place flow new joy in Christ, desire to make him Lord over the whole of life, understanding of the weak, care for the hurting, forgiveness for those who offend, and even love for the lost. In short, the Christian community becomes an instrument of grace because God's love becomes the substance of the church's soul. In such contexts, ministers thrive and their ministries become a blessing to all (including themselves and their families) rather than a burden. Without question, there will also be challenges and disappointments, but even these will not destroy the joy that God builds on a foundation of grace.

The necessity of grace for preaching that is true to the gospel leads to a basic question that all must answer in order to affirm that they are preaching the Christianity of the Bible: "Do I preach grace?" Would your sermons be perfectly acceptable in a synagogue or mosque because you are only encouraging better moral behavior that any major religion would find acceptable?[38] If this is so, the path to a better, more Christian message is not through preaching any less of Scripture, but rather through preaching more. Do not stop preaching until Christ has found his place in your sermon and his grace has found its way into the heart of your message. In this way, the people to whom you preach will walk with him, and his joy will be their strength to do his will.

---

36. Richard Lovelace, *Dynamics of Spiritual Life* (Downers Grove, IL: InterVarsity, 1979), 101.

37. Francis Schaeffer, *True Spirituality*, in *The Complete Works of Francis Schaeffer*, vol. 3 (Wheaton, IL: Crossway, 1982), 200; and *The God Who Is There* (Downers Grove, IL: InterVarsity, 1968), 134.

38. Jay Adams, *Preaching with Purpose: A Comprehensive Textbook on Biblical Preaching* (Grand Rapids: Baker Academic, 1982), 152.

21

BENEDICTIONS AND CHARGES

A Benediction (or Blessing) is the common close of a worship service. With these words the covenant people are reminded of the promises they have heard in worship so that they go into the world to do God's will with confidence in his promised care and enabling. As the final aspect of gospel-oriented worship, the Benediction is not merely a "closing" but rather is integral to the "sending" now appropriate for a forgiven, instructed, and blessed people. Consequently a Dismissal or Charge often accompanies the Benediction as those discipled for Christ's purposes in the worship service are dismissed with a Charge to do his will in the world. The Benediction is not simply a conclusion but is also a reminder to God's people that they start this new week with assurance of his Blessing. God will provide for them to accomplish all that he calls them to do. Christ's grace is not merely for the context of the church, but for all of life unfolding before his people until God's kingdom is on earth as it is in heaven.

In many churches the Benediction is voiced only by an ordained pastor with the understanding that the words (1) convey the official endorsement of the church on all that has proceeded and (2) carry Christ's own Blessing on his people for the work he now calls them to do. Since the one uttering such a Benediction speaks for both the church and for God, ensuring that the church has called and approved a person for such a pronouncement is certainly appropriate. At the same time, we should not presume that those called to such office in the church can never employ the gifts of others in communicating God's Blessing. Responsive readings, choral Benedictions, corporate hymns, and final prayers can also effectively "end and send."

We should also be careful not to suggest that some portions of Scripture are off limits for "regular people." If a layperson is asked to close worship, respect for the ordained office can still be shown by changing the second-person pronouns to first-person (e.g., "The Lord bless you and keep you . . ." can be said as, "May the Lord bless us and keep us . . .") or by making it clear that the Benediction is being taken from Scripture and is not being said with the authority of church office (e.g., "Hear what God's Word says in Hebrews 13:25 . . .").

Often ministers raise their hands toward the congregation during the Benediction as a gesture of blessing. Again, there are issues of church office and authority implicit even in such a gesture. In some traditions, three fingers are held together (or the thumb and first two fingers are held together) as a sign of the Trinity when hands are raised. In other traditions, the Bible is raised to indicate that the Blessing is based on the authority of God's Word. Some ministers walk toward the departure door and utter the final Blessing while touching the shoulders, hands, or heads of congregants along the aisle. Most pastors simply stand at the front of the church and raise open hands as a gesture of the wideness of God's mercy and the generosity of his heart. But probably none of these gestures is as important as the tonality of a voice tempered by the message that has preceded, the circumstances of the congregation, and the goodness of the gospel to communicate the compassion, tenderness, joy, and strength of God's care.

Receiving almost as much discussion in classic worship literature as the minister's gestures and expression is the proper deportment of congregants during the final Blessing. Some suggest a reverently bowed head, others want joyfully expectant and uplifted eyes, and still others want hands outstretched as a sign of receiving a blessing. The vigor and vehemence of these discussions underscore our almost infinite capacity to make a controversy out of our preferences or to make a superstition out of our habits. If we simply consider that a Benediction is God's blessing on his people, we will know that all of these postures can be (and should be) used by God's people depending on the nature of the service, circumstances, and heart. If we were to think of the Benediction as God's speaking to us, then sometimes we would bow in humble thanksgiving; other times we would look up and lean forward as toward the embrace of a loved one. Just as we may find it good at times to stretch our arms toward heaven in prayer, at other times to fall to our knees, and at other times to fall on our faces, so also Benedictions can be variously received and honored without any disrespect. It is better to inform God's people of the varieties of responses they have the privilege to express by his grace (and to lead them accordingly), rather than to require a posture Scripture does not.

A Benediction is not simply a Scripture verse with a nice sentiment or a summary of the Sermon's message. A verse praising God is certainly appropriate for the end of a service, but this, likewise, is not really a Benediction. A Benediction is a blessing. Verses that summarize the Sermon or praise God can often be turned into a Benediction by paraphrasing them or by adding words of blessing to them (see examples below). Since the Benediction is the promise of blessing for the tasks God calls his people to do, it is often followed by a Charge (e.g., "Go in his peace," or "Go now and serve God in this way with confidence that he goes with you to help you and to bless you"; see additional examples below). To such Charges and Benedictions the congregation or choir frequently responds with some kind of "Amen" spoken or sung (see suggestions below).

In common practice, a Benediction may simply be the perfunctory close to a worship service, but with skilled attention a Benediction can be a powerful instrument of pastoral care. With a Benediction, a pastor can communicate the care of the Heavenly Father with such tenderness and power that the worshipers leave the service full of confidence and joy for their work in the world. A Benediction can be one of the most memorable and meaningful elements of a worship service. Love pours from the eyes, strength from the hands, and grace from the voice of a pastor who understands the power of sending God's people out with the promise of divine pardon, presence, and peace.

Benediction Examples

Common Benedictions Pronounced by the Minister

1. The LORD bless you and keep you; the LORD make his face shine upon you and be gracious to you; the LORD turn his face toward you and give you peace.

   (Num. 6:24–26)

2. May the God of hope fill you with all joy and peace as you trust in him, so that you may overflow with hope by the power of the Holy Spirit.

   (Rom. 15:13)

3. The God of peace be with you all. Amen.
   (*Rom. 15:33*)

4. May the grace of the Lord Jesus Christ, and the love of God, and the fellowship of the Holy Spirit be with you all.
   (*2 Cor. 13:14*)

5. May God himself, the God of peace, sanctify you through and through. May your whole spirit, soul and body be kept blameless at the coming of our Lord Jesus Christ. The one who calls you is faithful and he will do it.
   (*1 Thess. 5:23–24*)

6. May our Lord Jesus Christ himself and God our Father, who loved us and by his grace gave us eternal encouragement and good hope, encourage your hearts and strengthen you in every good deed and word.
   (*2 Thess. 2:16–17*)

7. The grace of our Lord Jesus Christ be with you all.
   (*2 Thess. 3:18*)

8. May the God of peace, who through the blood of the eternal covenant brought back from the dead our Lord Jesus, that great Shepherd of the sheep, equip you with everything good for doing his will, and may he work in us what is pleasing to him, through Jesus Christ, to whom be glory for ever and ever. Amen.
   (*Heb. 13:20–21*)

9. Grace be with you all.
   (*Heb. 13:25*)

Alternative Suggestions

Benedictions can be developed from many additional texts, readings, hymns, songs, or key portions of the Sermon. Such sources can be adapted into meaningful Benedictions by introducing or following them with one of the following (or similar) phrases:

1. Now receive the Lord's Benediction . . .
2. People of God, now receive this promise of blessing from the God of grace . . .

3. As you prepare to go into the world with the message of the gospel, this is God's word of promised blessing . . .

4. Hear now God's blessing for you . . .

Examples of Scriptural Texts Combined for Benedictions

1. May the goodness and love of the Good Shepherd follow you all the days of your life.
   May He gather you in his arms and carry you close to his heart,
   so that you, too, can say, the Lord is my shepherd: I shall never be in want.
   (from Ps. 23:6; Isa. 40:11; Ps. 23:1)

2. May the God who blots out your transgressions, for his sake,
   and remembers your sins no more,
   continually free you from your burdens,
   so that you may praise his name;
   and so that you may gather with the righteous around the Lord,
   who has dealt so bountifully with you.
   (from Isa. 43:25; Ps. 73:5; 142:7)

3. May our Lord, who has stored up for you a hope in heaven where moth and rust do not destroy,
   keep you strong to the end, so that you will be blameless on the day of our Lord Jesus Christ.
   (from Col. 1:5; Matt. 6:19–20; 1 Cor. 1:8)

4. Peace be to you and love with faith from God the Father and the Lord Jesus Christ. Grace to all who love our Lord Jesus Christ with an undying love.
   (from Eph. 6:23–24)

Examples of Scriptural Texts Adapted for Benedictions

1. May the God who changes not,
   who has no shadow of turning
   and whose compassions never fail,
   preserve you by his lovingkindness
   so that you might know,
   great are his faithful acts, they are new every morning.
   (from Lam. 3:22–23)

2. May the Lord prosper your work and defend you,
   may his goodness and mercy daily attend you,
   may you ponder anew what the Almighty will do,
   may all that is within you forever adore him. Amen.

   (from Ps. 103, as in Joachim Neander's hymn,
   "Praise to the Lord, the Almighty")

3. May the God of Abraham, who reigns enthroned above,
   even the Ancient of everlasting days, the God of love,
   give you faith in him as your refuge and high tower
   so that you may believe he exists and that he rewards those who
   earnestly seek him.

   (from Ps. 61:3; Heb. 11:6; and Thomas Oliver's hymn,
   "The God of Abraham Praise")

4. May the God who did not spare his own Son
   but gave him to bear our sins on the cross
   always remind you of these things, even though you know them,
   so that you are firmly established in the truth you now have.

   (from Rom. 8:32; 1 Pet. 2:24; 2 Pet. 1:12)

Examples of Non-Scriptural Texts Adapted for Benedictions

1. May the Lord your God, our help in ages past,
   and our hope for years to come,
   be your guard while troubles last,
   and lead you to his eternal throne.

   (from Isaac Watts's hymn, "Our God, Our Help in Ages Past")

2. May the Lord grant you
   the love that leads the way,
   the faith that nothing can dismay,
   the hope no disappointments tire,
   and the passion that burns like fire.

   (as in Elizabeth Elliot's biography of Amy Carmichael,
   A Chance to Die [Baker, 1987])

3. Now may your rising soul survey
   the mercies of your God;
   may you be lost in wonder, love and praise,
   so that through every period of your life

his goodness you will pursue,
until our Lord comes again and makes all things new.
> *(from hymns, "Love Divine, All Loves Excelling" and "When All Your Mercies, O My God")*

4. May Christ be your shield today:
Christ before you; Christ behind you;
Christ beneath you; Christ above you;
Christ on your right; Christ on your left;
May Christ be with you, Christ be in you
    alone and in multitude,
    near and afar;
    for all you face and for all your life,
    that you may live in the protection and power of his blessing.
> *(from the "Breastplate" prayer of St. Patrick)*

Ascription (Doxology/Acclamation) Examples

Ministers often precede the Benediction with words that ascribe to God aspects of his nature or character (Ascription) that are the basis for God's blessing. These words of praise (Doxology) acclaim the goodness and greatness of God (Acclamation) as a fitting close to worship that sends God's people into the world with confidence in his power and care:

1. Oh, the depth of the riches of the wisdom and knowledge of God!
How unsearchable his judgments, and his paths beyond tracing out!
Who has known the mind of the Lord? Or who has been his counselor?
Who has ever given to God, that God should repay him?
For from him and through him and to him are all things. To him be the glory forever! Amen.
> *(Rom. 11:33–36)*

2. Now to him who is able to do immeasurably more than all we ask or imagine, according to his power that is at work within us, to him be glory in the church and in Christ Jesus throughout all generations, for ever and ever! Amen.
> *(Eph. 3:20–21)*

3. Now to the King eternal, immortal, invisible, the only God, be honor and glory for ever and ever. Amen.
> *(1 Tim. 1:17)*

4. To the only God our Savior be glory, majesty, power and authority, through Jesus Christ our Lord, before all ages, now and forevermore! Amen.

(Jude 25)

5. Grace and peace to you from him who is, and who was, and who is to come . . . Jesus Christ, who is the faithful witness, the firstborn from the dead, and the ruler of the kings of the earth. To him who loves us and has freed us from our sins by his blood, and has made us to be a kingdom and priests to serve his God and Father—to him be glory and power for ever and ever! Amen.

(Rev. 1:5–6)

6. Praise and glory and wisdom and thanks and honor and power and strength be to our God for ever and ever. Amen!

(Rev. 7:12)

Charge and Dismissal Examples

1. Go in peace.

2. Go now and serve your God in the confidence of his love and grace.

3. God has shown you what is good.
   And what does the Lord require of you?
   To act justly and to love mercy
   and to walk humbly with your God.

(from Mic. 6:8)

4. Someone asked Jesus,
   "Teacher, which is the greatest commandment in the Law?"
   Jesus replied:
   "Love the Lord your God
       with all your heart
       and with all your soul
       and with all your mind.
   This is the first and greatest commandment.
   And the second is like it:
   Love your neighbor as yourself.

All the Law and the Prophets hang on these two commandments."
Go in peace to do as Christ commands.
(from Matt. 22:36–40)

5. Go equipped by his grace,
and surrounded by salvation's walls.
Let nothing shake your sure repose,
for you have a sure foundation that nothing can shake.
That foundation is Jesus Christ.
*(from Isa. 28:16; 60:18; and 1 Cor. 3:11, with wording of the hymn,
"Glorious Things of Thee Are Spoken," by John Newton)*

6. Be on your guard; .
stand firm in the faith;
be of courage; be strong.
Do everything in love.
(from 1 Cor. 16:13–14)

7. And now forgetting what is behind and straining toward what is
ahead,
press on toward the goal for which God has called you heavenward
in Christ,
that you may exclaim with the psalmist:
I praise you, my God, for your love and faithfulness;
I praise you, O Lord, with all my heart.
(from Phil. 3:13–14; Ps. 138:1–2)

8. Live a life worthy of the calling you have received.
Be completely humble and gentle;
be patient, bearing with one another in love.
Make every effort to keep the unity of the Spirit through the bond
of peace.
There is one body and one Spirit—
just as you were called to one hope when you were called—
one Lord, one faith, one baptism,
one God and Father of all,
who is over all and through all and in all.
(from Eph. 4:1–6)

9. Whatever you do, whether in word or deed,
do it all in the name of the Lord Jesus,
giving thanks to God the Father through him.
(Col. 3:17)

Benediction/Charge Response Examples

Spoken Response Examples

Congregations often follow Benedictions with these or similar responses:

1. Alleluia.
   Alleluia, Amen.

2. Bless the Lord.
   We bless you, O Lord, our God.

3. Go in peace to love and serve the Lord.
   Thanks be to God.

4. Walk now in the love, peace, and power of your God. Amen.
   Amen.

Musical Response Examples

Such selections may be used as, before, or following a Benediction and Charge:

Traditional

"As You Go, Tell the World," anonymous, in *African American Heritage Hymnal*
"Doxology," by Thomas Ken
"Give Me Jesus," African American spiritual
"God Be with You Till We Meet Again," by Jeremiah Rankin
"Grace, Love and Fellowship," by Tom Fettke
"Lord Dismiss Us with Your Blessing," by John Fawcett
"May the Mind of Christ My Savior," by Kate Wilkinson
"Now May He Who from the Dead," by John Newton
"Savior, Again to Thy Dear Name," by John Ellerton
"The Lord Bless You and Keep You," from Numbers 6:24–26, by Peter Lutkin
"When This Song of Praise Shall Cease," by William Bradbury

Contemporary

"May the Peace of God," by Keith Getty and Stuart Townend
"O How He Loves You and Me," by Kurt Kaiser

Choral

"*Dona Nobis Pacem*"
"E'en So, Lord Jesus, Quickly Come," by Paul Manz
"God Be with You," by Ralph Vaughan Williams
"God Be with You," by John Rutter
"May the Grace of Christ, Our Savior," by John Newton, with music by Ludwig van Beethoven
"Now Unto the King," by William David Young
"The Lord Bless You and Keep You," from Numbers 6:24–26, by Peter Lutkin
"Give Me Jesus," African American spiritual, arranged by L. L. Fleming

Text Resources for Additional Benedictions and Charges

Book of Common Worship. Philadelphia: Board of Christian Education of the Presbyterian Church (USA), 1966, esp. 349–50.

Brink, Emily R., and John D. Witvliet, eds. *The Worship Sourcebook*. Grand Rapids: Calvin Institute of Christian Worship and Baker Books, 2004.

Old, Hughes Oliphant. *Leading in Prayer: A Workbook for Worship*. Grand Rapids: Eerdmans, 1995.

Vasholz, Robert I. *Benedictions: A Pocket Resource*. Ross-shire, Scotland: Christian Focus, 2007.

Music Resources for Benedictions and Charges

Hymnals often include useful texts also.

African American Heritage Hymnal. Chicago: GIA Publications, 2001.

Baptist Hymnal. Nashville: LifeWay, 2008.

Hymnal 1982 According to the Use of the Episcopal Church. New York: Church Publishing, 1985.

The Hymnal for Worship and Celebration. Waco: Word Music, 1986.

Lutheran Service Book. St. Louis: Concordia, 2006.

Psalter Hymnal. Grand Rapids: CRC Publications, 2007.

Songs of Fellowship. Vols. 1–4. Eastbourne, UK: Kingsway Music, 1991–2008.

Trinity Hymnal. Rev. ed. Philadelphia: Great Commission Publications, 1990.

Trinity Psalter. Philadelphia: Great Commission Publications, 1994.

The Worshipping Church. Edited by Don Hustad. Carol Stream, IL: Hope Publishing, 1990.

22

Worship Service Examples

Historic Reformed

This worship service suggested by Hughes Oliphant Old follows the general contours of John Calvin's liturgy with some additions informed by both earlier and later practice.[1] Old's tremendous contribution to the modern church has been to reacquaint us with the wisdom and riches of historical liturgies. In this example, the elements of praise are expanded in accord with practices later than Calvin, but the Confession of Sin remains early in the service (as Calvin designed) and the Assurance of Pardon is included (as Calvin wanted). Also included are multiple Scripture readings of the pre-Calvin eras that again have fallen from common practice outside high church traditions.

Most important to Old is a service reflecting the five elements of worship that the Reformers believed the Bible prescribed for worship: praises, confessions, petitions, intercessions, and thanksgivings.[2] For the Reformers, the machinations of the medieval Mass that sought to recapitulate the history of redemption in ritual were extreme and

---

1. Suggested order of worship (with slight alterations) by Hughes Oliphant Old in *Leading in Prayer: A Workbook for Worship* (Grand Rapids: Eerdmans, 1995), 369–70.
2. Ibid., 362.

superstitious. The altar had become a "passion play" in which Christ's victimization and victory were reenacted in elaborately coded movements. The Reformers found the drama theologically and aesthetically distasteful, believing it distracted from the message of grace and the primacy of the Word. Old reflects the Reformers' perspective by including the biblical elements in his worship service without explicit reference to retelling the gospel.

The re-presentation of the gospel is implicit in this liturgy, but commitment to the wisdom of the ancient liturgies is more the emphasis. For example, Old puts an Intercessory Prayer and Offering after the Sermon. The placement is more a way of honoring historic practice than fulfilling a gospel strategy. Traditionally the prayer and Offering would have been included with the weekly Communion that followed the Sermon. Without weekly Communion in common practice today, Old still wants to include these "communion" (i.e., community/family) dynamics as a way for the church to celebrate its corporate identity. In the absence of weekly Communion such priorities are commendable, but probably difficult to implement in most North American settings. If there is no Communion, almost everything that holds people after the Sermon will seem anti-climactic, prolonged, and—in the case of the Offering—possibly manipulative.

Most traditions that have chosen not to have weekly Communion have moved the Offering to avoid having the preacher seem to "preach for the plate." Instead, the Offering is often placed prior to the Sermon with a testimony or mission report. In this way the congregation not only gives an Offering as thanksgiving for God's grace (since thanksgiving naturally follows an Assurance of Pardon) but also logically connects the Offering to the ministries of the church. As an additional advantage, the preaching of the Word remains the sending force compelling God's people to take the gospel into the world when the Sermon (with the Closing Hymn and Benediction that echo its themes) climaxes the close of worship.

Prelude
Doxology

Invocation
Hymn of Praise

Psalm Read or Sung
Gloria Patri

Prayers of Confession and Supplication
   Confession (in unison)
   Petitions and Supplications
   Assurance of Pardon
   Doxology

Prayer for Illumination
Scripture Lesson(s)
   Old Testament
   New Testament
Hymn (or anthem that could also be sung between the Scripture readings)
Sermon
Hymn

Prayers of Intercession
   for the Church
   for the ministry
   for all peoples
   for the civil authority
   for those who suffer
Lord's Prayer

Collection of Tithes and Alms (an anthem of thanksgiving could be
   sung during the Collection)
Prayer of Thanksgiving
Hymn of Thanksgiving
Benediction
Doxology
Postlude

Modified Presbyterian

Here is a traditional Presbyterian service adapted to reflect the contours
of the gospel.[3] In this example from Redeemer Presbyterian Church of
New York City, the aspects of the gospel sequentially unfold in what the

---

3. This example is a conflation of alternative services presented in D. A. Carson's *Worship by the Book* (Grand Rapids: Zondervan, 2002), 173–74.

church identifies as "gospel reenactment": (1) praise resulting from God's revelation of himself; (2) renewal resulting from the Spirit's revelation of our sin and God's grace; and (3) commitment shown in expressions of prayer, faith, and care for one another.

Since Communion only occurs once a month, this thoughtful service (similar to the one previously suggested by Old) incorporates "communion" dynamics by placing the Offering after the Sermon. For reasons indicated in the previous discussion, this Offering placement may not be feasible for many churches—and there is a clear gospel strategy that can also explain placing the Offering after an Assurance of Grace prior to the Sermon. Also, note the use of testimony and ministry reports prior to the Sermon in this example and the one that follows (i.e., Independent Evangelical). These examples from wonderful and wise churches underscore the importance of giving congregational witness to the progress of the gospel as part of worship. Clearly this was a significant aspect of New Testament worship that the twenty-first-century church is re-discovering for great blessing (cf. Acts 4:23–33; 10:34–48; 13:15–41; 15:3–4; 1 Cor. 14:26; Rev. 1:1–2, 9–20).

This so-called "Center-City" model also makes significant use of congregational dialogue and musical excellence in a variety of styles to minister to those with strong appreciation for both the historical and aesthetic dimensions of worship.

Praise

    Preparation (printed Scripture reading for reflection)

    Praise Hymn

    Responsive Call to Worship (Scripture)

    Invocation

    Lord's Prayer

    Doxology

    Silent Adoration

Renewal

    Scripture (Call to Renewal)

    Prayer of Confession

    Silent Confession

    Confessional Response

    Words of Encouragement (Scripture of Assurance)

    Testimonies of God's Work (and/or membership vows, baptisms, ordinations, commissioning)

Intercessory Prayer (pastoral or prayers of the people)
Hymn

Commitment
Words of Welcome and Announcements
Scripture Reading
Sermon
Call to Offering
Offering and Offertory
Hymn
Exhortation/Charge
Benediction and Dismissal
Dismissal

Independent Evangelical

This service reflects the worship practice probably most familiar in evangelical churches throughout North America: the placement of the intercessory prayer and Offering prior to the Sermon; the balance of hymns to start the service, prepare for the Sermon, and close the service; the absence of multiple Scripture readings; and the typical placement of the Lord's Prayer, Doxology, and *Gloria Patri*.[4] Such an order is virtually standard across many denominations and regions. Without challenging their basic order, such services may experience great renewal and a restored sense of purpose with these gentle encouragements: (1) choose elements whose theological content will reflect a gospel development (then make this development clear with the rubrics that connect the elements), and (2) offer the elements in a variety of ways (e.g., a Doxology might be read responsively from a New Testament epistle in place of the regularly sung "Doxology" of Thomas Ken).

Prelude
Choral Call to Worship
Welcome
Hymn
Invocation

---

4. This is a slight conflation of worship services provided by the College Church of Wheaton, Illinois, in Carson's *Worship by the Book*, 173–74.

Doxology
Apostles' Creed
Hymn
Congregational Prayer/Lord's Prayer
Anthem and Offering
(Testimony or Report of God's Work)
Hymn
Scripture Reading
Gloria Patri
Sermon
Hymn
Benediction
Postlude

Blended Baptist

This service is identified on the church's Web site as intentionally "a blend of casual and formal, contemporary and traditional."[5] The highly effective ministry of Dr. John Piper is reflected in a very thoughtful integration of worship styles respectful of his church's tradition and sympathetic to contemporary tastes. The service progresses through a familiar order of elements for North American evangelical churches (i.e., a Call to Worship leads to an opening Hymn of Praise, followed by prayer, an Offering, more music, and a Sermon with a Benediction), but the music carries much of the freight of the worship's gospel message. Not only is the music designed to engage both traditionalists and those who appreciate contemporary worship music (though the bent is obviously toward the preferences of the Baby Boomer generation), but the contents of the songs and hymns form the gospel contours of the worship.

I have retained the titles of the musical selections in the order of service below to make apparent the redemptive flow of the worship. The opening song set includes songs that begin with praise ("The Glories of Calvary") but also include confession ("When I Survey"). Then praise and prayer acknowledge God's provision of grace. These are followed by a time of reflection on God's goodness ("Great is Thy Faithfulness"), preparing for thankful responses of Offering and praise for God's provision ("Shield About Me" and "*Agnus Dei*"). The acknowledgments of God's provision

5. This worship service is provided by Bethlehem Baptist Church in Minneapolis, Minnesota.

are also preparation for additional instruction from God's Word in the Sermon. Finally, a Benediction closes the service.

Those with high church preferences will be concerned with the lack of Scripture readings, corporate responses, and creedal affirmation, but this church serves those whose backgrounds would find these off-putting and, instead, does a masterful job of maintaining the gospel contours of worship through the content of its musical choices. The church is often much more specific about the gospel progression of its worship, giving the service segments titles such as "Adoration," "Confession," "Thanksgiving," "Word," and "Benediction." I chose this service instead to demonstrate how music can help the gospel take shape in a service with divisions more familiar to those of many Baptist, independent, and evangelical backgrounds.

Prelude
Gathering
   "Más Amor, Más Poder (More Love, More Power)" *Jude Del Hierro*
Welcome
Call to Worship
   Reading: 1 Peter 2:21–24
Praise
   "The Glories of Calvary" *Steve and Vikki Cook*
   "When I Survey the Wondrous Cross" *Watts/arranged by Mason*
   "We Declare Your Majesty" *Malcolm Du Plessis*
Prayer of Praise
Reflection
   Offertory *Instrumental*
   "Great Is Thy Faithfulness" *Thomas O. Chisholm/William M. Runyan*
Response
   "Shield About Me" *Donn Thomas*
   "*Agnus Dei*" *Michael W. Smith*
Word
   Sermon Text
   Sermon
Benediction
Postlude

African American Baptist

The transferable principles of Christ-centered worship are evident in this worship service from a traditional, rapidly growing African American church in St. Louis. Under the leadership of an able and wise pastor, Friendly Temple Missionary Baptist Church honors its heritage while also deepening its gospel emphases with energetic and thoughtful worship. Pastor Michael Jones utilizes music and worship forms familiar to generations of African Americans (his grandfather pastored this same church), while also setting an agenda for transforming the inner city through mercy, education, and housing ministries that are as innovative and courageous as any in this country. The church has rapidly become one of the largest in the city and has used its prestige to press gospel principles that are reclaiming neighborhoods from devastation, young people from crime and despair, and an older generation from cynicism and resignation.

The worship services of Friendly Temple are exuberant, inspiring, and dialogical. Worship includes songs and hymns that have been embraced by many African American congregations since the mid-twentieth century. This music is led by a large choir accompanied by both organ and praise band instrumentation now familiar in many urban churches. The music guides worshipers through the stages of the service, and often provides transition between elements, as well as acoustic emphasis to words spoken in rubrics, announcements, and occasionally the Sermon.

The emphasis on providing a traditionally black experience of worship definitely affects the style of worship, but also focuses the church's message. Embedded within the traditional "feel" of the service are song choices, Scripture readings, prayers, an Offering, a Bible-based Sermon, and a Benediction, all of which carefully reflect and develop gospel principles. Adoration begins with a choral Call to Worship that leads into a scriptural Call to Repentance followed by a Song of Assurance and Pastoral Prayer that includes both confession and petition. Familiar gospel contours further unfold through elements of thanksgiving, fellowship, instruction, Charge, and Benediction that progress through both pastoral and musical rubrics that are at times carefully orchestrated and at other times obviously extemporaneous. The service may appear free form, but the pastor and choir expertly navigate to their gospel destination with obvious knowledge and trust of each other's contributions and expectations.

Gathering Music
"We Bring the Sacrifice of Praise"

Choral Call to Worship
  "The Lord is Worthy of Praise"
Responsive Reading: Psalm 1
Song of Assurance
  "Welcome to this Place"
Pastoral Prayer for Church Needs
Preparation for Thanksgiving
  Reading: Malachi 3:8–12
Offering
  Collection
    with
  Choral and Congregational Songs of Thanksgiving
Announcements and Greeting of Guests
Choral Anthem
  "Praise to the Lord"
Choral and Congregational Preparation for the Word
  "Holy Spirit, Come Down"
Proclamation of the Gospel
  Prayer for Illumination
  Text Reading: Matthew 27:27–32
  Preaching from Matthew 27:27–32
Prayer of Consecration
Invitation to Discipleship
Benediction
Postlude

Emerging Church

This order of worship is gleaned from the worship of a rapidly growing, emerging church which primarily ministers to twenty-somethings.[6] As in many emerging churches, much of the appeal is to young people turned off by what they perceive as the lack of authenticity in traditional churches and the consumer mind-set of many contemporary churches. The longing for authenticity, relational connection, and cultural engagement means these

---

6. This worship service is provided by The Journey, an emerging church of the Acts 29 Network.

churches are intent on shedding themselves of cultural baggage (such as bulletins, formal dress, and church ceremony) in order to live authentically in their culture (ministering to the needy, deeply connecting with one another, and listening to God's Word "straight," i.e., with direct application and without embellishment).

Pastor Darrin Patrick is a master at reading the pulse of this "fatherless" generation (the children of divorce, absent fathers, and technology substitutes for relationships) while challenging it with great pastoral wisdom and biblical insight. Though there is no announced structure to the service, the worship proceeds along gospel contours through the content of the songs chosen, the Sermon, *and* weekly Communion. The ordinance that seems such a burden to so many in an older generation (delaying us from our Sunday brunches) has been re-embraced by a generation prioritizing relational connectedness and authentic engagement with the spiritual.

The music includes traditional hymns offered with contemporary instrumentation and new songs with cutting-edge sounds. There is a sincere desire to maintain continuity with the best of the historical church while connecting with younger tastes and expressions. The appeal to youth should not be misinterpreted as disengagement from gospel priorities. Because of the wisdom and commitments of the pastoral staff, the content of the musical choices progresses through historic gospel contours. The service begins with praise that recognizes the glory of God ("O Worship the King"), moves to confession ("At Your Feet"), offers assurance of God's gracious provision ("Prayer for Faith"), encourages worshipers to yield to God's instruction (Scripture reading and Sermon) and to respond in thankful obedience (Offering) and consecration (Communion that includes adoration, confession, assurance, and mutual commitment).

How well this progress is apprehended by worshipers largely depends on the transitions spoken by the worship leader, which underscores the importance of well-chosen rubrics (see chapter 17). Still, it is clear the intention is to pare down the worship to its gospel essentials. Though the informality and musical style seem far removed from historic Protestant worship, the spare liturgy is actually much closer in form to early Reformation practice than much of what is now considered "traditional" worship.

Worship Opening
   "O Worship the King"
   Greeting and Announcements

Worship Continuing
   "At Your Feet"
   "Prayer for Faith"
Scripture Reading
Sermon
Communion
   "Alas and Did My Savior Bleed"
Offering
Worship Closing
   "That We Might Live"

Examples of "Gospel-Shaped" Liturgies

The following orders of worship are offered as full examples of how to use different worship components to re-present the gospel. These liturgies lean toward the traditional (in order to make them familiar and acceptable for a broad range of Protestant churches) while also trying to incorporate thoughtful features of contemporary worship (that will help churches' outreach and preparations for their future). My intention is *not* to suggest "correct" liturgies, but rather to demonstrate how worship leaders can use various resources in creative ways while maintaining the gospel contours of worship.[7] For reading clarity, only the last example labels these contours

7. For other resources with order of worship examples, see the historic liturgies described in part 1 of this book; the Books of Common Worship or hymnals of the Anglican, Baptist, Lutheran, Presbyterian, and Methodist communions noted previously in the chapters of part 2 of this book; the internet resources provided in the appendix of this book; Carson, *Worship by the Book* (includes contemporary and classical Reformed, traditional evangelical, and Anglican liturgies); Howard Vanderwall, ed., *The Church of All Ages* (Herndon, VA: Alban Institute, 2008), with particular suggestions for cross-generational worship; Emily R. Brink and John D. Witvliet, eds., *The Worship Sourcebook* (Grand Rapids: Calvin Institute of Christian Worship and Baker Books, 2004), a monumental treasure trove of worship resources; Terry L. Johnson, ed., *Leading in Worship* (Oak Ridge, TN: Covenant Foundation, 1996), a classic Presbyterian approach; Jeffrey J. Myers, *The Lord's Service: The Grace of Covenantal Renewal Worship* (Moscow, ID: Canon, 2003), a Reformed perspective modified with understanding of continental, Lutheran, and patristic contributions; and the seminal contributions of Robert Webber, who reintroduced the evangelical church to the beauty of ancient forms in order to provide continuity for our future (e.g., *Ancient-Future Worship: Proclaiming and Enacting God's Narrative* [Grand Rapids: Baker Books, 2008]). Most of these sources have sought either to provide continuity within their traditions or to improve present practice with suggestions that help the church bridge its worship to the past and/or future. My intention has been to provide a Christ-centered rationale (demonstrated in the church through the ages) that equips worship leaders to make informed choices among these suggestions in accord with the gospel calling of their particular churches.

within the service bulletin, but it is important to note that each liturgy—while varying the order and worship components—consistently re-presents the aspects of Christ-centered worship (see marginal notes):

Aspects of Christ-Centered Worship

1. Adoration (recognition of God's greatness and grace)
2. Confession (acknowledgment of our sin and need for grace)
3. Assurance (affirmation of God's provision of grace)
4. Thanksgiving (expression of praise and thanks for God's grace)
5. Petition and Intercession (expression of dependence on God's grace)
6. Instruction (acquiring the knowledge to grow in grace)
7. Communion/Fellowship (celebrating the grace of union with Christ and his people)
8. Charge and Blessing (living for and in the light of God's grace)

Example 1: Liturgy of the Word with "Continental" Liturgy of the Upper Room[8]

Prelude and Pre-Worship Meditation   1. Adoration
"How Lovely Shines the Morning Star," by Philip Nicolai, 1597

How lovely shines the Morning Star!
The nations see and hail afar
The light in Judah shining.
Thou David's Son of Jacob's race,
My Bridegroom and my King of Grace,
For Thee my heart is pining.
Lowly, holy, great and glorious,
Thou victorious Prince of graces,
Filling all the heav'nly places.

Now richly to my waiting heart,
O Thou, my God, deign to impart
The grace of love undying.

---

8. This first of five "gospel-shaped" liturgies is adapted from a worship service provided by the Rev. Preston Graham Jr. of Christ Presbyterian Church in New Haven, Connecticut. For the remainder I am thankful for the ministry of the Rev. Dr. George Robertson, the Rev. Ryan Laughlin, and music director Kathleen Chapell whose years preparing Christ-centered worship have yielded such wonderful expressions of a grace-filled liturgy for Covenant Presbyterian Church in St. Louis.

In Thy blest body let me be,
E'en as the branch is in the tree,
Thy life my life supplying.
Sighing, crying, for the savor
Of Thy favor; resting never
Till I rest in Thee forever.

Worship through Invocation and Adoration
Call to Worship: Psalm 68:1–3, 32–35

Pastor: May God arise, may his enemies be scattered; may his foes flee before him.

People: **As smoke is blown away by the wind, may you blow them away; as wax melts before the fire, may the wicked perish before God.**

Pastor: But may the righteous be glad and rejoice before God; may they be happy and joyful.

People: **Sing to God, O kingdoms of the earth, sing praise to the Lord,**

Pastor: to him who rides the ancient skies above, who thunders with mighty voice.

People: **Proclaim the power of God, whose majesty is over Israel, whose power is in the skies.**

Pastor: You are awesome, O God, in your sanctuary; the God of Israel gives power and strength to his people.

People: **Praise be to God!**

Hymn of Praise: "Praise to the Lord, the Almighty"
Invocation and Prayer of Adoration
Old Testament Reading: Ezekiel 33:10–16
New Testament Reading: Revelation 1:4–8

Reader: This is the Word of the Lord!

People: **Thanks be to God!**

Doxology

Worship through Confession and Assurance   2. Confession
Corporate Confession

Leader: Let us confess our sins to God our Father.

People: O most great, most just and gracious God; you are of purer eyes than to behold iniquity; but you have promised mercy through Jesus Christ to all who repent and believe in him. Therefore, we confess that we are sinful by nature and that we have all sinned and come short of the glory of God. We have neglected and abused your holy worship and your holy name. We have dealt unjustly and uncharitably with our neighbors. We have not sought first your kingdom and righteousness. We have not been content with our daily bread.

You have revealed your wonderful love to us in Christ and offered us pardon and salvation in him; but we have turned away. We have run into temptation; and the sin that we should have hated, we have committed.

Have mercy upon us, most merciful Father! We confess you alone are our hope. Make us your children and give us the Spirit of your Son, our only Savior. Amen. (from a prayer of Richard Baxter, *The Savoy Liturgy*, 1661)

Private Confession   3. Assurance
Assurance of Pardon
"If we confess our sins, he is faithful and just and will forgive us our sins and purify us from all unrighteousness." (*1 John 1:9*)

Pastoral Prayer   4. Thanksgiving
Song of Response: "In Christ Alone"   5. Prayer/
                                                             Intercession

Worship through the Word   6. Instruction
Scripture Reading: 2 Timothy 2:1–2
Sermon: Grace Multiplied!

Worship through Sacrament   7. Communion
Introduction to the Lord's Table
Collection for the Ministry of God's People
Offertory and Preparation Hymn: "All People That on Earth Do Dwell"
Confession of Faith

Leader: Christians, what do you believe?

People: I believe in God the Father Almighty, Maker of heaven and earth, and in Jesus Christ, His only Son, our Lord, who was conceived by the Holy Spirit, born of the virgin Mary, suffered under Pontius Pilate, was crucified, dead, and buried; He descended into hell; the third day He rose again from the dead; He ascended into heaven, and is seated on the right hand of God the Father Almighty; from there He will come to judge the living and the dead. I believe in the Holy Spirit, the Holy Catholic Church,* the Communion of Saints, the forgiveness of sins, the resurrection of the body, and the life everlasting. Amen. (Apostles' Creed)

*That is, the true Christian church of all times and all places.

Prayer of Thanksgiving and Consecration
Words of Institution from 1 Corinthians 11:23–32
Invitation

Pastor: Let us proclaim the wonders of our faith:

All: Christ has died. Christ is risen. Christ will come again.

Pastor: Alleluia! Christ our Passover is sacrificed for us;

All: Therefore let us keep the feast. Alleluia!

Pastor: The Gifts of God for the People of God.

Take them in remembrance that Christ died for you, and feed on him in your hearts by faith, with thanksgiving.

Sharing the Bread and Cup

Prayers for those not communing:[9]
Prayer for those searching

Oh God, I am discovering that the more I have, the more I need to have, the more I am loved, the more I need to be loved, the more I achieve, the more I need to achieve. Nothing seems to satisfy me. "Nothing tastes." Could it be, as someone once said, that "Our hearts are restless until they find their rest in thee." Dear God, if this is true, and if as the Bible teaches there is life and life eternal in Christ alone, please guide me to him. Open me

9. Additional prayers for those not communing are offered by Tim Keller in Carson, *Worship by the Book*, 249.

to the reality of the one who alone can satisfy my restless heart.
Give me the courage to believe that which I cannot see but can
understand through your Word, sacraments and church family.
Lord I want to believe, please help me in my unbelief! Amen.

Prayer of belief

Lord God, I now see that I am weaker and more flawed than
I ever before believed, but in Christ, I am more loved and accepted than I ever dared hope. Even as I have not loved you or
my neighbor with all of my heart, you have shown your love for
me in that while I am still sinning, Christ died for me and took
upon himself the condemnation that I deserve. I now know that
You owe me nothing for my efforts, but you offer acceptance,
love and blessing into all eternity because of Christ's efforts
on my behalf. I therefore ask that you would enable me to turn
away from trusting in my own efforts to gain your acceptance
and forgiveness, and trust in the perfectly righteous efforts of
Christ on my behalf in order to be accepted by you and entered
into your holy family. And just as you raised Christ from the
dead, so too I ask that you would give me a new life in Christ,
one that will lead eventually to heaven itself. Thank you for
Christ, and the power of the Holy Spirit to believe in him alone
for my salvation. And as You have called us to follow You in
baptism and in a life of committed discipleship in Your church,
grant that I may take the necessary steps to be one with Your
people, and live in the fullness of Your Spirit. Amen.

Closing Hymn: "All Hail the Power of Jesus' Name!"   8. Charge and
Prayer of Thanksgiving   Blessing
Gloria Patri
Benediction

> Leader: Now may the Lord bless you, even as one who
> by the power at work within you is able to accomplish
> abundantly more than all we can ask or imagine. To
> him be glory in the church and in Christ Jesus to every
> generation forever and ever. Amen. *(from Ephesians
> 3:20)*

> People: **Thanks be to God! Hallelujah!**

Postlude

Example 2: Liturgy of the Word with "North American" Liturgy of the Upper Room

Greeting and Announcements

Psalm for Reflection: Psalm 25:1–7   1. Adoration

> To You, O LORD, I lift up my soul; in You I trust, O my God. Do not let me be put to shame, nor let my enemies triumph over me.

> No one whose hope is in You will ever be put to shame, but they will be put to shame who are treacherous without excuse.

> Show me Your ways, O LORD, teach me Your paths; guide me in Your truth and teach me, for You are God my Savior, and my hope is in You all day long.

> Remember, O LORD, Your great mercy and love, for they are from of old.

> Remember not the sins of my youth and my rebellious ways; according to Your love remember me, for You are good, O LORD.

Prelude: "Helmsley," by Philip Lane

Call to Worship: from Revelation 4

> Pastor: Holy, holy, holy is the Lord God Almighty, who was, and is, and is to come.

> **All: You are worthy, our Lord and God, to receive glory and honor and power, for You created all things, and by Your will they were created and have their being.**

Hymn of Adoration: "Crown Him with Many Crowns"

> Choir: Crown Him the Lord of love! Behold His hands and side,

> rich wounds, yet visible above, in beauty glorified:

> no angel in the sky can fully bear that sight, but downward

> bends his burning eye at mysteries so bright.

> Men: Crown Him with many crowns, the Lamb upon His throne;

> Hark! how the heavenly anthem drowns all music but its

own! Awake, my soul, and sing of Him who died for
thee,
and hail Him as thy matchless King through all eternity.

Women: Crown Him the Lord of life, who triumphed
o'er the grave,
and rose victorious in the strife for those He came to
save;
His glories now we sing who died and rose on high, who
died eternal life to bring, and lives that death may die.

All: Crown Him the Lord of years, the potentate of time,
Creator of the rolling spheres, ineffably sublime. All
hail, Redeemer, hail! for Thou hast died for me; Thy
praise shall never, never fail throughout eternity.

Choir: Crown Him with many crowns!

Pastoral Prayer of Invocation and Confession   2. Confession
Individual Silent Confession
Assurance of Pardon: Colossians 1:13   3. Assurance
    Pastor: He has rescued us from the dominion of dark-
    ness and brought us into the kingdom of the Son He
    loves, in whom we have redemption, the forgiveness
    of sins.
Response of Praise: from Revelation 19   4. Thanksgiving
    Pastor: Hallelujah! Salvation and glory and power belong
    to our God. Praise our God, all you His servants, you
    who fear Him, both small and great!
    All: **Hallelujah! For our Lord God Almighty reigns. Let
    us rejoice and be glad and give Him glory!**

Hymn of Thanksgiving: "Doxology"
Prayer of Intercession   5. Intercession
Offertory: "One Faith, One Hope, One Lord"
    Choir: There is one body, one spirit, as you were called
    to one hope.
    One Lord, baptism and faith, one God and Father of all,
    who is in you all.

One faith, one hope, one Lord, one church for which He
   died. One voice, one song we lift in praise to Him who
   was and is and shall be evermore.

Though we be many people, diverse with various gifts,
   we are given to each other for the unity of faith, that
   we grow in the knowledge of the Son of God, in the
   fullness of Christ.

One faith, one hope, one Lord, one church for which He
   died. One voice, one song, we lift in praise to Him who
   was and is and shall be evermore.

One faith, one hope, one Lord, one God.

Hymn of Preparation: "O Day of Rest and Gladness"   6. Instruction
Scripture Reading: Mark 2:23–3:6
Sermon: Made for Us
Hymn of Response: "How Deep the Father's Love for Us"

Celebration of the Lord's Supper   7. Communion
   Preparation
   Apostles' Creed
   Words of Institution
   Prayer of Consecration
   Communion
   Prayer of Dedication
Communion Hymn: "And Can It Be That I Should Gain"
Benediction   8. Blessing
Postlude: "Chorale," by Adolf Hesse

Example 3: Liturgy of the Word without Liturgy
of the Upper Room

Greeting and Announcements   7. Communion/
Psalm for Reflection: Psalm 27:1, 4–6   Fellowship
                                                           1. Adoration
   The LORD is my light and my salvation—whom shall I
      fear? The LORD is the stronghold of my life—of whom
      shall I be afraid?

   One thing I ask of the LORD, this is what I seek: that I
      may dwell in the house of the LORD all the days of my
      life, to gaze upon the beauty of the LORD and to seek
      Him in His temple.

For in the day of trouble He will keep me safe in His dwelling; He will hide me in the shelter of His tabernacle and set me high upon a rock.

Then my head will be exalted above the enemies who surround me; at His tabernacle will I sacrifice with shouts of joy; I will sing and make music to the Lord.

Prelude: "Solitude," by Harold DeCou

Call to Worship: Habakkuk 2:20

Pastor: The Lord is in His holy temple; let all the earth be silent before Him.

Silent Reflection

Hymn of Adoration: "God Himself Is with Us"

Invocation

Call to Confession: "Cast Thy Burden Upon the Lord"   2. Confession

Choir: Cast thy burden upon the Lord, and He shall sustain thee; He never will suffer the righteous to fall: He is at thy right hand. Thy mercy, Lord, is great and far above the heav'ns: Let none be made ashamed that wait upon Thee.

Corporate Confession of Sin

All: **Heavenly Father,**

You have made us as precious to you as Jesus.

You have made us as righteous as he by nailing our sin to his cross.

You pardoned us through his penalty;

Purchased us with his sacrifice;

Cleansed us with his blood;

And, now you assure us we are as treasured as he in your heart.

Yet, despite this amazing love we turn from you:

Our hearts go wandering into selfishness;

We neglect those who are hurting;

We excuse our unforgiveness; and,

We live as though you do not care.

Forgive us, we pray.

Humble our hearts through your mercy that makes living for Jesus our joy.

Displace our love for sin with greater love for Christ, Then help us to be in life what you have already made us for eternity: a holy people.

Silent Confession

Assurance of Pardon: Matthew 11:28–29

> Pastor: Come to Me, all you who are weary and burdened, and I will give you rest. Take My yoke upon you and learn from Me, for I am gentle and humble in heart, and you will find rest for your souls.

Profession of Faith: from Heidelberg Catechism, question 1

> All: I believe that I am not my own, but belong—body and soul, in life and in death—to my faithful Savior Jesus Christ. He has fully paid for all my sins with His precious blood, and has set me free from the tyranny of the devil. He also watches over me in such a way that not a hair can fall from my head without the will of my Father in heaven: in fact, all things must work together for my salvation. Because I belong to Him, Christ, by His Holy Spirit, assures me of eternal life and makes me wholeheartedly willing and ready from now on to live for Him.

Prayer of Intercession
Offertory and Offering

Hymn of Preparation: "Glorious Things of Thee Are Spoken"
Scripture Reading: Exodus 25:31–40
Sermon: The Lampstand
Hymn of Response: "Guide Me, O Thou Great Jehovah"

Benediction
Postlude: "And Can It Be?"

3. Assurance

4. Thanksgiving

5. Intercession
4. Thanksgiving

6. Instruction

8. Blessing

Example 4: Liturgy of the Word with Commissioning Service

Greeting and Announcements

Psalm for Reflection: Psalm 46   1. Adoration

> God is our refuge and strength, an ever-present help in trouble.
>
> Therefore we will not fear, though the earth give way and the mountains fall into the heart of the sea, though its waters roar and foam and the mountains quake with their surging.
>
> There is a river whose streams make glad the city of God, the holy place where the Most High dwells. God is within her, she will not fall; God will help her at break of day.
>
> Nations are in uproar, kingdoms fall; He lifts his voice, the earth melts. The LORD Almighty is with us; the God of Jacob is our fortress.
>
> Come and see the works of the LORD, the desolations He has brought on the earth.
>
> He makes wars cease to the ends of the earth; He breaks the bow and shatters the spear, He burns the shields with fire.
>
> "Be still, and know that I am God; I will be exalted among the nations, I will be exalted in the earth."
>
> The LORD Almighty is with us; the God of Jacob is our fortress.

Prelude: "Lovely Fields So Gentle," by C. W. Gluck

Call to Worship: Psalm 146

> Pastor: Praise the LORD.
>
> All: **Praise the LORD, O my soul. I will praise the LORD all my life; I will sing praise to my God as long as I live.**
>
> Pastor: Do not put your trust in princes, in mortal men, who cannot save. When their spirit departs, they return to the ground; on that very day their plans come to nothing.
>
> All: **Blessed is he whose help is the God of Jacob, whose hope is in the LORD his God, the Maker of heaven and**

earth, the sea, and everything in them—the LORD, who remains faithful forever.

Pastor: He upholds the cause of the oppressed and gives food to the hungry. The LORD sets prisoners free, the LORD gives sight to the blind, the LORD lifts up those who are bowed down, the LORD loves the righteous. The LORD watches over the alien and sustains the fatherless and the widow, but He frustrates the ways of the wicked.

All: The LORD reigns forever, your God, O Zion, for all generations. Praise the LORD.

Hymn of Adoration: "Hallelujah! Hallelujah!"
Invocation

Hymn of Confession: "Man of Sorrows! What a Name" (vv. 1–3)
Assurance of Pardon: Isaiah 53:5–6

Pastor: He was pierced for our transgressions, He was crushed for our iniquities; the punishment that brought us peace was upon Him, and by His wounds we are healed. We all, like sheep, have gone astray, each of us has turned to his own way; and the LORD has laid on Him the iniquity of us all.

Hymn of Thanksgiving: "Man of Sorrows" (vv. 4–5)

Testimonies from Mission Trip to Haiti
Elders' Commissioning of Missionaries to Ukraine
Prayers and Intercessions
Offering with Choral Anthem: "Shine, Jesus, Shine"

Scripture Reading: Luke 5:1–11
Sermon: Man Fishers
Hymn of Response: "Jesus Saves! Jesus Saves!"

Benediction
Postlude: "Come, Christians, Join to Sing," arranged by Don Wyrtzen

2. Confession
3. Assurance

4. Thanksgiving
7. Communion/
Fellowship

5. Intercession
4. Thanksgiving

6. Instruction

8. Blessing

Example 5: Liturgy of the Word with Baptism and
Gospel "Aspects" Identified

Adoration of Our Gracious God   1. Adoration

Psalm for Reflection: Psalm 105:1–5

> Give thanks to the LORD, call on His name; make known
> among the nations what He has done. Sing to Him,
> sing praise to Him; tell of all His wonderful acts.
>
> Glory in His holy name; let the hearts of those who seek
> the LORD rejoice.
>
> Look to the LORD and His strength; seek His face
> always.
>
> Remember the wonders He has done, His miracles, and
> the judgments He pronounced.

Prelude: "My Jesus, I Love Thee," arranged by Dale
Grotenhuis

Call to Worship: Psalm 105:1–3

> Pastor: Give thanks to the LORD, call on His name;
>
> All: **Make known among the nations what He has done.**
>
> Pastor: Sing to Him, sing praise to Him; tell of all His
> wonderful acts.
>
> All: **Glory in His holy name; let the hearts of those who**
> **seek the LORD rejoice.**

Hymn of Adoration: "Ye Servants of God, Your Master
Proclaim"

Invocation

Confession to the God of Grace   2. Confession

Corporate Confession of Sin

> All: **Almighty and most merciful Father,**
>
> **We have erred and strayed from Your ways like lost**
> **sheep.**
>
> **We have followed too much the devices and desires of**
> **our own hearts.**
>
> **We have offended against Your holy laws.**
>
> **We have left undone those things which we ought to**
> **have done.**
>
> **And we have done those things which we ought not to**
> **have done.**

But now we humbly seek You, O Lord, and ask for Your mercy, as you have urged us by your lovingkindness; Spare us, O God, as we confess our faults.

Restore all those who are penitent, according to Your promises declared in Christ Jesus, our Lord.

And grant, O merciful Father, for His sake that we may hereafter live a godly and righteous life; to the glory of Your holy name. Amen.

Individual Silent Confession

Assurance of God's Grace

3. Assurance

Pastor: How great is the love the Father has lavished on us, that we should be called children of God! And that is what we are! (*from 1 John 3:1*)

Song of Assurance: "Behold What Manner of Love"

Celebration of Baptism

7. Community/ Fellowship

Explanation of Baptism

Testimonies and Vows of Faith

Prayer of Consecration

Administration of Baptism

Welcome

Thanksgiving for God's Grace

4. Thanksgiving

Offering and Offertory Duet: "More Love to Thee, O Christ"

More love to Thee, O Christ, more love to Thee! Hear Thou the prayer I make on bended knee. This is my earnest plea:

"More love, O Christ, to Thee, more love to Thee, more love to Thee!"

Once earthly joy I craved, sought peace and rest; now Thee alone I seek; give what is best. This all my prayer shall be:

"More love, O Christ, to Thee, more love to Thee, more love to Thee!"

Then shall my latest breath whisper Thy praise; this be the parting cry my heart shall raise: "More love, O Christ, to Thee, more love to Thee!"

Petitions and Intercessions for God's Grace
Prayer Requests from the Congregation
Testimonies of God's Grace
Announcements for the Life of the Church
Pastoral Prayer of Intercession

Instruction in God's Grace
Hymn of Preparation: "Open Our Eyes Lord"
Scripture Reading: Ephesians 1:15–23
Sermon: Praying with Our Eyes Wide Open
Hymn of Response: "All Hail the Power of Jesus' Name!"

Pastoral Charge and Benediction

Postlude: "Our God, Our Help in Ages Past," arranged by Dale Grotenhuis

5. Petition/
Intercession
(7. Communion/
Fellowship)

6. Instruction

8. Blessing

Note: While it can certainly be argued that the sacrament of Communion is lacking in this service, we can also observe the "communion" of the saints being celebrated through the intentional integration of announcements, corporate affirmations, prayer requests, testimonies, and vows. And the entire liturgy is a sacramental reflection as it re-presents the aspects of the gospel.

23

COMMUNION SERVICES

The gospel message made apparent in the symbols of the Liturgy of the Upper Room is the same message communicated by the structure of the Liturgy of the Word. By the movements and elements of the sacrament, we acknowledge God's holiness, confess our sin, and celebrate his grace; we are nourished by his provision and, thus, are encouraged and enabled to live with his blessing. Scholars debate the origins, developments, efficacy, and appropriateness of virtually every expression, gesture, and element—and Christ's church has often divided over such—but there remain common features beneath the blizzard of differences in Communion observance across traditions, time, and territory.[1]

Common Denominators and Debates

While acknowledging historical anomalies, the common denominators include: an invitation for the faithful to partake, an Affirmation of Faith,

---

1. For example, Gregory Dix argues for the essential continuity and apostolic origin of Christian liturgy despite differences of time and region (see *The Shape of the Liturgy* [New York: Continuum International, 2005]), but Paul Bradshaw argues these differences indicate that the various traditions had few controls and were largely influenced by cultural factors (see *The Search for the Origins of Christian Worship: Sources and Methods for the Study of Early Liturgy*, 2nd ed. (Oxford: Oxford University Press, 2002). Neither argument negates the premise that the gospel forms liturgy among the faithful. Whether through internal controls or despite external influences, it remains apparent that there are continuities that ultimately unite the traditions in gospel expression.

prayer that includes Confession of Sin and need for sustaining grace, setting aside the elements from common use for a holy purpose, distribution of the elements, partaking of the elements, thanksgiving for God's provision, and declaration of God's peace and power through the gospel.

Debates rage over whether to partake "at rail or while seated," "at or about table," by elder service or personal procession, with separate or common cup, "in total or by tincture," with wine or juice, with loaf or wafer, and so on. Churches divide over whether the minister should elevate the host, practice Fraction, stand behind or before the table, and so on. Entire worship philosophies develop over the content and sequence of the eucharistic prayer, the order in which leaders serve and are served the elements, whether to require preparation services, how to fence the table, whether to allow Scripture reading or music during the distribution, whether to partake individually or corporately, when to serve the organist, and how to fold the cloth that covers the table prior to the distribution.

These last two matters are mentioned with only a little tongue in cheek. Churches really do debate such matters with vigor and apparent confidence that the Bible actually provides guidance to govern such matters. In one of my early pastorates, the ingredients of the Communion bread became the source for controversy. The sugary sweet recipe had been passed down for generations, and by honored tradition the elders' wives prepared a batch of the bread for each Communion Sunday. The problem was that the bread was so tasty that it tempted children to rush the altar after the service to grab handfuls. The church's leadership struggled with whether to allow such "desecration" of the elements that had just been used for the Lord's Supper. Some argued that there was nothing magical about the leftover bread and there was nothing wrong with letting the kids have it. Besides, it was argued, tasting the almost-candy bread would encourage the children to become members of the church so they could partake of the sweetness of Christ's grace during the service. Others wanted no such worldly allurements for this spiritual observance and urged that the elders' wives be ordered to use less sugar so the bread would be less tempting. Ultimately, we thought it unwise to *order* the wives to do anything and settled on hiding the bread after Communion.

Beyond the fun of telling this anecdote, my purpose is simply to demonstrate that what we are so ready to debate in Communion practice may have much more to do with our traditions and circumstances than it does with anything provable in the Bible. A verse cannot be cited with certainty to determine whether we should individually partake of the elements as we are served, to demonstrate personal devotion, or refrain from partaking until all have been served, to demonstrate our corporate solidarity. Our traditions, preferences, and circumstances largely determine the practices that enable us to express the common denominators of Communion. This becomes more apparent when we remember that today virtually no major church or denomination practices Communion as did first-century Christians.

Biblical Contexts

The Lord's Supper began in the context of a Passover meal (Matt. 26:17–29) but was also reflected in an evening meal (Luke 24:28–30) and an early breakfast (John 21:13). By the time Paul writes to the Corinthians, it is clear that New Testament Christians are regularly celebrating Communion within the context of a larger meal that is integral to their weekly worship (1 Cor. 11:20–22). Translating such biblical practice into the distribution of quarter-size wafers and plastic thimbles of juice, or into the practice of dipping pieces of *leavened* bread into a common cup, must be understood as a symbolic paraphrase of the original supper. We have extracted the essence of the first-century love feast and synthesized it into the Communion ordinances we now practice. This realization should keep us from being too adamant about our procedural preferences or too critical of others' practices.

Keeping a gracious spirit and historical perspective in healthy balance should keep us from being too hasty about innovation or too deferential to tradition regarding our Communion practices. The Lord's Supper should enable God's people to feast on the wonders of his mercy. A Communion service without familiar features robs God's people of the ability to enter into worship, but so does a service whose every feature has become routine.

Frequency Concerns

Two competing concerns drive the continuing controversy over the frequency of Communion: What should be required for the regular practice of biblical worship; and When does regular practice drift into the meaningless routine of insincere worship. As has been discussed earlier in this book, traditions vary over how often the Lord's Supper should be served. Though there is some debate, most historians agree that the common practice of the early church was weekly Communion. This may be implied by Paul's words (1 Cor. 11:20) and is mentioned as the regular practice of the church in the *Didache* (written in the late first or early second century.[2] However, during the Reformation, concerns about sacerdotalism (the idea that the mere practice of the sacraments communicates sanctifying grace) led many Protestants away from "ritualistic" practice of the Lord's Supper. For many of the Reformers, the routine practice of Communion too easily made its observance nominal for the impious or magical for the ignorant. To engage the heart authentically required making the Lord's Supper special, and that meant making it less frequent (monthly, quarterly, or annually).

So what should we do today? My own preference would be weekly observance. Those who are concerned that this would make the sacrament less "special," Robert Rayburn well answers:

> I have never heard any Christian say, "Let's be careful not to have our pastor preach the Word too often." All Christians recognize that it is through the Word that our Savior speaks to us today, but many seem not to understand that he speaks by the sacraments also. It is the very same message. Through the sacraments Christ ministers to his children, feeding them spiritually. It is difficult indeed, in the light of the spiritual benefits which are imparted with (not *in*) the Lord's Supper, not to agree with John Calvin, who insisted that the Lord's people should have the privilege of partaking of the sacrament every Lord's Day as the climactic part of their worship services. The elders of Geneva, who refused to allow him to provide weekly communion, were like many in our evangelical churches today who do not want the Lord's gracious ministry with the sacraments too often.[3]

The apparent practice of Scripture, the precedent of the ancient church, and appreciation for the ways Christ ministers the gospel to his people through the Lord's Supper persuade me of the efficacy of weekly celebration of the Lord's Supper—but my enthusiasm is measured.

Weekly Communion is my preference, but I do not consider it a mark of orthodoxy or a mandate of Scripture. In part, my lack of insistence comes from the awareness that few churches ever practice Communion as did the early church. There are numerous problems with insisting that *our* regular practice of Communion is mandated weekly by the Bible. First, even if we believe the Bible indicates the practice of the early church was weekly Communion, we must confess the Bible does not *command* weekly Communion. We may infer that the apostles intended for the early church's practice to be our own, but this is only an inference. There are many aspects

2. See *Didache*, 14. Written in the late first or early second century, "The Teaching—*Didache*—of the Apostles" is one of our earliest post-apostolic documents.
3. Robert G. Rayburn, *O Come, Let Us Worship: Corporate Worship in the Evangelical Church* (Grand Rapids: Baker Academic, 1980), 259.

of early church worship that were derivative of a Middle Eastern culture (e.g., greeting one another with a kiss). We should be cautious about insisting that an ancient church in a culture accustomed to communal meals intended for all churches in all cultures in all ages to commune just the same. A scriptural practice is not necessarily a scriptural mandate.

Second, as has already been mentioned, it would be very difficult to prove from biblical example that our forms of Communion should be practiced weekly. A first-century Christian accustomed to the New Testament love feasts would probably guffaw in amusement if told that our thimbles of wine and wafers of bread reflected the practices of the early church. But it is not simply the amount of bread and wine that differentiates our Communion from that of the early church. In the Bible, the Lord's Supper was practiced as a means of uniting the church around a common meal. People of different races, regions, and pasts came together to share their food, funds, prayers, and homes. They had to work past their differences, prejudices, and antipathies to engage in eating, conversation, and worship in the same space. How much of the meal was simply socializing and how much was distinguished as a symbolic ritual we don't really know. What is plain is that the meal was a meal and not just a ceremony—or, at least, the ceremony was in the context of a meal.

Integral versus Routine

I am not arguing that Communion should be a full meal. I am suggesting that many of our struggles over how often we should practice Communion result from our ceremonial distillation of the common experience of the early church. The Communion of the early church was not a routine ceremony; it was a natural and integral expression of living and worshiping together in Christ. The meal was not made special by layering it with ever-increasing details of ceremony, restriction, and formality. The meal cohered with the preached message of the gospel, and as people participated in the Lord's Supper they experienced and demonstrated what it meant to live the gospel. What kept Communion from being routine was the fact that it was part of living the gospel.

If Communion becomes too ceremonial—and by this I mean that we say the same words and use the same gestures, varying neither order, prayer, creed, nor song—then it will be humanly impossible for weekly Communion not to become a dull routine to endure or a magic ritual to perform. In order for the Lord's Supper to engage the human spirit weekly it must be expressed in ways that make it integral to the rest of the worship. In words of invitation, institution, or challenge, the minister may reflect ideas or themes developed in the Sermon.[4] The way in which the elements are distributed may vary to express important aspects of the life of the church—sometimes making the Lord's Supper formal, triumphant, or celebrative; other times making it informal, familial, or intimate. There are times to encourage individuals to partake of the elements individually in order to bare their souls before the Lord, and there are times to encourage partaking together in order to unite as the family of God. Awareness of different ways that Communion has been legitimately practiced within and among the traditions (e.g., processing forward, being served as families, being served individually, passing the elements to a circled congregation) can provide a variety of respectful expressions of the sacrament.

The size of the church, resources available, and resistance to change may make weekly Communion unfeasible or unwise. Again, weekly Communion should not be considered a mark of orthodoxy or superior piety. The Lord's Supper should represent the grace that alone makes us right before God. Insisting on weekly Communion in order to satisfy personal preference or prove superior status ultimately denies the gospel that the sacrament should be representing.

Reinforcing the Gospel

A church does not cease to be a church because it practices Communion less frequently than weekly. Christ can still powerfully minister to his people without weekly Communion. One benefit of Christ-centered worship is that the liturgy itself serves a sacramental function, as does the preaching of the Word. By reflecting the contours of the gospel in the Liturgy of the Word, the grace of Christ is proclaimed. Christ-centered preaching also makes his grace known to his people. When the preparation for the Word, the preaching of the Word, and the Liturgy of the Upper Room unite to present the gospel, the church employs each dimension of Christ's provision to experience his grace. Each should reinforce the other, but the lessened presence of one does not destroy the effectiveness of the others.

4. Hughes Oliphant Old offers helpful words about fencing the table (i.e., warning the unrepentant or unbelieving not to participate in the Lord's Supper). He reminds us that the biblical and historical emphasis is on encouraging the faithful to come to the table, and caring for the unrepentant. The table should have a strong communal and evangelistic dimension. Those who have properly understood this have used the table not simply to caution, but to woo the unbeliever. The consequence is that revivals have sprung from wise proclamation of the invitation always implicit in the Lord's Supper (see Old's *Leading in Prayer: A Workbook for Worship* [Grand Rapids: Eerdmans, 1995], 233).

The Reformers taught the primacy of the preached Word because they knew that without an understanding of the truths of Scripture, the significance of the liturgy and the sacraments would be lost. They had experienced the superstitious views of the sacraments and the nominal participation in the liturgy that were the inevitable consequences of a diminished emphasis on preaching. But they did not intend for the primacy of the Word to eclipse the other elements of worship. Grace preached was to be the context for understanding grace expressed in liturgy and sacrament. The grace presented in these would then work synergistically with the gospel proclaimed in the pulpit to lead the heart to more profound levels of spiritual understanding and appreciation. This should remain our goal.

If the liturgy and sacraments are not understood as expressions of grace—if we only practice them out of a sense of duty and propriety—then their gospel power will ebb and the church will increasingly turn to preaching alone for instruction and inspiration. The other alternative, of course, is that preaching will be deemphasized and the church will increasingly look to the proper performance of worship and sacrament as its means to acquire grace. But when the sacraments and liturgy are understood as expressions of grace that reinforce the gospel in the Word preached, then each is more appreciated at the same time it reinforces the others. These dynamics should encourage us that it is possible to coordinate the means of grace Christ has provided for his church so that each supports the gospel message of the other.

24

MUSICAL STYLES

Earlier in this book (chapters 9 and 10), I explained why it has never been
more important for church leaders to unite in a worship approach
that prioritizes gospel principles. Acting with these priorities will
require us to exegete the culture in which we minister in order to identify
the calling of our church in its specific setting. Prioritizing the honor of
Christ's name and the progress of his kingdom can create harmony around
a common mission that will enable us to unite in worship style choices
even when personal preferences vary. As noble as this ethic may sound,
however, I realize the stumbling block hindering many churches' progress
toward unity in worship is music.

At levels more deep than most of us can explain, music communicates
our values, anchors our feelings, and expresses our hearts. The music chosen to lead us to communion with heaven can create within us the deepest
experiences of either inspiration or isolation. Music can move us or repel
us. People may advocate a musical style because they find it appealing or
because they believe it appropriate. What makes it appropriate can be tradition, familiarity, a sense that a certain style communicates proper respect,
or a missional conviction that a style will appeal to a target generation or
people group. None of this can be proven by a Bible verse or a mathemati-
cal formula, so reactions to musical choices are often more visceral than
reasonable. We rely on personal judgment, past experience, advice from

experts, and expressions of appreciation or criticism, and we hope (and pray) for some level of consensus.

Articulating Gospel Principles

The most important strategy for church leaders to pursue in uniting the church in worship is clear and regular articulation of gospel principles. When leaders lock arms around the common purpose of re-presenting the gospel with respect, sensitivity, and intelligence to those God has called them to teach and reach, then the leaders can more readily explain and act on their worship approach. Regular teaching of gospel priorities can also help the people of existing churches learn to be accepting of differences and deferential to others' needs while simultaneously insisting on biblically sound content, God-honoring presentation, and respect for forebears. Leaders of new churches may have more opportunity simply to declare what worship style(s) will be best for their target constituency—but eventually all churches will have their own traditions that subsequent generations will challenge.

Unifying Strategies

One strategy for easing tensions when preferences vary widely is offering worship services with different styles at different times or locations (or with different languages). Such measures typically are only stopgap, and eventually will create separate worship communities rather than a unified church body. Unless the intention is to spin off a separate body of believers into a separate church, it is usually best to work toward consensus and help people learn the gospel value of serving one another's worship needs.

Some standard strategies can help build the consensus most church leaders desire. Obviously, the first is to introduce less-familiar music sparingly. The music may be unfamiliar because it is contemporary, because it is traditional (many contemporary churches are rediscovering the beauty and depth of traditional hymns), or because it is foreign (changing multicultural neighborhoods may require new worship styles for effective outreach). Until the new music becomes familiar or widely accepted it might be used every few weeks, or during less-formal services, or in specific portions of the worship service (such as in the gathering time). The goal is not to sneak in the new music, but to give people time to adjust, give feedback, and learn how to love one another.

New Tunes for Historical Lyrics

One strategy that can show respect for traditional preferences while introducing new styles is writing new tunes for historical lyrics. The ministries of James Ward (e.g., "O For a Thousand," "Rock of Ages"), Vikki Cook ("Before the Throne of God Above"), Indelible Grace ("Arise, My Soul, Arise," "God Be Merciful to Me"), Red Mountain Music ("The Love of Christ Is Rich and Free"), and Christ Community Church in Franklin, Tennessee, have excelled in this approach (for internet links to the latter three, see the appendix).

Similar Tunes and Lyrics

Another strategy is to use new songs that are similar in style to music already familiar in the church. The contemporary hymns of Graham Kendrick (e.g., "Shine, Jesus, Shine") and Keith Getty and Stuart Townend (e.g., "In Christ Alone," "How Deep the Father's Love," "Oh, to See the Dawn") are theologically rich and bridge both contemporary and traditional music styles. The same is true of Mark Lowry and Buddy Greene ("Mary, Did You Know").

New Lyrics to Traditional Tunes

The church may also choose to use new lyrics to secular music that is familiar and acceptable in style for the church culture. "Highland Cathedral" is a grand and noble bagpipe tune. Though it was recently written, the tune has become very familiar through its popular use in church ceremonies and weddings. Copyright restrictions will not allow publication of the tune with new words, but the music is so appropriate for worship that choirs, churches, and wedding parties have obtained local permission to sing the tune with the words to "Bought by the Blood" (see following pages). Churches can also encourage new generations and ethnicities of hymn writers by letting them write new lyrics to older tunes familiar in the church or culture. For example, the words to "Easter Dawn" (see following pages) can be sung to the tune of the familiar choral anthem "Creation Hymn," or to the tune of "An American Hymn" (re-popularized by Placido Domingo), from the secular film "East of Eden." New music is often the greater challenge to traditional sensibilities, so encouraging new lyrics for older tunes can provide opportunity for fresh contributions without rattling church foundations.[1]

   Every generation and people group needs to believe that it can contribute to the continuing life and worship of the church. If a church makes no

---

1. I would also encourage modern composers to write new tunes for lyrics such as these.

place for new contributions, it will lose the enthusiasm and participation of those who must ensure its continuing ministry. Singing new lyrics to familiar tunes can be an unintimidating way to encourage new contributions that maintain congregational vitality. In addition, allowing such opportunities may provide for new generations to re-discover and fall in love again with wonderful tunes resurrected from the history of the church (see following pages).

There are, of course, risks with each of these strategies. Persons in the church may believe that new tunes are not appropriate or respectful of "sacred" lyrics from history. Others may object that new words written for older tunes are not as good or fitting as the original lyrics. Finally, people may be concerned that music borrowed from secular culture has too much identification with inappropriate cultural values. These concerns may be apt, and should not be swept aside without consideration. At the same time, congregations will be helped by understanding that many of the tunes they are accustomed to singing were not originally attached to the words they know (e.g., "Amazing Grace").

The Reformers were willing to borrow musical forms from the secular culture to encourage congregational singing. And virtually every great mission effort has profited by allowing words in different languages to be used with traditional hymn tunes. All hymns were "contemporary" when they were written. Some hymns we now consider noble were considered edgy in their day (e.g., Isaac Watts's "When I Survey the Wondrous Cross"). Keeping the church rooted in its worship history and reaching toward its worship future is never without challenges, but those rooted in and reaching for gospel priorities will have the greatest potential for meeting those challenges.

Bought by the Blood
Lyrics by Bryan Chapell

Compatible with the tune of "Highland Cathedral," by M. Korb and U. Roever

1. Bought by the blood of heaven's perfect Lamb,
   Freed from the bonds of earth by pierced hand;
   He all my worthiness and I, His sin,
   Nailed to a cross by the pow'r of God's love.

Refrain
Though his call take me far away,
Though it cost my name, comfort and gain,
I will serve Him all my days,
My life now His, my Lord.

2. Bold I approach my King's eternal throne,
   Robed in a righteousness that's not my own,
   Filled with His Spirit for a holy cause,
   Bearing His cross by the pow'r of God's love.

Refrain

3. Lord, now grant me for the gospel strife,
   Grace for the morning and the fearful night;
   Strengthen my zeal for my dear Savior's reign,
   Raising His cross by the pow'r of God's love!

Refrain

Easter Dawn
Lyrics by Bryan Chapell

Compatible with the choral anthem "Creation Hymn," by B. Chapell and C. Courtney; or with the tune of "An American Hymn," by Lee Holdridge (from the secular film "East of Eden")

Angels watch a rising sun,
    Roll back the shadows of the dawn,
Revealing from the darkness of the night,
    A scene too strong for even Heaven's sight:

Beams atop a crimson hill,
    Now mark the place His blood was spilled.
Creation groans; its winds an awful sigh.
    Guilt-bound, the vaults of earth withhold reply.
        He is gone!

Bridge: Then with the morn, the angels said,
    "Why look for Him among the dead?"

"He lives! He's risen from the grave.
    Death's chains He broke with break of day.
Despair He turned to Heaven's victory;
    Your sins He conquered for eternity;
        They are gone!"

Bridge: Now with the morn my soul shall rise,
    In praise to Him who rules the skies.

He rose by power of grace divine
    The life He lives, by faith, is mine.
Redeemed, I claim the dawn of this new day,
    With hope the Son creates in me to say,
        "He arose!"

Calvary's Anthem

Bryan Chapell
(Adapted from *The Valley of Vision*)
Appalachian Song

6. The heart that knows Christ's holy light,
more splendor shows than lilies white.
That heart is mine by grace that's free,
secured by blood at Calvary.

7. Though now my will is weak and frail,
I know of blood that will not fail.
By faith I lean on Jesus' might,
to know His peace both day and night.

8. The One who gave His life for me,
now bids me rest at Calvary.
The blood once spilled for mercy's sake,
transports my soul through heaven's gate.

9. May hymns of praise for wondrous love,
soar with my soul to Christ above;
I'll join the anthem ever-long,
his blood for me, my lasting song.

I Watched My Savior

Bryan Chapell

KINGSFOLD
Traditional English Melody
(found in TH #79)

1. I watched my Sa-vior bleed a-way; Sin nailed Him to a cross. The sky turned black, though it was day; all thought His cause was lost. They put Him in a sin-ner's tomb, and sealed it with a stone. My hope des-cend-ed in that grave, all earth-ly plans un-done.

2. Three days then passed of ut-ter doubt; What good comes from the dead? The an-swer came with an-gel shout, "He a-rose just as He said!" The stone was moved; my Lord was gone, a-long with all my sin. My hope as-cend-ed with the Son; now I be-lieve in Him.

3. New life dawns in the Eas-ter light; He lives with-in my heart. The pow'r I need for dai-ly life, the Spir-it does im-part. The hand that nailed Him to the cross, now clasps the one once pierced. The beast that scourged His back and scoffed, knows mer-cy e'en more fierce.

4. That mer-cy like a might-y man fought Sa-tan for my soul; E'en Hea-ven turned its face a-way, so aw-ful was the toll; But love di-vine en-dured the pain, His pas-sion was for me; For on his cross he hung my crimes, and bled to set me free.

5. Sure grace now seals my heart to Christ, His blood has claimed my soul. Full vic-t'ry won by sac-ri-fice, has made my spir-it whole. No long-er can I doubt His love, nor ques-tion Heav-en's plan. King Je-sus lives, and so shall I, en-throned at God's right hand.

Jesus' Love

Ephesians 3:14-21

Words: Bryan Chapell

Tune: "My Hope is Built"

1. I kneel be - fore my Fa - ther's throne, awed by the name that's
2. Out of His glo - ry rich - es flow to strength- en me for
3. Lord, grant me pow'r to com - pre - hend the love of Christ that
4. Now un - to Him of pow'r so great, He does more than we

now my own. By grace I'm in His fam - i - ly, one
trials be - low; my in - ner be - ing filled with pow'r, the
dwells with - in; its length, its breadth, its height and depth, sur -
ask or think; to God be glo - ry in the church; through

with His Son e - ter - nal - ly.
Spir - it's gift for Sa - tan's hour. *What won - drous grace from*
pas - sing thought, more ful - ly blessed.
Christ, e - ter - nal praise on earth.

heav'n a-bove to fill my heart with Je- sus' love! My heart is full with Je- sus' love.

While Shepherds Slept

Bryan Chapell

St. Clement
C. Scholefield

1. While shep - herds slept, the heav'ns a - wak -ened, the sky was
2. The child who sleeps a - mid the cat - tle, yet rules the
3. This news then spread by shep-herds re - joic- ing, "Our Lord rests
4. Dear Child, my King, my Lord, my Sa - vior, please come a -
5. New hope by faith fresh birth with - in me; Then sing through

robed in ho - ly light; And an - gels sang a Sav - ior's
world made by His hand; The star that hails the babe's ar -
in a man - ger bed; A King so kind He'd bend to the
gain in - to my night; I need your love to pierce my
me the an - gels' song; Your love shall be the star that

sto - ry: peace on the earth has come this night.
riv - al, has pierced the dark at His com - mand.
brok- en, His grace the crown up - on His head."
dark- ness, your grace to shine its ho - ly light.
guides me; my heart shall be your last - ing throne.

Appendix

WORSHIP RESOURCES
ON THE INTERNET

Widely Used Resource Sites

http://www.biblegateway.com/ Many versions of the Bible are included on
this site. There are several searches possible, including topical, passage,
and word. Text can be copied and pasted.

http://www.calvin.edu/worship/ The Calvin Institute of Christian Worship provides many resources for the study and practice of Christian
worship. Devoted to the renewal of worship by continuity with the
great traditions of the church while respecting modern contributions,
the institute's *Worship Sourcebook* in print and CD form is the most
recommended single resource now available for worship service creation
in the Reformed tradition.

http://www.cpdl.org/wiki/index.php/Main_Page The choral public domain
library includes traditional church music that is in the public domain.
It can be copied without charge.

http://www.cyberhymnal.org Probably the most used and extensive Web
site for searching out hymns by title or text. Users can copy and paste

the text if they want to include it in their bulletin. They also have the ability to listen to the tune on the page on which the text appears. There are many other features available on this site that are helpful to worship planners and musicians.

http://www.dnah.org *Dictionary of North American Hymnody* searchable Web site with the contents of 4,876 hymnals published in North America between 1640 and 1978, including over one million hymns contained in these publications.

http://www.hymnary.org Seeks to combine the best features of numerous sites devoted to hymn study, sharing, and research.

http://www.igracemusic.com A collection of songs and resources from Reformed University Fellowship and Indelible Grace.

http://justus.anglican.org/resources/bcp/ Several versions of classic liturgy from The Book of Common Prayer are here in the Anglican tradition.

http://oremus.org/hymnal/ This online hymnal contains texts and MIDI files of tunes used in much of the English-speaking world, with particular emphasis on the Anglican tradition.

http://www.smithcreekmusic.com/Hymnology/index.html Smith Creek Music offers extensive resources and links for collecting and studying worship music, hymns, and texts.

http://www.worship.ca/sec7.html#hymns Evangelical Lutheran Church site devoted to worship from many traditions. A very extensive list of links to hymn and liturgy sites connects to everything from modern hymnody to Gregorian chants to handbell and choral resources to liturgical dance.

Fee-based Sites

http://www.ccli.com Christian Copyright Licensing International [CCLI] was established in 1988 to provide churches with simple, affordable ways to use copyrighted music legally.

http://www.praisecharts.com Provides for downloading and printing sheet music and chord charts from numerous contemporary worship sources.

http://worshipleader.com Many free reviews, articles, and resources, along with material for sale provided by *Worship Leader* magazine.

http://www.worshipmusic.com/ A worship site devoted to making praise and worship music available from a variety of well-known resources.

http://www.worshiptogether.com A contemporary worship site devoted to marketing contemporary praise and worship music with links to a variety of helpful resources.

Examples of Helpful Church Sites

http://www.cardiphonia.com/ The Web site of Redeemer Church in Indianapolis devoted to enhancing worship by sharing its many insights and resources regarding the aesthetics of ancient and modern worship.

http://www.christcommunity.org/ The Web site of Christ Community Church in Franklin, Tennessee, that includes many worship resources with a strong missional perspective at its "Worship and Arts" link.

http://www.redeemer2.com/rstore/category.cfm?Category=1 Redeemer Music is a resource for new Christian music in the jazz, classical, and folk traditions with texts that uphold the centrality of the gospel message. Originally created for worship services at Redeemer Presbyterian Church in New York City, this music is now heard at churches throughout the United States and overseas.

http://www.redmountainchurch.org Red Mountain Church in Birmingham, Alabama, has specialized in putting the texts of some excellent hymns—lost to modern use—to contemporary tunes, similar to much of the work of Reformed University Fellowship and Indelible Grace.

http://www.sovereigngraceministries.org/Worship/Worship.aspx The network of Sovereign Grace churches provides theologically rich, contemporary music resources—much of it free.

Many churches publish their bulletins online, which can provide ideas for designing services. Some larger churches have Webcast services that can be watched as models or as catalysts for creating orders of service (e.g., http://www.tenth.org/ [Tenth Presbyterian in Philadelphia]; http://www.firstevan.org/ [First Evangelical Church in Memphis, Tennessee]). First Evangelical is the home church of Ron Man, whose music and worship ministry has brought significant understanding of biblical principles for worship to churches in many nations (see http://www.worr.org/).

Some sites have specialized interests that can provide many helpful worship resources, such as http://books.google.com/books?id=omOqqHQ4ZEkC&dq=baird+presbyterian+liturgies (which makes available Charles W. Baird's classic work on Presbyterian liturgies).

BIBLIOGRAPHY

Adams, Jay. *Preaching with Purpose: A Comprehensive Textbook on Biblical Preaching.* Grand Rapids: Baker Academic, 1982.

Allen, Ronald, and Gordon Borror. *Worship: Rediscovering the Missing Jewel.* Portland, OR: Multnomah, 1982.

Armstrong, Chris. "The Future Lies in the Past: Why Evangelicals Are Connecting with the Early Church as They Move into the 21st Century." *Christianity Today,* February 2008, 22–29.

Armstrong, John H. "Thinking Out Loud (Again) on Worship." *Reformation and Revival Weekly Newsletter,* May 21, 2002.

Baird, Charles W. *The Presbyterian Liturgies.* Reprint, Grand Rapids: Baker Academic, 1960. Formerly published as *Eutaxia,* 1855.

Baker, Jonny, et al. *Alternative Worship: Resources from and for the Emerging Church.* Grand Rapids: Baker Books, 2004.

Bannerman, David D. *The Worship of the Presbyterian Church.* Edinburgh: Andrew Elliot, 1984.

Barkley, John M. *Worship of the Reformed Church.* Richmond, VA: John Knox, 1967.

Barraclough, Geoffrey, ed. "Calvinism: The Majesty of God." In *The Christian World:* *A Social and Cultural History,* 178–79. New York: Harry N. Abrams, Inc., 1981.

Bennett, Arthur, ed. *The Valley of Vision: A Collection of Puritan Prayers and Devotions.* Carlisle, PA: Banner of Truth Trust, 1975.

Book of Common Prayer, according to use in the Episcopal Church in the USA. San Francisco: HarperOne, 1983.

Book of Common Worship, approved by the General Assembly, Presbyterian Church (USA). The Board of Christian Education, Presbyterian Church (USA), 1966.

Brack, Harold A. *Effective Oral Interpretation for Religious Leaders.* Englewood Cliffs, NJ: Prentice-Hall, 1964.

Bradshaw, Paul F. *The Search for the Origins of Christian Worship: Sources and Methods for the Study of Early Liturgy.* 2nd ed. Oxford: Oxford University Press, 2002.

Branaugh, Matt. "Willow Creek's 'Huge Shift.'" *Christianity Today,* May 2008, 13.

Bridges, Jerry. *The Discipline of Grace: God's Role and Our Role in the Pursuit of Holiness.* Colorado Springs: NavPress, 1994.

Brink, Emily R., and John D. Witvliet, eds. *The Worship Sourcebook.* Grand Rapids: Calvin Institute of Christian Worship and Baker Books, 2004.

Broadus, John A. *On the Preparation and Delivery of Sermons.* Rev. ed. Edited by

Jesse B. Weatherspoon. London: Hodder and Stoughton, 1944.

Calhoun, Anne, and David Calhoun, eds. *Daily Prayers by F. B. Meyer*. Great Britain: Christian Focus, 2007.

Calvin, John. *Institutes of the Christian Religion*. Edited by John T. McNeill. Translated by Ford Lewis Battles. Library of Christian Classics. Philadelphia: Westminster, 1960.

Campbell, Paul N. *Oral Interpretation*. New York: Macmillan, 1966.

Carson, D. A., ed. *Worship by the Book*. Grand Rapids: Zondervan, 2002.

Chalmers, Thomas. "The Expulsive Power of a New Affection." Vol. 2 of *History and Repository of Pulpit Eloquence*. Edited by Henry C. Fish, 319–35. New York: Dodd, Mead and Co., 1856.

Chan, Simon. *Liturgical Theology: The Church as Worshiping Community*. Downers Grove, IL: InterVarsity, 2006.

Chapell, Bryan. *Christ-Centered Preaching: Redeeming the Expository Sermon*. 2nd ed. Grand Rapids: Baker Academic, 2005.

———. *Holiness by Grace*. Wheaton, IL: Crossway, 2001.

———. *In the Grip of Grace*. Grand Rapids: Baker Academic, 1992.

———. *Using Illustrations to Preach with Power*. Rev. ed. Wheaton, IL: Crossway, 2001.

Chapell, Bryan, John Frame, Joseph "Skip" Ryan, Roy Taylor, and Wade Williams. "MNA Guidelines for Church Planters on Principles and Practices of Worship." Presbyterian Church in America, October 2000.

Chiara, Peter A. *Liturgy and Laity*. Brooklyn, NY: Cofraternity of the Precious Blood, 1964.

Clowney, Edmund. "The Singing Savior." *Moody Monthly*, July–August 1979, 40–42.

———. *The Unfolding Mystery: Discovering Christ in the Old Testament*. Phillipsburg, NJ: Presbyterian and Reformed, 1988.

"Collect." References: Louis Weil. *Gathered to Pray: Understanding Liturgical Prayer*. Cambridge, MA: Crowley Publications, 1986. Wikipedia, http://en.wikipedia.org/wiki/Collect.

Crump, Geoffrey. *Speaking Poetry*. Rev. ed. London: Dennis Dobson, 1964.

Curry, S. S. *Vocal and Literary Interpretation of the Bible*. New York: Macmillan, 1903.

Dalbey, Mark L. "A Biblical, Historical, and Contemporary Look at the Regulative Principle of Worship." DMin diss., Covenant Theological Seminary, 1999.

Dargan, Edwin C. *A History of Preaching*, vol. 1. New York: Hodder and Stoughton, 1905.

Davies, Horton. *The Worship of the English Puritans*. London: Dacre Press, 1948. Reprint, Morgan, PA: Soli Deo Gloria Publications, 1997.

Dawn, Marva. *Reaching Out without Dumbing Down: A Theology of Worship for the Turn-of-the-century Culture*. Grand Rapids: Eerdmans, 1995.

Deddens, K. "A Missing Link in Reformed Liturgy." *Clarion* 37, nos. 15–19 (1998), http://www.spindleworks.com/library/deddens/missing.htm.

De Gruchy, John W. "Aesthetic Creativity, Eucharistic Celebration and Liturgical Renewal: With Special Reference to the Reformed Tradition." Paper for the Buvton Conference, Stellenbosch, South Africa, September 1, 2003.

De Jong, James A. *Into His Presence*. Grand Rapids: Board of Publications of the Christian Reformed Church, 1985.

Dix, Gregory. *The Shape of the Liturgy*. New York: Continuum International, 2005.

Edwards, Paul. "The Rise of Expression." In *Performance of Literature in Historical Perspectives*, edited by David W. Thompson, 529–48. Lanham, MD: University Press of America, 1983.

Erickson, Craig Douglas. *Participating in Worship: History, Theory, and Practice*. Louisville: Westminster John Knox, 1989.

Farley, Michael A. "Reforming Reformed Worship: Theological Method and Liturgical

Catholicity in American Presbyterianism, 1850–2005." PhD diss., St. Louis University, 2007.

Faust, Clarence H. and Thomas H. Johnson, eds. *Jonathan Edwards*. New York: American Book, 1935.

Finnegan, Ruth. *Oral Poetry*. Cambridge: Cambridge University Press, 1977.

Foster, Richard. *Streams of Living Water: Celebrating the Great Traditions of the Christian Faith*. New York: Harper, 1998.

Frame, John. *Contemporary Worship Music: A Biblical Defense*. Phillipsburg, NJ: Presbyterian and Reformed, 1997.

———. *Worship in Spirit and Truth*. Phillipsburg, NJ: Presbyterian and Reformed, 1996.

Frankforter, A. Daniel. *Stones for Bread: A Critique of Contemporary Worship*. Louisville: Westminster John Knox, 2001.

Furr, Gary A., and Milburn Price. *The Dialogue of Worship: Creating Space for Revelation and Response*. Macon, GA: Smyth and Helwys, 1998.

Gaddy, Welton C. *The Gift of Worship*. Nashville: Broadman, 1992.

Garside, Charles, Jr. *The Origins of Calvin's Theology of Music*. Transactions of the American Philosophical Society 69, pt. 4. Philadelphia: American Philosophical Society, 1979.

Garver, Joel. "Uniformity in This Kirk." http://www.joelgarver.com/writ/hist/uniform.htm.

Girardeau, John L. "The Discretionary Power of the Church." *The Blue Banner* 8, nos. 5–6 (May–June 1999): 1–15.

Godfrey, Robert W. "Worship: Evangelical or Reformed." *New Horizons* 23, no. 4 (April 2002): 11–12.

Goldsworthy, Graeme. *Preaching the Whole Bible as Christian Scripture*. Grand Rapids/Cambridge, UK: Eerdmans, 2000.

Gore, R. J., Jr. *Covenantal Worship: Reconsidering the Puritan Regulative Principle*. Phillipsburg, NJ: Presbyterian and Reformed, 2002.

"Gradual." Encyclopedia Britannica, Eleventh Edition; Catholic Encyclopedia of 1913. Wikipedia, http://en.wikipedia.org/wiki/Gradual.

Greidanus, Sidney. *The Modern Preacher and the Ancient Text: Intepreting and Preaching Biblical Literature*. Grand Rapids: Eerdmans, 1988.

———. *Preaching Christ from the Old Testament*. Grand Rapids: Eerdmans, 1999.

Hall, Christopher A. *Reading Scripture with the Church Fathers*. Downers Grove, IL: InterVarsity, 1998.

Hall, Edwin. *The Puritans and Their Principles*. 2nd ed. New York: Baker and Scribner, 1846.

Hamilton, Michael S. "The Triumph of the Praise Songs." *Christianity Today*, July 1999, 29–35.

Harper, John. *The Forms and Orders of Western Liturgy from the Tenth to the Eighteenth Century*. Oxford: Clarendon, 1991.

Harrell, William. *Concerning Worship: An Address Given at the Tidewater Reformed Minister's Fellowship in Suffolk, Virginia, on 6 May 1986*. Greenville, SC: A Press, 1987.

Harrison, R. K. "Deuteronomy." In *New Bible Commentary*, edited by D. Guthrie and J. A. Motyer, 201–29. Grand Rapids: Eerdmans, 1970.

Hart, D. G. "It May Be Refreshing, but Is It Reformed?" Review of *Worship in Spirit and Truth*, by John M. Frame. *Calvin Theological Journal* 32 (1997): 407–23.

Holck, Manfred, Jr., comp. *Dedications and Readings for Church Events*. Grand Rapids: Baker Books, 1991.

Hoon, Paul Waitman. *The Integrity of Worship: Ecumenical and Pastoral Studies in Liturgical Theology*. Nashville and New York: Abingdon, 1971.

Horton, Michael. *A Better Way: Rediscovering the Drama of God-Centered Worship*. Grand Rapids: Baker Books, 2002.

Hustad, Donald P. *True Worship: Reclaiming the Wonder and Majesty*. Wheaton, IL: Harold Shaw Publishers and Hope Publishing, 1998.

Hybels, Lynne. *The Joy of Personal Worship.* Wheaton, IL: Victor, 1984.

Johnson, Terry L., ed. *Leading in Worship.* Oak Ridge, TN: Covenant Foundation, 1996.

———, comp. and ed. *Trinity Psalter.* Pittsburgh: Crown and Covenant Publications, 1994.

Jones, Paul S. *Singing and Making Music: Issues in Church Music Today.* Phillipsburg, NJ: P&R, 2006.

Joseph, Bertram. "The Dramatic and Rhetorical Speaker's 'Person' and 'Action' in the English Renaissance," revised by Wallace Bacon. In *Performance of Literature in Historical Perspective,* edited by David W. Thompson, 459–75. Lanham, MD: University Press of America, 1983.

Jungman, Joseph A. *The Mass of the Roman Rite.* Rev. ed. Translated by Francis Brunner. New York: Benzinger Bros., 1950.

Kauflin, Bob. *Worship Matters: Leading Others to Encounter the Greatness of God.* Wheaton, IL: Crossway, 2008.

Kelderman, Duane, et al. *Authentic Worship in a Changing Culture.* Grand Rapids: CRC Publications, 1997.

Keller, Timothy J. "Reformed Worship in the Global City." In *Worship by the Book.* Edited by D. A. Carson, 193–249. Grand Rapids: Zondervan, 2002.

Kennedy, Gerald. *His Word through Preaching.* New York: Harper and Row, 1947.

Kline, Meredith. "Dynastic Covenant." *The Westminster Theological Journal* 23 (1960): 1–15.

Lachman, David, and Frank J. Smith, eds. *Worship in the Presence of God.* Greenville, SC: Greenville Seminary Press, 1992.

Lantz, J. Edward. *Reading the Bible Aloud.* New York: Macmillan, 1959.

Leithart, Peter. "For Whom Is Worship?" *New Horizons* 23, no. 4 (April 2002): 5.

Lewis, C. S. *Mere Christianity.* New York: Macmillan, 1952.

Litfin, Bryan M. *Getting to Know the Church Fathers: An Evangelical Introduction.* Grand Rapids: Brazos, 2007.

Lloyd, Dan S. *Leading Today's Funerals.* Grand Rapids: Baker Books, 1997.

Long, Thomas G. *Beyond the Worship Wars: Building Vital and Faithful Worship.* Herndon, VA: Alban Institute, 2001.

Lovelace, Richard. *Dynamics of Spiritual Life.* Downers Grove, IL: InterVarsity, 1979.

Lovette, Roger. *Come to Worship: Effective Approaches for Worship Planning.* Nashville: Broadman, 1990.

Lutheran Hymnal, authorized by the Evangelical Lutheran Synodical Conference of North America. St. Louis: Concordia, 1941.

Lutheran Worship, prepared by The Commission on Worship of the Lutheran Church–Missouri Synod. St. Louis: Concordia, 1982.

MacArthur, John. *The Ultimate Priority.* Chicago: Moody, 1983.

Macleod, Donald. *Presbyterian Worship: Its Meaning and Method.* Richmond, VA: John Knox, 1965.

Man, Ronald E. "Including Worship in the Seminary Curriculum." Unpublished manuscript, 1–47.

———. "Proclamation and Praise: Hebrews 2:12 and the Role of Christ in Worship." *Viewpoint,* July–August 2000, 6–8.

Manton, Thomas. *A Treatise of the Life of Faith.* Ross-shire, Scotland: Christian Focus, 1997.

Marshall, Walter. *The Gospel Mystery of Sanctification.* Grand Rapids: Reformation Heritage, 1999.

Martin, Ralph. *The Worship of God.* Grand Rapids: Eerdmans, 1982.

Maxwell, William D. *An Outline of Christian Worship: Its Development and Forms.* London: Oxford University Press, 1952.

McGinn, Donald J. *The Admonition Controversy.* New Brunswick, NJ: Rutgers University Press, 1949.

McIntosh, Gary L. *Church That Works: Your One-Stop Resource for Effective Ministry.* Grand Rapids: Baker Books, 2004.

Moore, Matthew R. "Dear Church Family." Distributed by Session to Briarwood Presbyterian Church, Birmingham, AL, January 27, 2002.

Morgan, Irvonwy. *The Godly Preachers of the Elizabethan Church*. London: Epworth, 1965.

Morganthaler, Sally. *Worship Evangelism: Inviting Unbelievers into the Presence of God*. Grand Rapids: Zondervan, 1995.

Moulton, Richard G. *The Literary Study of the Bible*. Boston: D. C. Heath, 1906.

Murray, John. "Christ Himself in the Assemblies of His People." *New Horizons* 23, no. 4 (April 2002): 3–4.

———. *The Collected Writings of John Murray*. Vol. 4. Edited by Iain H. Murray. Carlisle, PA: Banner of Truth Trust, 1982.

———. *Principles of Conduct*. Grand Rapids: Eerdmans, 1957.

Myers, Jeffrey J. *The Lord's Service: The Grace of Covenantal Renewal Worship*. Moscow, ID: Canon, 2003.

Myers, Warren, and Ruth Myers. *Praise, A Door to God's Presence*. Colorado Springs: NavPress, 1987.

Nichols, John Hastings. *Corporate Worship in the Reformed Tradition*. Philadelphia: Westminster, 1968.

Noll, Mark A. "We Are What We Sing." *Christianity Today*, July 1999, 37–41.

Old, Hughes Oliphant. *Leading in Prayer: A Workbook for Worship*. Grand Rapids: Eerdmans, 1995.

———. *The Patristic Roots of Reformed Worship*. Zurich: Theologischer Verlag, 1975.

———. *The Reading and Preaching of the Scriptures in the Worship of the Christian Church*. Vol. 1, *The Biblical Period*. Grand Rapids: Eerdmans, 1998.

———. *Themes and Variations for a Christian Doxology*. Grand Rapids: Eerdmans, 1992.

———. *Worship That Is Reformed According to Scripture*. Atlanta: John Knox, 1986.

Ortiz, Manuel. *One New People: Models for Developing a Multiethnic Church*. Downers Grove, IL: InterVarsity, 1996.

Ortlund, Anne. *Up with Worship*. Ventura, CA: Regal, 1975.

Our World Belongs to God: A Contemporary Testimony, Study Version, produced by the Contemporary Testimony Committee, and approved by the Christian Reformed Synod of 1986. Grand Rapids: Faith Alive Christian Resources, 1987.

Packer, J. I. *Rediscovering Holiness*. Ann Arbor: Servant Press, 1992.

Parrett, Gary A. "9.5 Theses on Worship: A Disputation on the Role of Music." *Christianity Today*, February 2005, 38–42.

Parsch, Pius. *The Liturgy of the Mass*. Translated by H. E. Winstone. 3rd ed. St. Louis: B. Herder, 1957.

Perry, Greg. "Reforming Worship." *Reformed Theological Review* 61, no. 1 (April 2002): 34–50.

Peterson, John W., comp. *Crowning Glory Hymnal*. Grand Rapids: Zondervan, 1965.

Pierson, Arthur T. *How to Read the Word of God Effectively*. Chicago: Moody Bible Institute, 1925.

Piper, John. *Gravity and Gladness on Sunday Morning: The Pursuit of God in Corporate Worship*. Minneapolis: Desiring God Ministries, 2000.

Rainsley, Glen E. *Words of Worship: Resources for Church and Home*. New York: Pilgrim Press, 1991.

Rayburn, Robert G. *O Come, Let Us Worship: Corporate Worship in the Evangelical Church*. Grand Rapids: Baker Academic, 1980.

Rice, Howard L., and James C. Huffstutler. *Reformed Worship*. Louisville: Geneva, 2001.

Ridderbos, H. *Paul: An Outline of His Theology*. Grand Rapids: Eerdmans, 1975.

Robertson, James D. *Minister's Worship Handbook*. Grand Rapids: Baker Books, 1974.

Roff, Lawrence. *Let Us Sing*. Philadelphia: Great Commission Publications, 1991.

Ross, Allen P. *Recalling the Hope of Glory: Biblical Worship from the Garden to the New Creation*. Grand Rapids: Kregel, 2006.

Ryken, Philip Graham. *Art for God's Sake: A Call to Recover the Arts*. Phillipsburg, NJ: Presbyterian and Reformed, 2006.

Ryken, Philip G., Derek W. Thomas, and J. Ligon Duncan. *Give Praise to God: A Vision* for *Reforming Worship*. Phillipsburg, NJ: Presbyterian and Reformed, 2003.

Ryle, J. C. *Worship: Its Priority, Principles and Practice*. Carlisle, PA: Banner of Truth Trust, 2005.

Schaeffer, Francis. *The God Who Is There*. Downers Grove, IL: InterVarsity, 1968.

———. *True Spirituality*. In *The Complete Works of Francis Schaeffer*. Vol. 3. Wheaton, IL: Crossway, 1982.

Scheub, Harold. "Performance of Oral Narrative." In *Frontiers of Folklore*, edited by William R. Bascom, 54–78. AAAS Selected Symposium 5. Boulder, CO: Westview, 1977.

Senn, Frank C. *Christian Liturgy: Catholic and Evangelical*. Philadelphia: Augsburg Fortress, 1997.

Shayon, Robert Lewis, and Nash Cox, comps. *Religion, Television, and the Information Superhighway: A Search for a Middle Way*. Philadelphia: Waymark, 1994.

Shubin, Russell G. "Worship That Moves the Soul: A Conversation with Robert King." *Mission Frontiers* 23, no. 2 (June 2001): 10–15.

Spencer, Donald A. *Hymn and Scripture Selection Guide*. Rev. ed. Grand Rapids: Baker Books, 1993.

Srawley, J. H. *The Early History of the Liturgy*. The Cambridge Handbooks of Liturgical Study. 2nd ed. Cambridge: Cambridge University Press, 1957.

St. Agnes Cathedral, Rockville Centre, New York. "Understanding the Catholic Mass." http://www.stagnescathedral.org/Parish/mass/mass.htm.

Stillinger, Jack, ed. *William Wordsworth: Selected Poems and Prefaces*. Boston: Houghton Mifflin, 1965.

Stupert, Calvin R. *A New Song for an Old World: Musical Thought in the Early Church*. Grand Rapids: Eerdmans, 2006.

Thompson, Bard. *Liturgies of the Western Church*. Philadelphia: Fortress, 2003.

Thompson, David W. "Interpretive Reading as Symbolic Action." *Quarterly Journal of Speech* 42, no. 4 (1956): 394.

Torrance, James B. *Worship, Community and the Triune God of Grace*. Downers Grove, IL: InterVarsity Academic, 1996.

Torrance, T. F. "The Mind of Christ in Worship: The Problem of Apollinarianism in the Liturgy." In *Theology in Reconciliation*, 139–214. Grand Rapids: Eerdmans, 1975.

Trinity Hymnal. Rev. ed. Philadelphia: Great Commission Publications, 1990.

Union Hagadah. Rev. ed. The Central Conference of American Rabbis, 1923.

Vanderwall, Howard, ed. *The Church of All Ages*. Herndon, VA: Alban Institute, 2008.

Vasholz, Robert I. *Benedictions: A Pocket Resource*. Ross-shire, Scotland: Christian Focus, 2007.

———. *Calls to Worship: A Pocket Resource*. Ross-shire, Scotland: Christian Focus, 2008.

Wainwright, Geoffrey, and Karen B. Westerfield, eds. *The Oxford History of Christian Worship*. Oxford: Oxford University Press, 2006.

Wallace, Peter J. "Worship: The Heavenly Pattern (The Geneva Liturgy of John Calvin—Heaven on Earth?)." Michiana Covenant Church, May 4, 2006, http://www.freerepublic.com/focus/f-religion/1626924/posts.

Webber, Robert E. *Ancient-Future Faith: Rethinking Evangelicalism for a Postmodern World*. Grand Rapids: Baker Academic, 1999.

———. *Ancient-Future Worship: Proclaiming and Enacting God's Narrative*. Grand Rapids: Baker Books, 2008.

———, ed. *The Complete Library of Christian Worship*. 3 vols. Peabody, MA: Hendrickson; Nashville: Star Song, 1993–94.

———. "How Will the Millennials Worship? A Snapshot of the Very Near Future." *Reformed Worship* 38, no. 2 (April–June 2001): 2–3.

———. *The New Worship Awakening: What's Old Is New Again*. Reprint, Peabody, MA: Hendrickson, 2007. Formerly published as *Blended Worship: Achieving Substance and Relevance in Worship* (Peabody, MA: Hendrickson, 1994).

———. *Worship Is a Verb*. Dallas: Word, 1985.

———. *Worship Old and New: A Biblical, Historical, and Practical Introduction*. Rev. ed. Grand Rapids: Zondervan, 1994.

Webber, Robert E., et al., eds. *Renew! Songs and Hymns for Blended Worship*. Carol Stream, IL: Hope Publishing, 1995.

Webster, Douglas. "Seeker-Sensitive, Not Consumer-Oriented." *Discernment*, Spring-Summer 2005, 8–9.

Whaley, Vernon M. *Understanding Music and Worship in the Local Church*. Wheaton, IL: Evangelical Training Association, 1995.

Wiersbe, Warren. *Real Worship*. Nashville: Oliver Nelson, 1986.

Willimon, William H. *The Service of God: How Worship and Ethics Are Related*. Nashville: Abingdon, 1983.

———. *Worship as Pastoral Care*. Nashville: Abingdon, 1990.

Winner, Lauren F. "New Song, Familiar Tune." *Christianity Today*, July 1999, 62–64.

Witvliet, John. "The Former Prophets and the Practice of Christian Worship." *Calvin Theological Journal* 37 (2002): 82–94.

Wolterstorff, Nicholas. "The Reformed Liturgy." In *Major Themes in the Reformed Tradition*, edited by Donald K. McKim, 273–304. Grand Rapids: Eerdmans, 1992.

Woolbert, C. H., and S. E. Nelson. *The Art of Interpretive Speech*. New York: F. S. Crofts, 1929.

Young, Karl. *The Drama of the Medieval Church*. Oxford: Clarendon, 1933.

INDEX